P9-ARJ-611

Fernald Library
Colby-Sawyer College
New London, New Hampshire

Presented by

MRS. JOHN SLOANE

CHAMPIONS OF PEACE

The story
of Alfred Nobel,
the Peace Prize and
the Laureates

CHAMPIONS OF PEACE

Tony Gray

PADDINGTON
PRESS LTD

THE TWO CONTINENTS
PUBLISHING GROUP

FERNALD LIBRARY
COLBY-SAWYER COLLEGE
NEW LONDON, N. H. 03257

JX
1962
A2
G7

Library of Congress Cataloging in Publication Data

Gray, Tony.
　Champions of peace.

　Bibliography: p.
　Includes index.
　1. Peace—Biography. 2. Nobel, Alfred Bernhard,
1833-1896. 3. Nobel prizes—History. I. Title.
JX1962.A2G7　　327'.172'0922　　76-3812
ISBN 0-8467-0143-X

© 1976 Paddington Press Ltd.
Photoset by Computer Photoset Ltd., Birmingham, England
Printed in the United States
Designed by Richard Johnson

IN THE USA
PADDINGTON PRESS LTD.
THE TWO CONTINENTS PUBLISHING GROUP LTD.

IN THE UK
PADDINGTON PRESS LTD.

71266

IN CANADA
Distributed by
RANDOM HOUSE OF CANADA LTD.

Unless otherwise noted, all photographs were provided
by courtesy of the Nobel Institute, Stockholm. All
quotations from the Nobel lectures and presentation
speeches are from *The Nobel Lectures 1901-1970*, ed.
Frederick W. Haberman, published in three volumes for
the Nobel Foundation by the Elsevier Publishing
Company (Amsterdam, London and New York) in 1972.

Contents

Acknowledgments

I would like to take this opportunity to express my gratitude to the Nobel Institutes in Stockholm and Oslo for their help in answering all my queries, and in providing me with much of the raw material for this book in the form of the presentation addresses, citations, biographies of the laureates and the text of their Nobel lectures. I would like at the same time to record my appreciation to them for their help in providing me with illustrative material. It is possible that they will not altogether agree with my comments on some of the laureates but I hope they understand that I was doing what I believed to be an objective book.

I would also like to thank the research staff at my local library in Richmond, Surrey, who, as always, have been of immense help; Eric Whitman, who helped me with some tricky German translations; and my editor at Paddington Press, Diane Flanel, who grappled magnificently with details most of which were away out of her period (and some of which were even out of mine).

Author's Note

THE FIRST PART of *Champions of Peace* deals with the life of Alfred Nobel, the circumstances surrounding his will and the establishment of the Peace Prize, and the changing nature of the prize over the course of its first seventy-five years.

In the remainder of the book I have dealt with the Peace Prize winners in chronological order, devoting a chapter to each decade. To establish the laureates in the context of the period in which their efforts for peace were made, I have prefaced each chapter with what amounts to a scrapbook for the decade, giving a brief run-down of the principal political events, especially those likely to affect war or peace. I have also included scientific advances, sociological changes and even a brief note on the plays and films of the decade in order to recapture something of the period's flavor. These summaries obviously cannot present any more than a skeleton impression of the period; but they may I hope, be sufficient to jog the memories of those who have lived through all or most of the decades and provide some useful if rough background material for the younger readers.

FOR MY SON MICHAEL

who, as a member of a CBS television news team, has seen terrible things in Israel, Syria, Beirut, Belfast and Angola and was himself wounded at Xuan Loc in Vietnam: with love and respect.

Introduction
War–and the Peace Prize

FOR THREE-QUARTERS of a century now a succession of committees appointed by the Norwegian parliament have been handing out considerable sums of money—around $100,000 dollars a year—to people and institutions who, in their view, have contributed most to the cause of peace on earth.

During these years we have had two major world wars in which well over fifty million people were killed and almost as many wounded; wars in Korea, Vietnam, Biafra, the Congo, India and Pakistan, Angola, Israel, Cyprus and the Lebanon; and a prolonged cold war between the Russian bloc and the Western allies which was accompanied by an arms race of such numbing proportions that the human mind is unable to grasp its full implications.

The full horror of the situation was crystallized by Linus Pauling, the 1962 Peace laureate, in a single nightmare statistic: by 1963 the nuclear powers between them had stockpiled enough weapons to reproduce the entire explosive power unleashed in World War II, day in and day out, for a total of 149 years; or, of course, it might all go up together on the same day—the first, and last, day of World War III. Now, needless to say, the stockpile is much larger.

We have seen the spread of nuclear weapons to China and India, and the proliferation of nuclear power for industrial use is now inevitable, since the world is rapidly running out of fossil fuels. But how can anybody possibly guarantee that nuclear materials and technology supplied for peaceful use will not be transformed into weapons of war?

We have seen the rise of dictators and learned the horrors of the concentration camps and the methodical eradication of six million Jews. We have seen the complete collapse of the old colonial system in Africa and Asia and parts of South America. Not many people will shed a tear on this score, perhaps, but the emergence of about seventy new nation-states has only too often meant their dazed entry into a state of revolution, anarchy, civil war and even genocide.

Since the end of World War II, men have been fighting continuously, without a day's respite, somewhere in the world—from the remotest jungles of Black Africa to the streets of Belfast and Detroit. There have been race riots, campus riots, civil disturbances, kidnappings and hijackings; and so much terrorism that violence has lost all its power to shock—real human blood flows as freely now on television news bulletins as fake blood in the "entertainment" sector.

And year after year, down all those dreadful years, the Nobel Peace Prize Committee in Norway—ordinary men and women from different walks of life—have been handing out *prizes for peace.*

And if that thought isn't sufficiently staggering in itself, consider some of the recipients of the Peace Prize.

There was Gustave Stresemann (1926), who before Germany was defeated in World War I urged unrestricted submarine warfare and was in favor of annexing as much territory as Germany could get its hands on.

There was George Marshall (1953), architect and commander of the greatest army the world had ever seen and a member of the policy committee which supervised the construction of the first atomic bomb.

There was Dag Hammarskjöld (1961)—widely regarded as a knight in shining armor—who misguidedly added to the Congo's almost insoluble difficulties by sending in a United Nations "peace-keeping" force which immediately joined in the fighting.

And there was Henry Kissinger (1973) who, before he concluded a cease-fire in Vietnam that wasn't really a cease-fire at all, had been adviser to Richard Nixon at a time when the president was ordering intensified bombing of North Vietnam in an effort to achieve "peace with honor"—even if it meant killing and maiming thousands of innocent civilians and totally devastating the terrain, largely destroying whatever agricultural potential the land may have had.

Since 1901, the year of the first award, fifty-six men, three women and eight institutions have accepted the prize for their contributions to world peace and their efforts in promoting fraternity between peoples. Only one man has turned it down on moral grounds: Le Duc Tho, Kissinger's North Vietnamese counterpart in the Vietnam peace negotiations, who did so because he felt that a real peace had not yet been achieved in Vietnam.

To be fair, many of the laureates have accepted the prize with great humility and without any illusions about the limits of their achievements. Woodrow Wilson (1919), for example, genuinely believed that his League of Nations could provide the answer to the world's dilemma, but realized that the organization could easily encounter grave difficulties. "It is the better part of our wisdom to consider our work as only begun," he said. "It will be a continuing labor."

René Cassin (1968), author of the United Nations Declaration of Human Rights, knew that the declaration was merely a blue-print and probably could have anticipated that even in some of the countries which ratified it, people would still be interned without trial and tortured for their beliefs.

Gandhi, the first to employ nonviolent protest in a political context, was never awarded the Peace Prize—a curious omission—but men like Albert Luthuli (1960), who applied his principles in South Africa, and Martin Luther King, Jr., (1964), who used Gandhi's "weapon" to fight racism in the South, both realized that for all their efforts violence still lay perilously close to the surface. King himself was to die violently, long before his work was accomplished.

Neither the laureates nor the committees who have selected them have ever given any indication that they thought the business of promoting peace, or the task of determining who (if anyone) had made the biggest contributions towards peace, was an easy one. There have been years, even, when the prize was not awarded at all: during the two world wars and at other periods when world tension was so unbearably high that to award anyone a prize for peace would have seemed manifestly absurd.

It is not surprising, therefore, that the Nobel Committee has sometimes encountered problems in finding suitable recipients for their prizes. The committee has been forced to confront the fundamental question of whether or not it is possible, on any basis whatever, to award a prize for a "meaningful" contribution to world peace.

If you take an organization like the League of Nations or the United Nations as the nearest approach to a system of settling international disputes amicably, there remains the problem of enforcing the decisions reached by a majority sitting in session. Léon Bourgeois, the 1920 Peace laureate and the "spiritual father" of the League of Nations, saw this difficulty even before the League came into existence; he believed that international justice would have to be enforced by means of sanctions—diplomatic, economic and, if necessary, *military.* So here, immediately, is a contradiction in terms: in order to enforce justice and secure peace, the League would have to be prepared to go to war. And, to make certain that its military sanctions were successful, it would have to be prepared to use enough power to win any war it decided to wage.

True pacifists like Bertha von Suttner (1905) and Ludwig Quidde (1927) were largely ineffectual because their books were read mainly by those already committed to the cause of peace. But if even a handful of people were shaken out of their complacency, the committee must have reasoned, then their work was not altogether in vain.

To award the prize to the International Committee of the Red Cross (1917, 1944 and 1963) or to the Office of the United Nations High Commissioner for Refugees (1954) is also, in a sense, admitting defeat. The Red Cross, by its very terms of reference, accepts war as inevitable and concentrates on alleviating the sufferings of the participants and their innocent victims. And the men and organizations concerned with the problems of resettling the homeless refugees of two world wars—men like Nansen (1922) and Father Pire of Belgium (1958)—however humanitarian and worthwhile their contributions may have been, could not strictly speaking be said to have been working for peace.

The money that the committee distributes comes from a foundation set up under the terms of the will of Alfred Nobel, the Swedish multimillionaire explosives expert; he stipulated that the interest on his fortune was to be divided into five equal prizes—one each for literature, physics, chemistry, and medicine or physiology, and one for peace. In the words of the will, the Peace Prize was to go to "the person who shall have done the most or the best work for fraternity between peoples, for the abolition of standing armies and for the holding and promotion of peace conferences."

As time went by and the anomaly of the whole concept of an award for peace became more marked, the committee tended to interpret these terms of reference more flexibly. Since there is not really anything these days that any individual can do to abolish standing armies, and since the United Nations incorporates all the machinery necessary for the holding and promotion of what amount to peace congresses, the committee has been forced to fall back on that phrase "fraternity between peoples."

And it is under this heading that the Peace Prize has sometimes been awarded to organizations like UNICEF (1965) or to men like Norman Borlaug (1970)—whose "green revolution" produced millions of acres of wheat where none would grow before—on the general principle that people with well-filled bellies are less likely to go to war with their neighbors than people who are starving, or to some powerful spokesmen against the hazards of nuclear technology like Linus Pauling or Andrei Sakharov (1975), who are not to blame if their warnings have not been more widely heeded.

BUT THE WHOLE concept of the Peace Prize is an anomaly based on an anomaly, for the money came, in the first place, from a financial empire based on the invention of dynamite, gelignite and cordite by a man who, in his day, probably did more than any other single human being to make possible the horrors of prenuclear warfare. Indeed, Nobel's inventions comprised the basic ingredients of the holocausts of the two world wars and they remain the standard stock-in-trade of terrorists everywhere.

True, a large proportion of Nobel's wealth came from the use of explosives intended for civil engineering projects. It would not be an exaggeration to say that his inventions changed the face of the world by enabling man to exploit the mineral resources of this planet at an unprecedented and ever-accelerating rate, and blast his way through the very fabric of the earth to clear canals and harbors and build roads and railways to places which would otherwise have remained inaccessible.

It is also true that an inventor cannot fairly be held responsible for the base uses to which men later put his inventions; Orville and Wilbur Wright cannot be blamed for the Stuka dive bomber or the B47. Yet in Nobel's case, it is not quite as simple as that.

The Nobel family were all connected with armaments and there can be no doubt that Alfred Nobel's invention of ballistite—known as cordite in many countries—was dictated purely by contemporary military requirements; it was in fact specifically designed as the perfect explosive for war purposes.

There is, however, some evidence that Nobel believed in the concept of what is now known as "the ultimate deterrent."

"My factories," he once wrote to Bertha von Suttner, "may well put an end to war sooner than your congresses. . . . The day when two army corps can annihilate one another in one second, all civilized nations, it is to be hoped, will recoil from war and discharge their troops."

It might be easier to believe that this was Nobel's principal motivation in continuing to work on ever more effective guns and explosives almost until the moment of his death if it were not for the vast fortune that he amassed, a great deal of it from the manufacture and sale of arms and ammunition of all types, and if it were not for the alacrity with which he went hopping around the world taking out patents on each new death-dealing innovation. Indeed, by the end of his career he held a total of 355 industrial and scientific patents, had built up 80 companies in 20 different countries and was one of Europe's richest men.

It is difficult to see what Nobel hoped to achieve with his Peace Prize. Did he think of it as a carrot which would encourage venal statesmen to work more diligently towards a peaceful solution of their problems in the hope of winning what was and still is a quite considerable sum of money? Or did he think of the prize more in the light of a reward, an additional bonus, for good men who would have done their best for humanity anyway?

In effect, Tim Greve, director of the Nobel Peace Prize Committee in Oslo, told me that in his opinion the award works in several ways. It gives the recipient an increased status which enables him to redouble his efforts; it puts a heavy responsibility on him to do so; and in the years when a statesman feels that he is in the running for the Peace Prize, the kudos, if not the thought of the money, may indeed act as a sort of incentive to induce him to make that extra effort.

To many people—not least to Nobel's fellow-Swedes—it has always seemed strange that the Norwegian parliament should have been singled out to appoint a committee to adjudicate on the world's peace-makers. In Nobel's time Norway and Sweden were united, though uneasily, under the same monarchy, and it has been suggested that the choice of the Norwegian Storting may have been Nobel's gesture of conciliation towards Norway, made in the hope of healing the developing breach.

But except in a very few instances, the committee cannot be said to have taken a parochial attitude and in view of the near-impossibility of choosing "champions of peace"—as Nobel referred to them in his will—the Norwegian committee has over the years done as well (or as badly) as any other committee might have done. They have picked out some interesting members of the human race; and some of the things the laureates have had to say on the subject of world peace make interesting if depressing reading—depressing, because for all their fine words and worthy deeds, we seem to be no nearer to peace today, in a world that is rapidly running out of food and fuel and, above all, faith in any kind of a future.

Alfred Nobel, King of Dynamite

THE NAME NOBEL comes from a parish in the southern tip of Sweden called Nöbbelöv. It was adopted by the first member of an old Scandian family of farmers who was lucky enough to make it to university. In the usual manner of the seventeenth century, he called himself Nobelius: Petrus Olavi Nobelius. After graduating from Uppsala University, he married his patron's daughter, became a judge and founded the family which later shortened its name to Nobel.

Alfred's father Immanuel was an original, an eccentric character with boundless energy who fluctuated wildly all his life between poverty and prosperity, fame and bankruptcy. He had little formal education, knew no foreign languages and could barely read or write—and yet he was always brimming over with inventive ideas.

He was born in 1801 in Gävle in northern Sweden and when he was fourteen years of age was sent to sea; many of his relatives, on his mother's side, were sea-faring folk. He spent three years voyaging around the Mediterranean and the Near East, first as a cabin boy and then before the mast, returning to Gävle in 1818. He was next apprenticed to a builder. Within a year he had moved to Stockholm, still as a builder's apprentice, but there he was able to put his spare time to good advantage, attending classes in architecture and mechanics at the Academy of Art.

Before long he was trying out new techniques, in conjunction with established builders and on his own, experimenting with such novelties as "moveable timber houses" and floating pontoon bridges. He also tried his hand at patenting and manufacturing machine tools of various kinds. Both Immanuel Nobel and his son Alfred were almost obsessively concerned with taking out patents on their inventions, however uncommercial they might seem to be.

Other innovations followed, among them a combined soldier's knapsack, mattress and inflatable lifesaving jacket of elastic rubber. In

1835 Immanuel founded Sweden's first rubber factory for the manufacture of elastic cloths for surgical, military and industrial use.

In 1827 he had married Carolina Andriette Ahlsell, and they had eight children of whom only three, Alfred and his elder brothers Robert and Ludvig, lived beyond the age of twenty-one. In the early days of the marriage, the family lived in extreme poverty, moving from house to house on the outskirts of Stockholm, where the rents were cheapest, always on the brink of disaster and forever burdened with debts.

In addition to his activities as an inventor, Immanuel set himself up in business as a building contractor, and in this he was to prove signally unsuccessful. In 1833, the year that Alfred was born, he went bankrupt and before very long removed himself first to Finland and thence to Russia, partly to escape his creditors and partly because he thought the opportunities there would be greater. He left his family behind in Stockholm, and although he probably sent home whatever money he could spare, for five years the family was supported mainly by the meager earnings of a small dairy and vegetable shop run by Alfred's mother, which was initially financed by sympathetic friends of the family.

Before he left Sweden, Immanuel had tried to interest the Swedish authorities in land and sea mines, which he had invented for the defense of his fatherland since it possessed neither a strong army nor a navy and could not hope to defend itself otherwise. But Sweden was not interested in either device.

On his arrival in St. Petersburg he repeated the demonstrations for the benefit of the Russian military authorities and found them far more receptive. Russia decided to plant a number of mines around the coast, and awarded Immanuel Nobel a sum of money to develop his mines on a factory scale. He acquired a partner and set up an engineering workshop. Here, in addition to land and sea mines, he turned out a well-known lathe—the "wheel-hub cutter, Nobel model"—as well as gun carriages and machine tools of various kinds. Among the other products of this workshop were Russia's first hot-water central-heating pipes, based on another Nobel invention.

In 1842 Immanuel had become sufficiently prosperous to send for his family. They joined him, traveling by ship across the Åland Sea and then by stage coach over very primitive roads from Turku to St. Petersburg.

IN THE MEANTIME, Alfred had been nursed through the first nine years of his life; a weak and sickly child, he was kept alive only by the relentless care and devotion of his mother, a fact which he acknowledged in a poem, written in English, when he was eighteen:

My cradle looked a death bed, and for years
a mother watched with ever anxious care,
so little chance, to save the flickering light.
I scarce could muster strength to drain the breast,
and then convulsions followed, till I gasped
upon the brink of nothingness—my frame
a school for agony with death for goal.

Alfred, quiet and introspective, spent his first eight years in the intensive care of his mother and attended school for only one year, at the age of eight, when he was admitted to first grade in St. Jakob's Higher Apologist School in Stockholm. The following year the move to St. Petersburg took place and he was forced to leave. In Russia all three sons were instructed by a private tutor. Alfred never went back to school and never attended a university. He received no degree of any kind during his whole lifetime, and his tutorial instruction—which must have been very thorough—came to an end when he was sixteen.

By now his father was prospering sufficiently to send his son Alfred abroad, to widen his outlook. The trip lasted two years and included a sojourn in the United States as well as visits to Italy and Germany; but the greater part of his time was spent in Paris, where Alfred studied chemistry, though informally, at some small, unknown laboratory.

On his return to Russia he joined his father and brothers in the engineering workshop which had been expanded yet again and was now known as Fonderies & Ateliers Mécaniques Nobel & Fils.

By this time the Nobels had a house of their own in a fairly fashionable part of St. Petersburg, and Immanuel had paid off his Swedish creditors to the last penny. The young man who rejoined his father's firm had learned a great deal from his journeying abroad where, among other things, he had observed with great interest the flourishing gunpowder industry of Henry Du Pont in the United States.

"It is plain," writes one of his biographers, Professor Henrik Schück, "that Alfred Nobel was already head and shoulders above his age group, both in knowledge and in mental maturity. He was a scientifically trained chemist [this is perhaps overstating the case a bit; one way and another, he had picked up a good working knowledge of chemistry, but he was far from being "scientifically trained"]; he was an excellent linguist with a mastery of German, English and French, as well as Swedish and Russian; he had a strong literary bent . . . and the basic features of his outlook on life were already fully developed. Letters from this period give us a picture of a precocious, intelligent but sickly, dreamy and introspective young man who preferred solitude."

Alfred Nobel in his early twenties

His father, Immanuel

His mother, Carolina Andriette

His elder brothers Robert and Ludvig

His younger brother Emil around the time of his death, aged twenty

When the Crimean War broke out in 1853, Russia's armed forces were in dire need of modernization and wanted all the modern equipment that they could lay their hands on. Large state orders poured into the Fonderies & Ateliers Mécaniques Nobel & Fils, and despite the difficulties of finding skilled labor in what was then a very backward country, Immanuel Nobel and his sons succeeded in turning out vast quantities of war materials, partly to Immanuel's own designs, made with machine tools of his own manufacture in a workshop expanded with borrowed money. Foremen were imported from Sweden, and the Nobel family supervised the whole operation. Components for Russia's first railways, rapid-firing guns and marine engines for the navy's first propellor-driven ships were among the goods turned out, as well as sea mines, which were used to block off the Finnish ports and the entrance to the fortress of Kronstadt, the key to St. Petersburg. Immanuel Nobel—who had been awarded a gold medal for his services to Russian industry—never doubted for a moment that this prosperity would continue indefinitely.

However, with the Treaty of Paris in 1856, the war came to an end and Russia canceled all existing orders, leaving Immanuel Nobel with considerable debts, a vast factory and over one thousand employees with nothing for them to do. The firm was rapidly reorganized to concentrate on marine steam engines, and Immanuel planned and delivered twenty engines for the first regular steamboat services on the Volga River and the Caspian Sea. But this was not enough to stave off disaster. A last-minute effort by Alfred, chosen because of his fluency in foreign languages, to raise money from the bankers of London and Paris proved unfruitful, and in 1859 Immanuel Nobel went bankrupt again. He moved back to Sweden as poor as he had been when he first arrived in Russia. With him were his wife and the only surviving child of three born in Russia, the youngest son Emil, who was to die tragically in 1864.

Alfred and his two elder brothers stayed on in Russia to see what could be salvaged from the factory. Robert and Ludvig appear to have devoted themselves principally to sorting out the firm's finances. Alfred, meanwhile, engaged himself in various mechanical and chemical experiments; while in St. Petersburg he took out three patents: one on a device for measuring gas, another on a new type of liquid measure, and a third on an improved barometer, none of which ever came to anything.

INSTALLED IN STOCKHOLM, Immanuel set up a small laboratory at his home at Heleneborg on the outskirts of the city, where he began to experiment, using nitroglycerin as an explosive. This explosive was not his invention; it had been discovered in 1847 by an Italian, Ascanio Sobrero, and while the Nobels were in St. Petersburg, two Russian scientists, Nikolai Zinin, previously Alfred's tutor, and the pharmacologist Yuli Trapp, had drawn their attention to this new and extremely powerful explosive as a possible material for charging their land and sea mines.

Shortage of money now prevented Immanuel from experimenting on any large scale—which is just as well perhaps, in view of the inherent instability of the material and his own extremely shaky knowledge of scientific matters, chemistry particularly.

In 1861 Alfred was sent to Paris again, to try to raise some money to finance his father's experiments with nitroglycerin; this time he succeeded in persuading the Societé Générale de Crédit Mobilier to lend the family 100,000 francs towards the exploitation of the new explosive. With this capital, Immanuel was able to start manufacture on a factory scale, using Sobrero's formula. By adding 10 percent nitroglycerin to ordinary black gunpowder, he produced what he called a "reinforced blasting powder" which, his biographer Erik Bergengren remarks laconically, "he succeeded sporadically in igniting with portfire, and which he considered excellent both for firearms and rock blasting. Experienced though he was in this field, he had no real scientific training and his efforts to bring about an explosion in a controlled manner were fruitless. In the meantime his family and neighbors lived as though on a volcano."

It was not until Alfred joined him at Heleneborg in 1863 that any useful or practical results were achieved. Before he left Russia, Alfred had himself already been working on the two principal problems connected with nitroglycerin as an explosive. One was the basic instability of the material and the difficulty of transporting this highly explosive oil without solidifying it in some way or another and, in the process, drastically reducing its explosive properties. The other was the difficulty and danger of igniting it.

Alfred had been thinking along completely different lines from his father. Instead of mixing the gunpowder and nitroglycerin, he was experimenting with various methods of using gunpowder as a means of igniting the nitroglycerin. After about fifty carefully controlled experiments in his father's laboratory, he came up with what he called "Nobel's Patent Detonator," a comparatively safe method of exploding nitroglycerin or indeed any high explosive.

His method was to isolate the nitroglycerin in a metal casing or a blocked-up bore hole and then let a smaller charge of gunpowder down into this, in a wooden cap with a fuse attached. When the fuse leading only to the gunpowder was lit, there was time to retire to a safe distance before the gunpowder went off (enough was known about the properties of gunpowder to control an explosion extremely accurately), and this

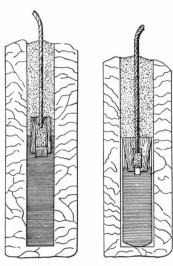

Drawings showing variants of Nobel's Initial Ignition Principle. Instead of attempting to ignite the highly unstable liquid nitroglycerin in the bottom of the casing directly, Nobel used either a metal (left) or a wooden (right) cap filled with ordinary black gunpowder. A slow-burning fuse, leading through noninflammable packing to the cap, gave the operators time to retire to a safe distance before the gunpowder went off, in turn exploding the nitroglycerin around it.

in turn set off the far less predictable and much more dangerous nitroglycerin charge.

Although he patented this system in various countries in 1864 and 1865, Alfred continued to work on it, later substituting a metal cap charged with detonating mercury for the wooden cap charged with black gunpowder. But the basic principle behind it, the so-called initial ignition principle, became standard to the whole technique of explosives and fundamental to all subsequent developments in the field. It was Alfred Nobel's first contribution to the science of explosives. Not only did it make possible the use of nitroglycerin and later even more violent explosives, but it also became possible to produce controlled explosions and to study the explosive properties of the chemicals being tested.

This initial ignition principle has been described as the greatest advance in the science of explosives since the invention of gunpowder." Ragnar Sohlman, Alfred Nobel's assistant during the final years of his life and the author of a book on Nobel's will, wrote: "People in general regard Alfred Nobel chiefly as the inventor of dynamite. But in reality his invention of the blasting cap and the initial ignition of explosives should, from a purely inventive point of view, and as regards technical importance, be placed well ahead of dynamite." And as recently as 1955, in *A History of Research in the Nobel Division of ICI,* F. D. Miles wrote: "The application of the percussion cap to the initiation of blasting explosive, made with a clear perception of the nature of the detonating shock wave, is certainly the greatest discovery ever made in both the principle and practice of explosives. On it the whole of the modern practice of blasting has been built."

This invention could not have come at a more opportune time. The new discoveries made in Europe in the first half of the nineteenth century in chemistry, physics and mechanics were beginning to be applied in a practical way in industry, the building trade and transport. But with the increasing speed of technological advance came an ever-increasing demand for coal and metals of all sorts, which in turn called for improved methods of mining them. At the same time, ambitious new engineering projects were crying out for more effective explosive agents to blast all obstacles out of the path of the pioneering engineers who dreamed of spanning continents with their railroads and cutting canals to connect the oceans. Nobel's discovery seemed, at first glance, to make all this possible; it enabled engineers to use nitroglycerin, by far the most violent and effective explosive the world had seen, with comparative ease and safety.

But however it was ignited, nitroglycerin remained a material that was always potentially hazardous. On September 3, 1864, the Nobel laboratory at Heleneborg was wiped out in an explosion that killed five people, among them Immanuel Nobel's youngest son, Emil; he was only twenty years old and had just matriculated. He had been helping his father and his elder brothers with their experimental work, and was already showing great promise. The disaster caused alarm and concern not only in Stockholm and all over Sweden, but throughout the world among engineers and scientists who had been following Alfred Nobel's innovations with high hopes. It now seemed that these hopes were dashed.

The tragedy deeply affected Immanuel Nobel. He suffered a stroke from which he never recovered; for all practical purposes, he was bedridden until his death, eight years later.

Alfred Nobel, on the other hand, reacted characteristically by immediately organizing a new Swedish company for the development of a nitroglycerin of a less dangerous type, and shortly after that he set up a Norwegian subsidiary. He then went abroad to take out patents on his discoveries and to prepare the way for companies which would later exploit them on a worldwide scale. Thus, despite the accident, and despite a widespread and deep distrust of so volatile a substance, the manufacture of nitroglycerin explosives developed, within a few years, into a world industry. So great became the demand for an effective blasting agent, that engineers were everywhere prepared to run the risk of an accidental explosion if it meant carrying through their projects more rapidly and more economically.

THE ORGANIZATIONAL WORK entailed in taking out patents and establishing companies abroad to exploit his inventions meant that Alfred

However carefully it was handled, nitroglycerin always remained a potentially hazardous material and there were frequent disasters in the Nobel factories. Heleneborg after one such accident in 1863.

Nobel spent most of his time traveling, demonstrating, arguing and promoting. In addition, he continued with his experiments. In fact, at the very time when he was canvassing engineers everywhere and trying to persuade them to adopt nitroglycerin as a solution to their blasting problems, he was working on its successor—an explosive which would have all or most of the power of nitroglycerin, without its fatal instability. But Nobel was a businessman first and foremost; he never flagged in his almost fanatical, if slightly cynical, promotion of nitroglycerin as the perfect explosive, until he had a safer replacement ready for the market.

Despite the tragedy at Heleneborg, in October 1864, after a series of demonstrations Nobel persuaded the construction board of the Swedish State Railways that nitroglycerin manufactured according to his process was far superior to the ordinary black gunpowder they had been using, and relatively safe. It was officially approved and put into use for blasting tunnels in Stockholm. Manufacture on an industrial scale was now essential but, understandably enough, the public reaction to stories about the new explosive made it extremely difficult for him to acquire factory premises or even a site. "No one," as Erik Bergengren put it, "wanted such a neighbor."

But Nobel, again characteristically, found a solution: within a month he was manufacturing his Nobel's Patent Blasting Oil on a covered barge moored in the middle of a lake called Mälaren outside Stockholm.

He next found a backer, a far-sighted and open-minded Stockholm merchant, J. W. Smitt, who had made a fortune in South America and was able to see far beyond the confines of suburban Stockholm. With Smitt, Nobel formed the world's first limited liability company in this field, Nitroglycerin Ltd., and obtained permission to build, on an isolated spot called Vinterviken, a factory which for over fifty years manufactured explosives of all kinds, with a capacity that expanded with every year that passed. Erik Bergengren reports: "Records show that, in the early stages, Nobel was not only the company's managing director but also its works engineer, traveler, advertising manager and treasurer." By now, Nobel's promotional work—and he was among the first manufacturers to use what is now called mail-order advertising to acquaint engineers and other interested parties abroad with the progress of his new industry—was beginning to bear fruit, and more and more firms abroad were making inquiries about the properties and potentialities of the new nitroglycerin blasting oil. It was used successfully to solve one of the biggest engineering problems of the era: the building of the Central Pacific Railroad right across the Sierra Nevada mountains. Nobel's discovery that nitroglycerin could be (comparatively) safely ignited saved millions of dollars for that one corporation alone.

This was a good beginning, but there were plenty of troubles ahead, due not only to the risks inherent in handling such an unstable material, but also to the ignorance of customers and transporters who often didn't bother to read the instructions which accompanied every consignment of the potentially lethal brew. Hair-raising reports of death and destruction were soon pouring in from all over the world. But blasting oil had everywhere proved far more effective and economical than gunpowder, and engineers all over the world were clamoring for it, regardless of the risks involved.

Inevitably there were terrible accidents in warehouses, in factories and on the engineering sites. Lives were lost and both the public and the authorities began to demand stricter controls. Several countries banned its import altogether.

The problems were indeed formidable. By now Nobel had another flourishing factory at Krümmel in Germany from which he could readily export supplies of nitroglycerin via the port of Hamburg. To send it by ship direct from Hamburg across the Atlantic was simple and safe enough, but to get it out to San Francisco or to the Midwest involved appalling risks. The cargo could, of course, go all the way by sea, around Cape Horn and all the way up the western coast of South America, but that was

A barge moored in the middle of Lake Malaren near Stockholm was, for a time, the only factory Nobel was allowed to use.

painfully slow. If it was sent via the Caribbean to the east coast of the Isthmus of Panama—there was no canal in those days—it had to be unloaded and reloaded onto small wagons, to be carted over the bumpy jungle roads right across the isthmus to the western coast, there to be loaded onto another ship for transport up the Pacific Coast.

Not surprisingly, the native laborers who were employed to handle the material in transit had no inkling of its true nature, and the most terrifying episodes were reported. There were tales of nitroglycerin—which looked very much like any other oil—being used as lamp oil, or to grease the axles of a covered wagon ("This," remarks Bergengren, still as deadpan as ever, "was seldom done more than once by the same person.") Nobel himself reported that he once had to deal with a drum of nitroglycerin that was frozen into the snow, and that he *dug it out* with a joiner's adze, remarking that he suffered from a bad headache after the operation. On another occasion, he wrote, "We got a message from the stationmaster to go down to the railway station to see one of the drums of nitroglycerin that was leaking. The stationmaster was told to turn the drum up on its end and we would be down to see about it in the morning. When we arrived next day, the stationmaster said: 'It was leaking so badly that I could not wait till you came so I just got the local plumber to put a patch on it.' " There was also, naturally, frantic opposition to the new blasting oil from the big American gunpowder manufacturing combines, notably the firm of Du Pont de Nemours of Wilmington, Delaware, who saw their markets menaced at what for them was their big boom period. It was very easy for Henry Du Pont, with his tremendous political power, to point to all the accidents that had happened and to tell the press, again and again, that if a man chose to use nitroglycerin, it was only a matter of time until he would lose his life.

Nevertheless, in spite of all the accidents and all the opposition, Alfred

Nobel—who knew very well how dangerous his invention was and who was working against the clock to produce a safer and more stable blasting agent to replace it—managed to found a company in America with New York shareholders, known as the United States Blasting Oil Company. After many vicissitudes this developed into the Giant Powder Company with a factory in California that could supply the Californian market locally, instead of having to import the material all the way from Krümmel in Germany, as previously. The name was taken from the nickname given to the new explosives by the Californian goldminers—"Giant Powder"—though most of the explosives were not powders at all. Later an Atlantic Giant Powder Company was formed to meet New York's needs.

Clandestine manufacturers were another big worry for Nobel. The new, powerful explosives were so urgently needed for tunneling, building, mining, quarrying and road building, that the official channels could not supply the engineers' needs. There was no shortage of pirate manufacturers prepared to turn out an approximation of Nobel's blasting oil. The pirated versions were often even more hazardous than his own, and did nothing at all for the reputation of the new explosive.

THEN CAME ANOTHER blow. In 1866, while Alfred Nobel was in New York publicizing the virtues of his new "safe" nitrogylcerin, his factory at Krümmel was destroyed, with the loss of many lives—how many, nobody seems to know as the records have disappeared. The situation suddenly became critical; despite the ever-increasing demand for nitroglycerin, there was a continuous clamor in the press about the intolerable accidents associated with its manufacture, transportation and use, and more and more governments were being pressed by public opinion to ban it altogether. As usual, Nobel was prepared.

"As early as 1863," he wrote, "I was fully aware of the disadvantages of nitroglycerin in its fluid form." All the time he had been busy promoting and selling nitroglycerin, he had been equally busy experimenting with ways of making it more stable and less dangerous, without substantially lessening its destructive power.

He had tried mixing it with black gunpowder, as his father had done, with gun cotton and paper powder, and later had had the idea of allowing it to be absorbed in a highly porous, nonexplosive substance which would not have any effect on the character of the nitroglycerin. He tried porous silica, paper, paper pulp, wood waste, brick dust, coal, dry clay and gypsum. Finally he settled for kieselguhr, a natural, inert, infusorial earth found in large quantities in various parts of the world. Kieselguhr is almost completely lacking in chemical reactivity and is extremely porous. He found that three parts of nitroglycerin absorbed into one part of calcined and sifted kieselguhr produced a solid, plastic explosive, roughly 25 percent less effective than pure nitroglycerin, but much easier and safer to handle and transport.

He called it "dynamite," after the Greek *dynamis*, meaning power. Like the initial ignition principle, this latter invention in turn formed the basis of all future explosives until the arrival of the atomic bomb.

From a makeshift laboratory constructed among the ruins of the Krümmel factory, during a period of extreme nervous strain, Nobel, now thirty years of age, had given the world an engineering tool of the utmost importance. Vast, hitherto unthinkable enterprises in the field of mining, industry, transportation and communications could now be safely carried out. Some examples of the gigantic projects undertaken even during his own lifetime include the nineteen-mile railway tunnel between Andermatt and Airolo in the Alps, built between 1872 and 1882; the clearing of the Danube at the Iron Gates between 1890 and 1896; the 295-foot-deep, four-mile-long channel of the Corinth Canal in Greece, built between 1881 and 1893; and the removal of the underwater Hellgate rocks in New York harbor.

Guhr dynamite, as it was then commonly known, increased in popularity with every passing month, despite the natural conservatism of many mining engineers who were prepared to risk the hazards of nitroglycerin in blasting-oil form because it was cheaper and more destructive. There were also difficulties about obtaining patents on a material which, once discovered, could very easily be imitated with slight variations, a problem that was to dog Nobel all his life. The many close copies of his kieselguhr dynamite meant that he was drawn into a number of complicated negotiations with lawyers.

Nobel's invention of dynamite led the Royal Swedish Academy of Sciences to recognize the achievements of the Nobel family. In 1868 Immanuel and Alfred Nobel were jointly awarded the academy's Letterstedt Gold Medal, for "outstanding original work in the realm of art, literature or science, or for important discoveries of practical value to mankind." Immanuel was cited "for his services in connection with the use of nitroglycerin as an explosive in general," and Alfred "more particularly for the invention of dynamite." Immanuel died four years later, in 1872.

Ascanio Sobrero, the Italian who actually discovered nitro-glycerin—though not in a form in which it could be put to any practical use—was overlooked by the Swedish Academy of Sciences, but Alfred acknowledged the Nobels' debt to him. He engaged Sobrero as

Nobel's dynamite made possible such engineering projects as the cutting of the Corinth Canal in Greece and the clearing of the Danube River at the Iron Gates. Dynamite could also be used for underwater explosions, such as the removal of the notoriously dangerous Hellgate rocks that blocked New York Harbor, shown in the drawing above. Below: a contemporary artist's impression of the Hellgate explosion.

adviser to his Swiss-Italian subsidiary, a sinecure of a post in which the Italian scientist enjoyed a good salary until his death.

NOBEL WAS FOREVER traveling and spent long periods abroad, more in fact than he ever spent at home. Not that he had a home, at first. A complete cosmopolitan, he once remarked, "my homeland is wherever I'm working, and I work everywhere." Between 1865 and 1873 while he was peddling his products, his laboratory and the focal point of his business was in Germany. But by 1873 things were going smoothly enough for the forty-year-old Nobel to leave Krümmel for good and settle down—to the extent that he ever settled down anywhere—in Paris, where he bought an elegant mansion in the Avenue Malakoff not far from the Place d'Etoile.

In addition to his factories at Vinterviken, Sweden, and Krümmel (twice demolished by terrible explosions: in 1866, as we have seen, and again in 1870), Nobel now had factories at Ardeer in Scotland; subsidiaries in South Africa, Australia, East Asia and South America; and interests in firms in Japan and Belgium. He had formed an association in France with the firm Barbe, Père et Fils et Cie. On the outbreak of the Franco-Prussian War of 1870-71, when the French generals discovered to their horror that the Germans were using the dynamite they had previously scorned to blow up French forts and villages, Barbe, Père et Fils et Cie soon acquired contracts to produce all the dynamite needed for the French war effort. Nobel also established plants in Norway, the United States, Austria, Finland, Spain, Switzerland, Portugal and what is now Czechoslovakia.

America went crazy over dynamite. It was adopted like any other new fad or discovery and was tried out on a fantastic range of projects: as part of a new humane killer for the meat industry, at one end of the scale; and as a rain-making device, at the other. In New York a severe drought in the late 1880s was brought to an end by exploding two hundred pounds of dynamite, slung from a balloon over the city; in Texas a series of dynamite explosions at ten-minute intervals resulted in "a sharp clap of thunder followed by heavy rain."

Dynamite had "arrived"—and Alfred Nobel made a fortune from it.

The Lonely Millionaire

ALFRED NOBEL'S HOUSE in the Avenue Malakoff was lavishly but not ostentatiously furnished and decorated in the style of the period. It had very handsome reception rooms, a winter garden with hothouses for his orchids and stables for his carriage horses.

The house also had a small laboratory where he worked, between trips abroad, to improve on his earlier discoveries, particularly kieselguhr dynamite. Despite its huge worldwide success, dynamite had, as he was very well aware, some serious weaknesses. The inert kieselguhr reduced the explosive power of the nitroglycerin by roughly one-quarter, and there was a dangerous tendency for the liquid nitroglycerin to be exuded from the guhr in certain circumstances—in conditions of extreme pressure or moisture, for example. What he was really looking for was an explosive combining the power of pure nitroglycerin—which was still being used in certain mines where the recalcitrant nature of the rock called for an exceptionally powerful explosive—with the safe and easy-handling properties of dynamite.

In 1875, in his private laboratory, he found the answer: blasting gelatin, or gelignite. This was a colloidal solution of nitrocellulose (gun cotton) in nitroglycerin. He had earlier considered the possibility of using gun cotton, but its power to absorb nitroglycerin proved negligible. Then one day while working in his laboratory, he happened to cut his finger and applied collodion. During the night he couldn't sleep because his finger was aching, and he began to ponder the possibilities of using nitrocellulose of a lower degree of nitration—the very kind present in the collodion he had put on his finger, in fact. He got out of bed at four o'clock in the morning and set to work. By the time his laboratory assistant, Georges Fehrenbach, arrived at nine o'clock, he was ready to demonstrate the first blasting gelatin, soon like all his other inventions to be patented.

The idea of combining the two most powerful explosives then known to man aroused great interest among scientists. Gelignite proved to be the ideal explosive for civil-engineering purposes: it was slightly more powerful than pure nitroglycerin; more or less insensitive to shock; strongly resistant to moisture and even to water, which meant that it could be more effectively used for submarine blasting; and its production costs could be kept comparatively low.

Gelignite—also put on the market under various other names such as Nobel's extra dynamite, express dynamite, blasting gelatin and saxonite—was an instantaneous success, and in the year of its discovery was being made in most of Nobel's factories. Only Great Britain, which had a very restrictive explosives legislation, hesitated a long time. Nobel's biggest factory, at Ardeer in Scotland—later to become the nucleus of Imperial Chemical Industries (ICI)—had to wait for a manufacturing license until 1884 when Frederick Abel, the eminent English professor of chemistry, pronounced it "in every respect the most perfect explosive known."

THE NOBELS WERE an extraordinary family. While Alfred was developing dynamite, and subsequently gelignite, his two elder brothers, Robert and Ludvig, who had stayed on in Russia to salvage what they could of Immanuel's business, now had their own flourishing armament industry. Ludvig's gun and rifle factory kept the imperial Russian armies supplied with small arms during the reigns of Alexander II and III, and provided the capital necessary for his brother Robert to develop an oil refinery at Baku, on the Caspian Sea, where he had taken out concessions on what turned out to be an apparently inexhaustible source of crude oil. The Nobel company was soon incomparably the biggest firm operating that oil field, drilling 50 percent of the total oil and employing 7,000 workers.

Paraffin, oil, petroleum and all the by-products of naptha were produced from the crude oil. The machinery necessary for all the operations involved, as well as the chemicals used in the various refining processes, were all produced on the site. The company also built its own gas- and electricity-generating stations, engineering shops and laboratories. Pipes made on the oil field were soon carrying the oil overland to Swedish-built tankers, the first in the world, plying the River Volga and the Caspian and Black seas as early as 1878.

Curiously enough, no nitroglycerin or dynamite factory was built in Russia during the brothers' lifetime. One possible explanation is that Ludvig Nobel held the general agency for his brother's explosives in Russia, and he imported these, at a considerable profit both to himself and to Alfred, not only for his own use on the oil fields but also on behalf of the imperial Russian government.

Ludvig Nobel lectured on explosives and demonstrated dynamite all over Russia and was largely responsible for its adoption there, despite some initial opposition from the government, who feared a repetition of the American accidents, especially since it would have to be transported over vast distances in a backward country with few serviceable roads.

For a few years around the turn of the century, the Nobel oil production at Baku exceeded that of the whole United States, and the Russian-based branch of the family became very rich indeed. Their empire, however, tottered with that of the Romanoffs in 1918. When the last tsar abdicated, all the Nobel enterprises were confiscated and nationalized by the Communists. The remaining members of the family were forced to leave everything behind them and flee the country.

IN THE MEANTIME, Alfred was again continuing with his experiments. In the 1880s, several European governments were looking around for a new explosive to replace the ordinary black gunpowder which had been the standard military explosive for five hundred years—and indeed the only known explosive of any practical value until Nobel's nitroglycerin.

Very little is known about the discovery of gunpowder. From ancient times, as early as 500 B.C., inflammable materials were used in warfare; "fire and the sword" was no empty cliché. A device known as "Greek fire" had featured in the defense of Byzantium against the Turks; it was probably based on an inflammable liquid distillate from coal tar or even wood. There were probably a number of different versions of Greek fire, and it was the Chinese who discovered, around the eleventh century, that it would burn even more fiercely if saltpeter were added.

Saltpeter gives off oxygen when it is heated, and the oxygen it creates is in turn ignited, augmenting the sum total of heat produced. But it does more; because it releases oxygen, saltpeter in conjunction with other inflammable materials can be made to burn without air. This in turn means that it can be burned in a confined space, such as the breech of a gun, where the hot air soon builds up a tremendous pressure and eventually causes an explosion. It is not known when the right mixture for creating such an explosion was stumbled upon, but Roger Bacon, in the thirteenth century, was able to describe a gunpowder which hardly differed at all from the gunpowder in use until the end of the nineteenth century—a mixture of saltpeter, sulfur and charcoal.

Artillery came into being around the thirteenth century and Crécy was probably the first European battle in which it was used on a large scale. Initially, gunpowder was not very successful, whether used in cannons or in light arms, such as the earliest forms of musket like the matchlock

71266

FERNALD LIBRARY
COLBY-SAWYER COLLEGE
NEW LONDON, N. H. 03257

arquebus. The trouble with it so far as artillery was concerned, was that the breech of the gun could not always be counted upon to contain the force of the explosion. When it was contained, the missile shot out of the barrel—but never very fast, nor very far. If it wasn't contained, the gun went up like a monster grenade and wiped out the entire gun crew.

The principal trouble with the musket in all its early versions was that it took a terribly long time to reload. In his heyday the British archer could dispatch some fifteen arrows per minute with his longbow; it was this high-speed delivery which had given him such an immense superiority over his continental opponents, armed with the theoretically more lethal, but far more cumbersome crossbow. When the British army replaced the longbow with the earliest form of musket, the rate of fire went down to one soft bullet every quarter-hour or so, if all went well. During the time that the musketeer was reloading—painfully slowly, step by step, on the instructions of an officer—he was extremely vulnerable and had to be protected by the cavalry and the pikemen. In addition, the early muskets were highly inaccurate and the bullets traveled so slowly that almost any form of light armor was protection enough against them.

In time, of course, muskets and cannons were greatly improved in design and construction: they all became far more accurate, delivered their missiles at a much greater velocity and the cannons rarely if ever exploded in the face of their crews. But in one respect they hadn't improved at all: they all made smoke, and lots of it.

"One hazard often overlooked," writes Jock Haswell in *The British Army*, ". . . was smoke. Depending on the strength of the wind, battlefields were usually shrouded in a thick, choking pall of smoke from the black powder used in every firearm, and . . . it was almost impossible for a soldier to see the effect of his fire or a commander to see what was happening. . . ."

WHAT WAS THUS desperately required was a smokeless explosive powder. Only this would enable the heavy artillery to keep up a prolonged, heavy and accurate bombardment, the sort of bombardment that was perhaps the most dreaded feature of the fighting in Flanders and on the whole Western Front during World War I. And it was Alfred Nobel—the inventor of gelignite, the perfect explosive for civil-engineering purposes—who now set out, deliberately and determinedly, to perfect the smokeless or near-smokeless high explosive that, in the aftermath of the Franco-Prussian War, was in such urgent demand among the war-mongering nations of Europe. In 1887 he produced it—ballistite: equal parts of nitroglycerin and nitrocellulose with 10 percent camphor, celluloid as a rule—and immediately all the horrors of modern "conventional" warfare became possible. (I put "conventional" in quotation marks because it seems to me such a tame word to use for something so horrific.)

Nobel's new military explosive had a great many advantages apart from the fact that it was virtually smokeless: it was far more powerful than ordinary gunpowder; it left no deposit; it could be stored indefinitely; and it was cheap to manufacture. It was available, too, in a plastic form: the mixture could be passed between hot rollers and compressed, under heat, into string, tube shapes or various other forms.

Because he was living mainly in France at this juncture, Nobel offered his invention to the French gunpowder monopoly, l'Administration des Poudres et Saltpetres, but they rejected it on the grounds that P. M. E. Vieille, a French professor of chemistry, working on completely different principles, had discovered another near-smokeless powder, which they had already accepted. Nobel went elsewhere with his wares, and the first country to accept ballistite was Italy.

Immediately there was a storm of protest in the French press against Nobel. He was, of course, in a somewhat delicate position. He was living in Paris and carrying out his experiments in his laboratory in the Avenue Malakoff—not all that far, as it happens, from the research laboratories of the French gunpowder monoply. More to the point, he was selling a new and powerful war weapon to a foreign power. He was accused of stealing secrets from the monopoly's research laboratories and threatened with imprisonment. His laboratory was broken into and ransacked; his licenses for firearms and experiments were withdrawn; the Nobel factory at Honfleur was forbidden to manufacture ballistite; and all his test stocks were confiscated.

As a consequence of this harrassment, Nobel decided to quit the country where he had lived for eighteen years—the nearest he ever came to having a permanent home anywhere, in fact—and leaving his house in the Avenue Malakoff exactly as it was, he moved to Italy in 1891, taking with him only whatever scientific equipment had not been seized. He bought a villa in San Remo on the Italian Riviera; it had a large park around it and was situated in an orange grove overlooking the Mediterranean. It had been called *Mio Nido,* but when someone pointed out to Nobel that "My Nest" was a singularly inappropriate title for a house belonging to a fifty-eight-year-old man who had never displayed even the slightest intention of nesting, he changed it to Villa Nobel, a name the house bears to this day.

IT WAS NOT ALTOGETHER true that Nobel had shown no signs of nesting; in fact, at this period of his life he was going through a particularly bad time, emotionally. He had begun to regard Paris as his permanent home, and the dispute with the French authorities upset him dreadfully. His brother Ludvig had died in 1888, and his mother the following year.

But the real cause of his blues—which he referred to as "visits from the spirits of Niflheim"—was the termination of the only long-term love affair of his life, a sad and often sordid entanglement with a Viennese flowergirl, young enough to be his daughter.

In the autumn of 1876, when he had been on a business trip to Austria, the forty-three-year-old millionaire-inventor met Sophie Hess, a petite, twenty-year-old beauty of Jewish extraction from a lower-class home in Vienna, from which she had fled to escape an unkind stepmother.

Previously, Nobel had been on remotely close terms with only two women: his beloved mother and Bertha von Suttner, who in the same year, 1876, as Countess Bertha Kinsky, applied for a job as his secretary and then left after a very short period to get married.

There may, in fact, have been a third woman before Sophie. In one of the few books about Nobel, Michael Evlanoff and Marjorie Fluor's *Alfred Nobel: The Loneliest Millionaire,* there is a reference to another, earlier tragic love affair. It occurred at the height of the Second Empire of Napoleon III and his dazzling Spanish Empress Eugénie, they say, when Paris was full of finery and riches from all over the world—oriental silks, Brussels laces, Maltese fringes, Irish linens, Paisley shawls, ladies fluttering by in crinolines with bare shoulders, curls cascading down flushed cheeks among fluttering fans and dainty nosegays, as laughing gentlemen followed them in nipped-in tail coats, satin vests and pointed shoes of soft kid leather. Having set this voluptuous and glamorous scene, the authors go on to recount how Nobel, dressed in somber colors was watching the passing show with gloomy disdain when a charming young girl addressed him, asking whether Monsieur had just lost someone dear to him.

The fragile girl, more simply dressed than all the others of her age and wealth, had, we are told, pale gold hair that fell in ringlets around her shoulders. This gave her a natural loveliness which in Nobel's eyes made her more dazzling than all the sophisticated beauties about her.

He answered—and I quote—"with the melancholy statement that his loss was greater than the loss of one dear to him. He had lost his dreams and illusions."

Not put off by this, as a more modern girl would have been, the authors tell us, she showed him a delicate and tender concern. They found a quiet place where they could talk together and Alfred, all his restraints swept away by her gentle probing into what distressed him, confided to her all the miseries of his young life. He told her of his loneliness, of how he mistrusted the motives of the people he met, of his feeling that he would never find the happiness he yearned for. The girl was convinced that life could be a good and wonderful experience. She had faith in the gifts life offered those who would reach out and seize them. She encouraged him to take full advantage of his mind and make his mark on the world.

They seem to have been together until dawn, according to the authors, and Alfred later wrote that he "had become a supremely happy and better man" and that "they had sealed their love with a chaste and hallowed kiss."

In the weeks that followed, Nobel, they say, saw a good deal of the girl and knew he had found the love he cherished and wanted—this was the kind of "noble" love that appealed to him. Then the girl died suddenly.

From the fact that no account of this affair appears in any of the other books on Nobel, and from the general tone of the writing—not to mention that details are included which the authors couldn't possibly have known unless they heard them from Nobel or got them from a letter or diary which nobody else seems to have seen, I was inclined to discount the whole story as a romantic fiction. But when in Stockholm I discussed it with a staff member of the Nobel Institute, who told me that whether the details were accurate or not, it was always understood within the Nobel family that there had been such a tragic love affair in Nobel's youth.

If so, it may explain his sudden infatuation at the age of forty-three with fraulein Sophie Hess. His relationship with Sophie was a classic story: the innocent, almost naive, high-minded millionaire-scientist, and the lazy, worthless, grasping good-time girl, who was prepared—for a time anyway—to forego the company of men her own age for the sake of the money, clothes and position in society that Nobel could offer her.

After two years of repeated visits to Vienna, Nobel installed his Sofiechen—later known as "The Troll" in his correspondence and, above all, his accounts—in a fine apartment in Paris, not far from his house in the Avenue Malakoff. There she had every luxury that even her insatiable appetites could demand. She was, however, bored during his frequent absences, and as time went by she became more and more rapacious, not only on her own behalf but on the part of her impoverished and grasping parents. Alfred's brother Ludvig warned him about the woman and urged him to break it off.

Not content with Paris, she began to frequent the fashionable watering places of Europe, traveling as Madame Nobel, where she was now seen with a string of young and handsome admirers. Nobel paid for her hats and her furs, her carriages and jewels, and all her hotel bills; he even bought her a villa in Ischl, the Austrian health resort. His letters to Sophie are all sweetness and light, and he leaned over backwards to avoid censuring her. Only to his private cashbook did he confide his real feelings in entries like: "Hats, the Troll, 300 francs; Wine, the Troll, 600 francs."

Year after year, as her behavior grew increasingly outrageous and intolerable, he continued to humor her. He provided her with a French companion, and introduced her to his circle of acquaintances in Paris—among them the writer Victor Hugo—and tried, not very successfully, to bring her into the Nobel family circle.

From time to time, with an inconsistency that often characterizes such affairs, he exhorted her to leave him and find someone her own age (in fact she was having no difficulty at all in finding young men). "Try to win the sincere, lasting and deep affection of a simple, upright man and unite with him in the true and genuine ties of family which cannot be associated with a warped relationship," he wrote. And again, later: "My whole life turns to bitter gall when I am forced to act the nanny to a grown-up child and be the butt of all my acquaintances."

But the woman who was to have been the hoped-for life companion had turned into a costly and embarrassing encumbrance. He continued to support her generously, even after he had moved to San Remo, but visited her very seldom. She moved in gay, fast circles where he felt distinctly uncomfortable, and everywhere she went she ran up vast debts in his name.

Then the inevitable happened: in the spring of 1891 he received a letter from her telling him that she was pregnant; the father was a young Hungarian officer. Nobel immediately gave her a very considerable annuity.

Sophie's marriage was only a matter of form. She never lived with her husband, but continued her former life, even after the child, a daughter, was born; and the two of them, husband and wife, proceeded in their different ways, to extort large sums of money from Nobel until his death. Indeed, even after his death she would not let him be, threatening to sell for publication the 216 love letters he had written to her if she were not given more money than the will had stipulated. The executors bought the letters from her on conditions that precluded publication and safeguarded them from any further blackmail threats.

ANOTHER OF NOBEL'S worries at this period of his life—shortly after he had moved down to San Remo—was the British cordite lawsuit.

As we have seen, scientists in many parts of the world had been searching for a smokeless explosive and had been exchanging information on their discoveries in the normal way. For about ten years Nobel had been swapping technical information of all sorts with Professor Frederick

Abel, the British scientist, and Professor James Dewar, a Scottish physicist and close friend of Abel.

In 1888 the British government appointed an explosives commission "to investigate new discoveries, especially such as affected the use of military explosives and to submit to the War Office proposals for the introduction of any technical improvements in the field that the commission could recommend." Among the members of this commission were Professors Abel and Dewar, and on its behalf they immediately got in touch with Nobel and requested him to give the commission, confidentially, the fullest possible information about his new invention of ballistite and the history of its development.

Convinced that the commission, when it had the facts, would recommend ballistite to the War Office, Nobel sent off full details of the substance and the process by which it was manufactured. Armed with this information, Professors Abel and Dewar now proceeded to vary the formula slightly and produce their own form of ballistite, which was pressed out into the form of cords and was consequently known as cordite. This they immediately patented in England and several other countries, and then persuaded the other members of the commission to recommend its exclusive use in the British Army and Navy. The Nobel company saw this as a breach of their patent and protested, but to no avail, and the matter was taken to court.

The action was heard in the Chancery Division in 1892 and was later submitted both to the Court of Appeal and to the Lords in 1895. All these courts overruled the company's and Nobel's claims for damages, and the plaintiff, Nobel's explosives company, had to pay the costs, which amounted to over $695,685 (in today's terms). A certain vagueness in the wording of the original letters of patent proved his undoing since it could be interpreted in a number of ways.

The loss of the money worried Nobel far less than the feeling that Abel and Dewar had betrayed his trust. He was morally vindicated, however, when one of the judges, Lord Justice Key, said that he was forced on purely legal grounds to agree with his two colleagues on the bench in overruling the plaintiff's case, but added: "It is quite obvious that a dwarf who has been allowed to climb up the back of a giant can see further than the giant himself. . . . In this case I cannot but sympathize with the holder of the original patent. Mr. Nobel made a great invention, which in theory was something extraordinary, a really great innovation—and then two clever chemists got hold of his specifications for the patent, read them carefully, and after that, with the aid of their own thorough knowledge of chemistry, discovered that they could use practically the same substances with a difference as to one of them, and produce the same results. . . .

Nobel relieved his feelings by writing a parody of the lawsuit called *The Patent Bacillus,* poking fun at justice and the law generally and mentioning the cordite suit specifically, but without naming any names; it was not published and the only copy is in his own hand. In a letter he commented: "I can afford to be indifferent to the pecuniary side of the case, but I cannot get over my intense disgust with the shabbiness displayed."

Nobel's ballistite was adopted in Italy, the Austro-Hungarian Empire, Germany, Norway and Sweden. England, Japan and some South American states took cordite, while France, Russia and the United States preferred the French "Poudre B" based on Vieille's discovery. From the countries which adopted ballistite, Nobel received considerable sums of money in license fees for several years, and his English company soon began to produce cordite as well as ballistite, both for the United Kingdom and for export; in fact, to use the current expression, he had the whole explosives business so neatly sewn up that he stood to profit whatever happened.

BUT THE EVENTS of a hectic life were beginning to show their effects on Nobel, now sixty and living in San Remo. In 1893 he engaged as his assistant a twenty-three-year-old Swedish explosives chemist, Ragnar Sohlman, who had just returned from the United States. This proved to be a very important step; not only did Sohlman become one of Nobel's closest friends during the final years of his life, but he was later to be chief executor of the will.

Nobel's final discovery in the long series of blasting powders and high explosives that he had been working on all his life was what he called a *"progressive* smokeless powder." It was a further development of ballistite, made in his laboratory at San Remo, with the object of increasing the muzzle velocity of projectiles without increasing the maximum pressure within the breach of a gun. He achieved this by inducing a progressive increase in the rate of burning of the powder, so that the pressure was evenly maintained as the projectile moved along the barrel. This progressive powder—which had no function at all, other than in connection with armaments— was manufactured and tested at several of the Nobel factories.

At this period of his life, from the late 1880s onwards, Alfred Nobel was increasingly involved with improvements in the performance of firearms. He told Sohlman and others that this particular field of study interested him chiefly as an intellectual problem and maintained that he was, nevertheless, implacably opposed to the practical use of such inventions. "For my part," he wrote, "I wish all guns with their belongings and

Nobel's villa at San Remo on the Italian Riviera.

The lonely millionaire at San Remo.

The iron jetty Nobel built at San Remo to conduct his experiments with new explosives; these activities were highly unpopular with his neighbors who had come to the Riviera for peace and quiet.

everything could be sent to hell, which is the proper place for their exhibition and use." At the same time, he continued to work on experiments which resulted in many "improvements" in the realm of armaments, such as a fuse cord containing nitroglycerin and a series of silent-firing rifles and guns of all sorts. He also invented a new type of rocket for rescue at sea.

He was, moreover, working on various substitutes for rubber, gutta-percha and leather made from raw materials closely related to the manufacture of explosives; he developed a varnish based on nitroglycerin in various solvents and pioneered some of the ingredients which are the basis of today's paints and varnishes of the nitrocellulose type. His work in these fields stimulated the manufacture of artificial rubber and leather as well as artificial silk, or rayon. Artificial silk goods have been made since the beginning of this century in Germany, Great Britain, Italy and France. Nobel's companies were associated with many of these enterprises, and in the early days of the development of artificial silk, he had assisted both with ideas and capital.

Nobel had also interested himself in experiments for the improvement of what was then known as the gramophone or phonograph, the telephone, electric batteries, incandescent lamps and even the synthetic production of precious and semiprecious stones from fused alumina.

He was also keenly interested in the prospects and possibilities of flying. In 1896 he helped to finance the attempt by the Swedish balloonist A. A. Andrée to reach the North Pole in a dirigible. But even as early as that, he foresaw that the future of flight lay, not in the direction of balloons and airships, but in the development of a rapid propellor-driven, heavier-than-air machine. In 1892, ten years before the Wright brothers' first flight at Kitty Hawk, he had written: "Aviation excites me, but we must not think of solving this problem by means of balloons. Once a bird has attained high speed, it is able to overcome gravity by only a slight movement of its wings. It is not done by magic. What a bird can do, man can do. We have to have floating rafts driven forward at great speed. . . ."

He even foresaw man's future preoccupation with the atom. "Since electricity," he wrote, "and in its wake, thought, circle the earth in a quarter of a second, I have acquired a sublime contempt for the paltry dimensions of our globe, and take the most interest in a much smaller world body, namely the atom. . . . Its form, movements and destinies, both as an individual and as a contributing cell in the life of the universe, occupy my thoughts more than they decently ought to."

"If I have a thousand ideas a year," he once said, "and only one turns out to be good, I'm satisfied."

IN THE EARLY 1890s Nobel began to think about returning to his homeland, where he had had no fixed abode since he emigrated in 1842 at the age of nine, with the exception of one brief period in 1863-64 when he was experimenting at Heleneborg.

There were several reasons for this decision. San Remo, though very beneficial to his health, had many disadvantages. All the apparatus and chemicals he required for his experiments, right down to the smallest and most elementary accessories, had to be imported from Germany. Local workmen with the necessary skill were unobtainable, and there were—not unnaturally—endless complaints from his wealthy neighbors about the constant explosions which shattered the peace of their idyllic coastline, as he conducted his tests on the end of a jetty built for the purpose. It was becoming more difficult for Nobel to find anywhere to go. He wouldn't go to England because of the bitterness he still felt about the cordite law suit; nor to France because of his conflicts with the French powder monopoly. He didn't like Wilhelm II's Germany because of its internal political unrest and its arrogant militarism. Eventually he decided it was time to return home.

However, instead of buying or building a mansion as most other multimillionaires would have done, he bought an industry: the A. B. Bofors-Gullspång Company, with its famous ironworks and munitions factory at Bofors in Varmland. He acquired an adjacent manor house at Björneborg in Varmland, where he proposed to continue the development of the blast furnaces, steel works and rolling mills already there. Sohlman was put in charge of his new Swedish operations.

Next he purchased a nearby waterfall at Karås so that he could exploit the possibilities of hydroelectric power, today Sweden's most vital source of energy, but then only in its experimental stage.

Nobel's health was not good—it had never been robust—and he found the harsh northern climate far too much for him after his Mediterranean sojourn. As a result, he only visited and personally directed this new group of factories during the summer and autumn months of the next few years, which were to be his last; the winter and early spring he always spent in Italy. The only relaxation the aging Nobel allowed himself was an occasional outing in his small, light carriage, drawn by two spirited Orloff stallions. He had equipped the wheels with rubber bands—another innovation—so that the only sound that could be heard was the clatter of the horses' hooves. He had also fitted up a telephone so that he could communicate with the coachman from the interior of his coupé, which was lit by electricity from accumulators. As one Swedish newspaper put it: "Thus the Lord of Dynamite sped along . . . [his] equipage flying silently through the dark, blazing with light. . . ."

The manor at Björkborn, Sweden, which Nobel rented towards the end of his life.

The exterior of his last laboratory at Björkborn.

There seems to be some evidence that Nobel's conscience troubled him a bit about the purchase of the Bofors armaments factory. "If there is one branch of industry which should be entirely independent of supplies from abroad," he wrote defensively, "then that is manifestly the defense branch, and as there are munitions factories in Sweden it is both pitiful and absurd not to keep them going. . . . *We accept orders so as to live,* but our aim is to create, and not to walk in our great-grandfather's footsteps." The italics are mine; for a man as rich as Nobel to talk about "accepting orders so as to live" is manifestly absurd and can only be an attempt to justify the fact that he was fully aware that a large proportion of the output of the Bofors factory was being sold to belligerent nations with no thought of defense in their heads.

Nobel spent his last summer and autumn, in 1896, in Sweden with Sohlman, directing the extensive modernization of the plants at Björkborn and Bofors. He seemed, in the process, to regain some of his old energy. Then in September his elder brother Robert, who had retired from Russia to Sweden many years earlier, died. Alfred again began to suffer from "repeated visits from the spirits of Niflheim"—severe attacks of migraine and vascular cramp—and went to Paris to consult specialists. He was informed that he had acute angina pectoris and that he must have absolute rest. In fact, in veiled words, he was being warned that it was time to put his affairs in order.

HIS LAST WILL and testament, in the form known to the world, had already been drawn up in 1895, during an earlier bout of illness. It had superseded two earlier versions and had been deposited in a bank in Stockholm, the city of his birth; but he discussed it again in detail with his nephew Emanuel, Ludvig's son, who was now head of the Naphtha Company of St. Petersburg and happened to be on a business trip to Paris at the time.

Despite the verdict of the specialists, it does not seem that Nobel's thoughts were unduly concerned with death at this period; he personally supervised the details of a villa for the Sohlman family which was then under construction in the park of his villa at San Remo, and while in Paris he sold his three San Remo carriage horses and bought new ones, with elegant trappings, to replace them.

He returned to San Remo from Paris but continued to correspond with Sohlman almost daily on the most minute details of the Bofors operation. In one letter he casually remarked: "It sounds like an irony of fate that I should be ordered to take nitroglycerin internally. They call it trinitin, so as not to scare the pharmacists and the public."

His final letter, also addressed to Sohlman, is dated December 7, 1896, at San Remo, where he had arrived a fortnight earlier. It deals with technical matters about yet another new nitroglycerin blasting powder which he was working on, and ends: "Unfortunately my health is again so poor that it is with difficulty I write these lines, but as soon as I can I shall return to the subjects which interest us. Your sincere friend, A. Nobel."

The letter lay unposted on his desk; a few hours after he completed it, he had a cerebral hemorrhage and collapsed. He died at two o'clock in the morning on December 10, 1896, after a harrowing struggle.

His final hours were deeply tragic. The fears that he had expressed in several of his letters turned out to be fully justified. He died alone, surrounded by his French servants without, as he had once put it, any "close friend or relative whose kind hand would one day close one's eyes and whisper in one's ear a gentle and sincere word of comfort."

From his study the staff had carried him up to his bedroom on the second floor of the villa; they then sent for his Italian doctor who prescribed absolute rest and confinement to bed. He appears to have lost some of his powers of speech and all memory of languages other than that of his childhood; his oldest servant and butler, Auguste, said later that Nobel had only used a few words that were intelligible to the staff. They gathered, however, that he wanted them to get in touch with his family and so Auguste sent off telegrams to Nobel's two nephews, Emanuel and Hjalmar, as well as one to Sohlman asking him to inform the rest of the family.

"At Bofors I read the telegram . . ." Sohlman writes, "and after communicating with Hjalmar and Ludvig Nobel, I decided to set out for San Remo at once in order to be of service, if possible, during my employer's illness. Hjalmar Nobel, too, decided to go; we met on the way and arrived at San Remo together on the evening of December 10, but too late to find Alfred Nobel alive. While on our way we had in fact received a telegram announcing his death. Emanuel Nobel, who like us had set out immediately after the first telegram, arrived ahead of us on December 10, but was also too late. Alfred Nobel had ended his life as much alone as he had usually lived."

The Will and the Way

ON DECEMBER 11, the day after Nobel's death, there were present at the villa in San Remo two of his nephews, Hjalmar and Emanuel, and Ragnar Sohlman, who had been Nobel's personal assistant for the previous three years.

After a brief service in the villa on December 17, the coffin was taken to the local railway station to be sent to Stockholm. There, a more formal funeral service was held on December 29 in the old Stockholm cathedral, Storkyran. After the ceremony the coffin was taken to the new cemetery, where, in accordance with a wish expressed by Nobel in his will, the body was cremated, an unusual request for those days. The will had also stipulated that his veins be opened and that not until this had been done, and his death verified by qualified physicians, were the remains to be cremated.

These instructions had reached Sohlman and the two Nobel brothers before they left San Remo. On the evening of December 15, two days before the ceremony at Nobel's bier, Sohlman had been visited in his hotel room in San Remo by Emanuel and Hjalmar, who told him that they had received a telegram from Stockholm informing them that their uncle's will had just been opened at the Enskilda Bank. They added that Sohlman and Rudolf Lilljeqvist, a Swedish industrialist, had been appointed sole executors. The telegram contained no other details of the contents of the will apart from Nobel's instructions for the disposal of his remains.

The unnecessarily elaborate precautions he outlined came from deep-seated fears of being buried alive which had haunted Alfred Nobel all his life, as they had haunted his father before him.* In any event, he need not

---

*Alfred's father, Immanuel, had patented a new kind of chipboard and among its possible uses had actually suggested that it could be used "for coffins which, while combining cheapness and lightness with tasteful construction, could be made so that a person coming to life in one of them could lift the lid from inside, the lid being provided with airholes for breathing, and with a cord attached to a bell."

have worried; the operation had already been performed as part of the embalming process, and even given the crass fallibility of the medical profession, since he was not cremated until nineteen days after his death, it is unlikely that any mistakes could have been made.

A day or so after the brief ceremony in San Remo, Sohlman received a letter containing the full text of the will. He showed it to the two Nobel nephews who were very upset, particularly Emanuel. While making a preliminary investigation of the papers in the house, Emanuel had come across one of the earlier wills, dated March 4, 1893, with a note saying it had been canceled in favor of one drawn up on November 29, 1895. Emanuel couldn't help being disappointed at the changes made in the later version, which greatly reduced the bequests to himself and the other members of his family in order to provide a fund for annual prizes to be awarded to persons who, in the words of the will, "shall have conferred the greatest benefit on mankind" in the preceding year. He was also distressed at the fact that he himself had been dropped as an executor. But what worried him most of all—as it worried both Sohlman and Hjalmar—was the sheer impossibility of the task, as it seemed to them, which Nobel had set before his executors.

The will began in the ordinary way by listing bequests to relatives, friends, employees and servants, and to the two executors. Frau Sophie Kapy von Kapivar (Sophie Hess's married name) was to get an immediate payment of 150,000 Austrian florins (almost $300,000 in today's terms) and an annuity of 6,000 Austrian florins for the rest of her life. Bequests to members of the family varied between 100,000 and 400,000 Swedish kroner (or, between $135,000 and $540,000 in today's terms), and smaller sums were left to business associates, employees, his valet, gardeners and chemical assistants.

Then came the relevant part:

> The whole of my remaining estate shall be dealt with in safe securities and shall constitute a fund, the interest on which shall be annually distributed in the form of prizes to those who, in the preceding year, shall have conferred the greatest benefit on mankind. The said interest shall be divided into five equal parts, which shall be apportioned as follows: one part to the person who shall have made the most important discovery or invention within the field of physics; one part to the person who shall have made the most important chemical discovery or improvement; one part to the person who shall have made the most important discovery within the domain of physiology or medicine; one part to the person who shall have produced in the field of literature the most

Testament

Jag undertecknad Alfred Bernhard Nobel förklarar härmed efter moget betänkande min yttersta vilja i afseende i den egendom jag vid min död kan efterlemna vara följande:

Öfver hela min återstående realiserbara förmögenhet förfogas på följande sätt: Kapitalet, af utredningsmännen realiseradt till säkra värdepapper, skall utgöra en fond hvars ränta årligen utdelas som prisbelöning åt dem som under det förlupne året hafva gjort menniskligheten den största nytta. Räntan delas i fem lika delar som tillfalla: en del den som inom fysikens område har gjort den vigtigaste upptäckt eller uppfinning; en del den som har gjort den vigtigaste kemiska upptäckt eller förbättring; en del den som har gjort den vigtigaste upptäckt inom fysiologiens eller medicinens domän; en del den som inom literaturen har producerat det utmärktaste i idealisk rigtning; och en del åt den som har verkat mest eller bäst för folkens förbrödrande och afskaffande eller minskning af stående armeer samt bildande och spridande af fredskongresser. Prisen för fysik och kemi utdelas af Svenska Vetenskapsakademien; för fysiologiska eller medicinska arbeten af Carolinska Institutet i Stockholm; för literatur af Akademien i Stockholm samt för fredsförfäktare af ett utskott af fem personer som väljas af Norska Stortinget. Det är min uttryckliga vilja att vid prisutdelningarne intet afseende fästes vid någon slags nationalitetstillhörighet sålunda att den värdigaste erhåller priset antingen han är skandinav eller ej.

Detta testamente är hittills det enda giltiga och upphäfver alla mina föregående testamentariska bestämmelser om sådane skulle förefinnas efter min död.

Slutligen anordnar jag såsom varande min uttryckliga önskan och vilja att efter min död pulsådrorna uppskäras och att sedan detta skett och tydliga dödstecken af kompetente läkare intygats liket förbrännes i såkallad kremationsugn.

Paris den 27 November 1895

Alfred Bernhard Nobel

outstanding work of an idealistic tendency; and one part to the person who shall have done the most or the best work for fraternity among nations, for the abolition or reduction of standing armies and for the holding and promotion of peace congresses.

The prizes for physics and chemistry shall be awarded by the Swedish Academy of Sciences; that for physiological or medical works by the Caroline Institute in Stockholm; that for literature by the Academy in Stockholm; and that for champions of peace by a committee of five persons to be elected by the Norwegian Storting. It is my express wish that in awarding the prizes no consideration whatever be given to the nationality of the candidates, so that the most worthy shall receive the prize, whether he be Scandinavian or not.

What worried Sohlman and Nobel's two nephews most was the fact that the principal legatee, the future Nobel Foundation, did not even exist as yet, and would have to be organized. Emanuel was also deeply concerned over what was to happen to the Nobel Brothers' Naptha Company of Baku; he was, in effect, running the company, but the stock owned by Alfred amounted to a controlling interest. Despite this huge question mark over his entire future, Emanuel, right from the outset, was inclined to do everything possible to respect his uncle's wishes.

To Sohlman, who as chief executor represented interests which might be regarded as running directly counter to his own, Emanuel said: "You must always remember the obligation implied in the Russian word for the executor of a will: *dushe privashshik,* which means 'spokesman for the soul.' You must try to act accordingly."

Sohlman wrote: ". . . I must confess that the first reading of Nobel's will caused me genuine disappointment and worry. I had become deeply absorbed in the experiments I had performed for Nobel . . . and had concluded that, in some form or other, they were to be continued after his death. I also felt concerned about the future of Bofors [in Sweden] after Nobel's strong financial support and technical experience were no longer available, and the idea of having to sell it off or otherwise break up his large share of the Bofors company, as well as the Nobel Dynamite Trust Company [in Great Britain] and the Naphtha Company [in Russia] did not appeal to me at all."

Sohlman went home for Christmas to Bofors and then to Stockholm for the funeral; there for the first time, he met Rudolf Lilljeqvist, the other executor, a man about fourteen years his senior and far less influenced by personal considerations or by any connection with the Nobel family and factories.

ON JANUARY 2, four days after the funeral, and four days after the remainder of the Nobel family had been informed of the contents of the will, a Stockholm newspaper published the text of the most important part of it—that section relating to the prizes—welcoming it as "a gift to mankind intended to further its development and promote its welfare, as well as to serve purely idealistic purposes—probably the most magnificent one of its kind that a private person has ever had both the desire and the ability to make."

This eulogy was against the main trend of opinion, even that of the executors who thought that it was undesirable to publish the terms of the will so early on; they had been hoping to find among Nobel's papers some more detailed instructions as to how precisely they were to go about the implementation of the will and the organization of the awards.

There were all sorts of other problems. The main legatee, the fund and its administration as we have seen, would have to be handled by an institution which would have to be established. Furthermore, the institutions already in existence which had been singled out to appoint the prizewinners in certain fields were bound to be subjected to a great deal of trouble in the process, and no provision had been made for their compensation. There were no directions as to what should be done if, in any year, no suitable candidate could be found or agreed upon. A final difficulty was that as Nobel had never lived for long in any one place, there was the problem of establishing which of his houses had been his official legal residence and what judicial tribunal should rule on the validity of the will and on such questions as the inventory of his estates and the administration of his property. Also the publication of part of the will had started rumors of a forced sale of Nobel's assets which had adverse effects on the shares of the companies concerned, notably the naphtha operation in Russia.

The press now began to have second thoughts. From several quarters bitter attacks were mounted on the fundamental thinking behind the bequest. Also criticized were the purely formal defects in the will which Nobel had foolishly drawn up himself, without legal advice; the flaws were seen more and more as sound reasons for having the whole idea declared invalid. A violent press campaign, undoubtedly inspired by some of Alfred Nobel's closest relatives in Sweden, urged the relatives to contest the will in favor of a compromise by which the total assets would simply be divided up between the relatives themselves and the various Swedish institutions designated as prize juries.

It was argued that it was downright unpatriotic for a Swede to overlook Swedish interests in favor of international activities; that it would be impossible for the Swedish prize juries to fulfill the task allotted to them satisfactorarily; that the task would interfere with their real work and expose them to accusations of bribery and corruption; and that the choice of the Norwegian Storting for the task of awarding the Peace Prize would cause grave damage to Sweden and to her relations with Norway, at a time when these were already sorely strained.

The fortune which Alfred Nobel had amassed from the invention, manufacture and sale of high explosives was enormous by contemporary standards: nearly $50 million in today's terms.

As time went by more and more newspapers expressed their doubts as to the possibility or even the wisdom of approving the will and putting it into effect. Criticism came not only from the conservative Right, but also from the socialist Left; and among the will's most implacable opponents was Hjalmar Branting, the Swedish Social-Democratic leader who, as it happened, won the Peace Prize himself in 1921.

Branting claimed that while Nobel was alive, the latter had shown no special interest in social welfare nor had he ever indicated "how these assets, which are the products of both nature and labor, may benefit everybody." "And these tremendous prizes have been offered," he argued, "so far along the course of human endeavor that those who may receive them will in any case obtain all the fame and wealth our civilization can offer."

"The only way to peace," Branting went on, focusing on the Peace Prize, "is through an international organization of the working classes in all countries, both in a political and an economic sense. From that it follows that really effective work for peace can never be performed by a single individual; that being so, the masses ought certainly to have a share in the sums which the Nobel Foundation may be able to disburse for this purpose and then use them to promote a steady and increasingly intensive peace propaganda." Indeed, Branting, a Marxist, resented the whole concept of the prizes. "A millionaire who makes a donation may be worth every respect," he said. "But it would be better to be rid of both millionaires and donations."

APART FROM THE fact that the rights and duties of the two executors had not at that time been definitely established in Swedish law, they faced formidable problems. The will had not been properly drawn up. There were tremendous difficulties about the liquidation of the property and reinvestment of all the proceeds from it in "first-class securities" as specified; and there was the problem of organizing a proper administrative body for the permanent management of the endowment fund and for the formulation of rules for the annual distribution of the prizes, covering matters which had been altogether omitted from the will—such as what was to be done if no suitable recipient could be found, or if the prize-awarding bodies could not agree on a suitable candidate.

The legal problems facing them included, on the one hand, certain purely formal but essential steps that had to be taken in the various countries in which Nobel had owned property; and, on the other, a number of highly involved problems regarding the differences of opinion and even legal disputes that could be expected to arise. The first category of problems included the tedious business of filing and proving the will; the securing of legal authority for the executors to take over all the assets and to make inventories in all the countries in which such assets could be located, as well as collecting whatever income might have accrued from these assets; and finally, the question of liquidating the Nobel estate.

Basically, the problem of jurisdiction revolved around the still-unresolved question of Nobel's legal residence. At the time of his death, he had two houses, one in Paris and another at San Remo, as well as the right to occupy the manor at Björkborn, which he had renovated and rebuilt, although it was legally owned by the Swedish Bofors-Gullspång Company in which Nobel had owned a controlling interest. Since his ninth year, however, when he had left Sweden with his mother and brothers to settle in Russia, he had never been a legal resident of any country; he had, in fact, been described as "Europe's wealthiest tramp."

Strictly speaking, jurisdiction over matters concerning his will and the estate could be exercised only by the court authorities in the country in which he had last seen a resident, which in this case was Sweden. Accordingly, Carl Lindhagen, the executors' legal expert—he was at the time deputy justice of the Swedish Court of Appeals—took steps to have the will proved in the Swedish capital, fully aware that this could be disputed on the grounds that he had been a resident, for a much longer period, both in France and in Italy.

Rudolf Lilljeqvist was at the time fully engaged on the construction of a new electrochemical factory at Bengtsfors, and had to leave it to his co-executor Sohlman to go first to Christiania (Oslo) to see whether the Norwegian Storting would be willing to undertake the administration of the Peace Prize.

"I first called upon Sievert Nielsen, president of the Storting," Sohlman wrote. ". . . I also met a few more of the leading parliamentarians of Norway, and they all expressed themselves as favorably disposed towards the assignment given in the will to the Storting, namely the selection of the Peace Prize laureates." Sohlman next went to Paris and set himself up in a family hotel not far from Nobel's house in the Avenue Malakoff. As he half expected, there were no notes of any kind among Nobel's effects clarifying the various matters in the will that were still in doubt. But by questioning people Nobel had known while he was in Paris, and the Parisian friends who had witnessed the will, he was able to get a clearer picture of Nobel's general intentions. In any event, Sohlman had known Nobel very well in the years immediately before the latter's death and was quite used to the way in which, in all his business dealings, Nobel had applied the principle of merely giving a general outline of his intentions and leaving it to others to work out the details. Sohlman now came to the conclusion that Nobel probably wished his will to be interpreted and implemented in the same way—by other people, using their common sense.

To put matters on a formal basis, Sohlman and Lilljeqvist now sent identical letters to the various Swedish institutions mentioned in the will, asking them if they would be willing to assume responsibility for assisting in the selection of prizewinners. They agreed, suggesting that a committee consisting of two representatives from the Academy of Sciences and one each from the Caroline Institute and the Swedish Academy should draw up proposals to be approved by the institutions and then submitted to the Swedish king for sanction.

At the same time Sohlman and Lilljeqvist sent a formal request to the Norwegian Storting, asking them to accept the responsibility of selecting a Peace Prize laureate. Within a month, on April 26, 1897, the Storting adopted a resolution accepting the task. At the same time Lilljeqvist and Sohlman had an audience with the king and presented him with a copy of the will.

SOHLMAN NOW HAD to hurry to Paris because he had heard from Gustaf Nordling, the Swedish consul general there, that Hjalmar and Ludvig Nobel, together with their brother-in-law, Count Ridderstolpe, husband of their sister Ingeborg, had arrived in Paris to investigate the situation with a view to contesting the will.

Immediately upon his arrival, Sohlman, assisted by Carl Lindhagen, their lawyer, started to take into his own possession all the documents and securities which had been deposited in the various French banks and private banking firms in Paris used by Nobel, to forestall possible legal attachment on behalf of the relatives. On the strength of a document signed by Nordling, all the securities formerly owned by Alfred Nobel were surreptitiously withdrawn from the various open-deposit accounts and placed in three large strongboxes in the Comptoir National d'Escompte to await a suitable opportunity to spirit them out of France to a safer storage place. This process took about three weeks, and Nordling took over when Sohlman left for England to engage a lawyer and arrange for the sale of Nobel's English and Scottish securities. On his return to Paris he found that all the securities which had been kept in open deposit at the Comptoir d'Escompte and elsewhere, and which represented the bulk of Nobel's estate in France, had been transferred to the vaults in the names of the two executors and of Nordling.

In Sweden the will was submitted for probate in Stockholm and also before the county court of Karlskoga, the court within whose jurisdiction both Bofors and Björkborn lay.

While the courts were considering the test cases which had been brought, all the Nobel securities in Paris were being transferred, partly to London and partly to Stockholm, in postal packages insured by the banking firm of Rothschild, since the French post office could not insure any packages worth more than 20,000 francs. The Rothschild firm stipulated that shipments on any single day should not exceed 2.5 million francs, so for a week or more, securities worth that amount were drawn every day from the vaults in Paris and posted to London or Stockholm. The actual method of transfer was a real James Bond operation, with Sohlman seated in a horse cab with a loaded revolver in his hand, fully prepared to defend the suitcase he was taking to the Swedish Consulate for packaging and dispatch to the Gare du Nord ("in case a collision with another carriage had been arranged by robbers").

"In retrospect," he wrote, "it may seem rather odd that we proceeded that way instead of simply instructing the bank to make the transfers itself in the usual manner. But we feared that under the circumstances such an order would attract undue attention and lead to objections from, for example, the French tax authorities—Le Fisc—particularly in view of the still unsettled question as to whether death duties were to be paid in France on all the securities stored there, or only on those of French origin—a problem connected with Nobel's [still-unsettled] residence."

When the last package had been dispatched, Nordling, as consul general for Sweden, expressed the view that he had been placed in a slightly compromising position and suggested to Sohlman that he should now inform the relatives of what had been done. Sohlman invited them all to a "peace and reconciliation" dinner, held at the famous old Noel Peter Restaurant in the Passage des Princes in Paris. At this dinner, the relatives, particularly Hjalmar Nobel, were inclined to argue that since Alfred Nobel had lived in Paris for seventeen years, the proper tribunal to try his will would be a French court. Sohlman then told them what he had done: although the matter was still open to discussion, he said, it was now only a matter of form, since all Nobel's important securities had been moved out of the jurisdiction of the French courts.

This seemingly high-handed and precipitate action had been taken, he explained, because a French court decision to the effect that Nobel's legal domicile had been Paris would not only have meant that all his assets would have become taxable in France, no matter where they were located, but also that his will might have been declared invalid, in view of its formal defects, and this would have nullified his entire bequest. This, Sohlman argued, was clearly not Alfred Nobel's intention. When he wrote his last will in Swedish and selected Swedish countrymen as witnesses and executors, and chose Swedish institutes to adjudicate on the awards, he must have been thinking of himself as a Swede, and must have taken it for granted that it would be a Swedish judicial authority which would make the final decision on his will. If he had foreseen any problems arising out of the fact that Paris might be held to have been his formal place of residence, he would himself have moved his securities out of the jurisdiction of the French courts, just as his executors had done.

The immediate result of this announcement was a burst of fresh activity on the part of Hjalmar Nobel and his French lawyers. On their advice, Hjalmar now asked for a court attachment on whatever property of Alfred Nobel's was still left in Paris. In this way he prevented the sale of the house on the Avenue Malakoff, causing a considerable loss to the estate.

He also went to Germany and Britain with the same object, but without success. The executors began to prepare themselves for a French court case.

In the spring of 1897, the courts at Stockholm and Karlskoga debated the will and the decision in both cases favored the county court of Karlskoga. The will was submitted for probate at Karlskoga county court, not only by the executors but also on behalf of the Swedish government, as well as the Swedish Academy of Sciences, the Swedish Academy, the Caroline Institute and the Norwegian Storting. The Swedish government in May 1897 formally instructed the attorney general to have the will declared valid and to give such help as might be needed by the Swedish institutions named by Nobel.

But the relatives continued to contest the will vigorously and not all of the prize-awarding institutions were happy about the arrangements, which they felt could do them damage. At the Caroline Institute, certain members wanted the plan to be remodeled so that each institute which was named as a prize adjudicator could use the Nobel bequest as it saw fit—an aim which, of course, could only be achieved with the assistance of the relatives and by supporting them in their efforts to have the will declared invalid.

There ensued a protracted and complicated series of negotiations between the executors and the most influential members of the institutes involved, some of whom were against the whole idea of the endowment. In a report dated May 7, 1897, the committee recommended acceptance provided that sufficient clarifications could be made to obviate all obstacles to the practical application of the will.

When the subject came up before the Academy of Sciences, however, Hans Forssell, president of the Swedish Academy, succeeded in having the committee's report rejected and in persuading the Academy of Sciences not to commit itself until the will had been legally proved. But in order to get the will proved, it was necessary for the prize-awarding bodies to accept their assignments in advance, and if one of the institutes refused even to appoint delegates to discuss the terms on which it would accept such a responsibility, a complete deadlock would be reached.

This situation forced the executors to consider some sort of a compromise with the relatives. Sohlman was in favor of this; Lilljeqvist remained skeptical both of the possibility of arriving at a satisfactory compromise, and also of the executors' right to commit the estate, and ultimately the Nobel Foundation, to a deal which might unfavorably affect the interest of future Nobel laureates.

To settle the matter, the executors invited the foreign legal advisers of the estate to meet them in Stockholm in July 1897. Maître Coulet from France and Timothy Warren from the United Kingdom gave assurances that there was no further danger of any action against the legality of the will in those countries; Dr. Wesphal of Germany recommended compromise with the relatives.

The inventory was completed and submitted to the country court at Karlskoga on November 9, 1897. Nobel's estate, which was found to total 33,233,792 kroner (almost $45 million today) after the deduction of death duties of more than 51 million kroner divided between Sweden, Norway, Germany, Austria, France, Scotland, England, Italy and Russia.

After the inventory had been filed, Sohlman made yet another trip abroad, visiting England, Germany and Russia to discuss the question of the disposal of Nobel's remaining assets and the possibility of transferring, on behalf of the family, his shares in the Russian Naphtha Company to Emanuel Nobel.

When Sohlman got back to Stockholm, he tried to find a way to break the deadlock caused by the refusal of the Academy of Sciences even to appoint delegates to consult with them. He and Lilljeqvist decided to invite the delegates of the Swedish Academy and the Caroline Institute to confer with them and their lawyer, Carl Lindhagen, without waiting any longer for the Academy of Sciences to make up its mind. At six meetings between January and February 1898, they discussed certain elaborations and additions to the will which they felt should be incorporated in the statutes of the future Nobel Foundation. As voluntary but unofficial representatives of the Academy of Sciences, Professors L. F. Nilson and Otto Pettersen also attended and the establishment of a scientific institution to be known as the Nobel Institute was proposed.

Emanuel Nobel attended the last two meetings as representative of the Nobel relatives living in Russia. In that capacity, he made a statement on February 14 which was to be decisive in the acceptance of the will and the foundation of the Nobel Institute. He told the meeting that he wished to respect his late uncle's wishes as expressed in the will in every way and consequently did not intend to dispute its terms any further, but added that he didn't think any alternations or additions to the will could be made without the consent of all the heirs. He asked to be informed of any contemplated changes or additions, so that he could decide whether he and his nearest relatives could approve of them. This was agreed.

Only ten days earlier the Nobel relatives living in Sweden had started a legal action against the will. Their complaint, signed on February 1, 1898, had been submitted to the county court of Karlskoga; it was directed against the executors of the will, the Swedish government, the three Swedish institutes concerned and the Norwegian Storting. The plaintiffs represented twelve of the twenty relatives entitled to a share in the estate, and their arguments were based on technical defects of the will and on the uncertainty about Nobel's legal place of residence. In view of these uncertainties, they argued that the property should be turned over to the relatives, and the executors made accountable, in the first place, to them. If the institutes designated as prize-awarding bodies should prove willing to adjudicate on, and distribute, these prizes, the relatives should have charge of the capital fund; given that, they would do what they could to carry out Nobel's wishes.

Because of the long delay in answering to which the Norwegian Storting was entitled as a foreign defendant, the first hearing could not take place until September 29, 1898, and by that time the case had been settled out of court.

Before that compromise was reached, however, Emanuel Nobel, as spokesman for the Russian branch of the family, had been subjected to strong pressures to join with his relatives in Sweden in their opposition to the will. These pressures came not only from the Nobel family themselves but from the highest and most influential circles in Stockholm.

Emanuel Nobel was in a very difficult situation. Primarily, he felt obliged to look after the best interests of his younger brothers and sisters. He called them together, explained the situation, and asked for their support for the attitude he had taken towards the will. They were all agreed and consented to his proposals.

Emanuel was against any idea of trying to interfere with his uncle's disposition of his property, or of participating in any radical changes such as the proposed division of the estate between the relatives and the award-giving institutions. His only personal interest lay in a wish to acquire for his family the controlling interest in the Nobel Brothers' Naptha Company in Baku, which his uncle had owned, in order to keep the management of the concern in the hands of the Nobel relatives.

There was a certain animosity between Emanuel Nobel and his cousins, the children of Robert Nobel. Robert had been the first to propose that the Nobel brothers should enter the oil business in Baku, and for a number of years had been local manager before ill health had forced him to retire to Sweden, where he died in August 1896. After Robert's retirement, the company had been run by his younger brother, Ludvig, and after the latter's death in 1888, by Ludvig's eldest son, Emanuel.

As a result of verbal negotiations, the executors—aware of the dilemma facing Emanuel Nobel—agreed to sell him, as representative of the heirs of Ludvig Nobel, all the stock that had been held by Alfred Nobel in the Nobel Brothers' Naptha Company, at the value at which, on the recommendation of the Stockholm stockbrokers, these securities had been listed in the inventory of the estate, though it was considerably less than their current stock exchange value. As far as Emanuel Nobel was concerned, this arrangement seemed adequate to safeguard the interests of his family.

However, pressure on him to make a common cause with his relatives in Sweden did not cease, and one day while he was in Stockholm in February 1898, he was summoned by King Oscar II for an audience.

The king apparently began by urging Emanuel, as the foremost representative of the family, to bring about a change in his uncle's will, particularly in reference to the Peace Prize, which could only lead, he feared, to controversies and diverse complications. "Your uncle has been influenced by peace fanatics," the king said. "And particularly by women."

The king went on to say that as the will was defective in form it would be hard to implement, and that this had caused the prize-awarding institutions to feel doubtful about it. The Royal Academy of Sciences, in particular, had declined to have anything to do with the matter until changes had been made. To this Emanuel replied that he had just had discussions with the prize-awarding juries' representatives and that an agreement had been reached.

"Well, of course," the king said, "one cannot prevent people from getting together and talking, but they are not able to make any binding agreements. In any case, it is your duty to your sisters and brothers, who are your wards, to see that their interests are not neglected in favor of some fantastic ideas of your uncle." Emanuel replied that he would not care to expose his sisters and brothers to the risk of being reproached, in the future, by distinguished scientists for having appropriated funds which properly belonged to them.

Later, Emanuel recounted the conversation to his Russian lawyer who warned him to leave Stockholm immediately for St. Petersburg lest he be arrested for *lèse majesté*.

However, once the will had gone through and the Nobel Foundation had been established the king supported it throughout his life, personally presenting the prizes.

EMANUEL NOBEL'S DECISION to support his uncle's will gave the executors an opportunity to renew their attempts to come to terms with the other relatives and greatly facilitated the settlement of the lawsuit they had begun. On May 29, 1898, an agreement was reached with two of the legatees and on June 5, 1898, the other relatives signed a document before the notary public in Stockholm declaring that they accepted Alfred Nobel's will both on their own behalf and on behalf of their descendants. They agreed not to make any further claim on the estate beyond what was stipulated in the agreement and also to surrender all rights to share in the management of the residuary fund or to make any further objections to any future interpretations of the will. In return for these concessions they received the entire interest on the assets for the year 1897, which amounted to a considerable sum.

While these negotiations were going on, the discussions with the prize-awarding bodies were renewed. Letters were sent to the institutions with the minutes of the meetings in February which had been attended by Emanuel Nobel. In the letter to the Royal Academy of Sciences—which alone had refused to appoint any delegates until the will had been proved, but which had been represented informally at the meetings by two of its members—the executors added a note to the effect that since Emanuel Nobel was supporting his uncle's will there could no longer be any doubt that it would be proved. In view of this change in the situation, the academy was again asked to appoint official delegates to take part in the drawing up of the statutes of a future Nobel Foundation. On May 11, 1898, the academy replied that they had appointed Professors L. F. Nilson and B. Hasselberg as its official representatives in all matters concerning the will and the future rules.

As soon as the agreement was made with the legatees, it was approved by the Swedish government and by all the prize-adjudicating institutions which had been made defendants in the action. The Caroline Institute, the Swedish Academy and the Academy of Sciences all gave their approval to the agreement in June 1898.

As regards the Norwegian Storting, the situation was slightly different. Special discussions turned out to be necessary to inform the delegates it had selected about what had been done to settle the various disputes over the will. The Norwegian Storting appointed a committee to study and, if they saw fit, to approve the compromise agreement with the Nobel relatives. The executors of the will, and Carl Lindhagen and Judge Santesson—who had already represented the Storting in negotiations concerning the Nobel will—were invited to the Norwegian capital, to discuss it. After a conference lasting several days, the Norwegians decided on July 4, 1898, to accept the agreement and become party to it. On September 9 the Swedish government gave its formal approval.

When the will had been admitted to probate, a new conference was called to draw up rules as to how the winners were to be selected. The rules regarding the Peace Prize were left to the Norwegian Storting. This plan caused some hesitation in Swedish circles—because of the hostility between Norway and Sweden—and it was argued that all the special statutes should be submitted to the Swedish government for approval, including any relating to the Peace Prize. The Norwegians objected to this as it would have placed the Norwegian Nobel Committee under the jurisdiction of the Swedish authority. Though still in union with Sweden, Norway had been a self-governing country for a century. It was then decided that the Norwegian Nobel Committee could draw up its own regulations. There has never been any conflict on this matter since.

The definitive text of the proposed "Statutes of the Nobel Foundation" as agreed upon by the committee members, was finally approved on April 27 and 28, 1899, and was submitted to the Swedish government for formal sanction. It contained clarification of certain points in the will including the following:

a. A prize might be divided between two works, each of which had been adjudged worthy of a prize, or it could be divided between two or more persons who had performed a piece of work together.

b. Prize-money which it had not been found possible to distribute might be returned to the main fund or placed in special funds to be used to further Nobel's ultimate purposes in other ways other than by prize awards.

c. To help them in the preliminary investigation of works proposed for awards, the Swedish prize-adjudicating institutes were to appoint Nobel committees of between three and five members; for their part the Norwegian Storting would appoint a special committee to make the investigations required for the award of the Peace Prize.

d. To assist them in investigations connected with the selection of prizewinners, the prize adjudicators should have the right to organize scientific institutions and other establishments. These institutions, which were to belong to the Nobel Foundation, were to be known as "Nobel Institutes."

On June 29, 1900, the statutes were approved by the Swedish government and officially promulgated as a government decree.

The long battle over Alfred Nobel's will was over.

Posthumous bust of Alfred Nobel
by the Swedish sculptor Christian Eriksson.

Choosing the Champions

WITH THE DISPUTE over the will out of the way, it was now possible to consider the final objective: the setting up and staffing of permanent organizations to implement Nobel's wishes. To insure that the claims of all candidates were fully examined and the money properly invested, it was first necessary to establish the overall administrative machinery. This took the form of a Nobel Foundation, governed by a board of five members and three deputies. The chairman of the board and his deputy were chosen by the Swedish government, and the other four members with their two deputies by special trustees appointed by the prize-awarding institutions. It was further decided that out of the latter's share of the annual income from the main fund, each of them should have the right to deduct one-fourth to cover expenses in connection with the selection of the winners and the expenses of the Nobel Institute itself.

On September 25, 1900, the trustees of the Nobel Foundation met for the first time. One of their first actions was to appoint an executive director of the foundation. The unanimous choice was Ragnar Sohlman, who had done so much to have the will proved and put into effect, in the face of all obstacles.

As soon as the machinery for the administration of the foundation and the various institutes had been set up, the institutes began to lay down the precise procedures by which the candidates would be weeded out and a final selection made.

In the case of the Peace Prize, the composition of the panel of referees has changed slightly over the years, but basically the system has followed the original pattern. Initially the secretary of the committee of five appointed by the Norwegian Storting prepared statements as a basis for judging the candidates worth further investigation and the final decision was made by the committee. After 1904, when the Norwegian Nobel Institute was fully operative, a research staff was available to prepare preliminary material.

The procedure today is roughly as follows:

Every autumn the Norwegian Nobel Institute sends out invitations requesting nominations. These invitations go to members and former members of the Nobel Committee of the Norwegian Storting; advisers appointed by the Norwegian Nobel Institute; members of legislative bodies and other high-ranking government officials; as well as members of the Interparliamentary Union; members of the International Arbitration Court at The Hague; members of the Council of the International Peace Bureau; members and associate members of the Institute of International Law; select university professors of political science, law, history and philosophy; and all living Nobel Peace Prize laureates. All act as *individuals* and their proposals, with full documentary evidence in support, must be submitted by February 1 of the following year. The committee of five then spends the time between February and October or November, studying and weighing up every detail in the career of the suggested candidates, reaching their conclusions with the help of the research staff of the Nobel Institute and the institute's extensive library. The committee consists of Norwegians from different walks of life: at the moment they include a woman economist, a member of the Norwegian Storting who was formerly editor of a small newspaper, a university professor of modern history, a bank director and an agricultural expert.

As the long list of categories suggests, there are literally thousands who are eligible to put forward their own choice for the Peace Prize. In addition, the Nobel Institute in Oslo receives hundreds of letters from people not in any way qualified to make suggestions. Some people even write in putting forward their own names (which is against the rules, in any event) and setting out grandiose schemes which they propose to carry out with the money in the cause of peace.

"A lot of the letters are from nuts, obviously," Tim Greve, secretary of the Norwegian Nobel Institute told me. "But we get some very moving ones too—about some relative who has been unusually saintly and kind, or a doctor who has created peace in someone's mind. We get a lot of letters, too, from mystics and religious fanatics of all sorts. What they're after, of course, is money to spread their particular brand of faith which, they are convinced, will bring peace to mankind. We're in a situation here where literally anybody from some nurse in India to the Pope can be nominated." He added that in an average year the committee receives about fifty serious suggestions from a total of some two to three hundred people among the thousands entitled to nominate candidates.

Nothing is revealed to the public until the final decision is made in October or November. The deliberations and votes are kept secret, and the decision is always final, without appeal. The Peace Prize is awarded in Oslo on December 10, the anniversary of Nobel's death, simultaneously with the awarding of the other prizes in Stockholm. The Peace Prize, like the four other awards, consists of a gold medal, a diploma and a sum of money representing one-fifth of the interest on the main fund, minus a deduction for expenses. The main fund—about 28 million Swedish kroner (almost $40 million in today's terms), left out of a total bequest of 31 million kroner after initial deductions for building and organization, is also augmented from time to time by undistributed prize money, which remains in the fund and earns additional interest.

Nobel's capital was originally invested in so-called gilt-edged securities. However, as time passed, and the world's economy patterns changed, inflation began to eat into the value of the main fund. Consequently, in 1953, changes were made in the statutes of the Nobel Foundation to enable the money to be invested in more profitable stocks, mortgage loans and real estate.

Each year, the proceeds of the main fund are divided into five equal shares and distributed to the prize-awarding bodies. They hold back a quarter of each share to meet their expenses, and the remaining three-quarters of each share constitutes the prize money.

The first prizes distributed in 1901 amounted to about 150,800 Swedish kroner each (very approximately, worth $25,000 today), tax free, a very considerable sum. Since 1953, when the foundation changed its system of investment, the value of the prize has risen from 171,134 Swedish kroner in 1953 (about $81,000 in today's terms) to 630,000 in 1975 (about $167,000), or by 268 percent, which represents an increase of 40 percent when inflation is taken into account.

I have already alluded briefly to Nobel's ideas on the subject of peace. It seems that his first ideas on the question came from his interest in literature, and particularly from his enthusiasm for the English poet Shelley. It was not, however, until much later in life that he began to think about the problem in practical terms, whatever his motivation may have been, and to look around for some way of putting his ideas into practice.

In a letter to Bertha von Suttner on October 31, 1891, quoted by August Schou in his remarks on the Peace Prize in the definitive *Nobel, the Man and His Prizes,* edited by the Nobel Foundation and published by Elsevier, Nobel argued that if any practical results in bringing about a lasting peace were to be achieved, it would be necessary to proceed gradually and

The Nobel Peace Prize medal in gold has three figures representing peace and fraternity among nations on the face and a bas-relief portrait of Nobel on the obverse.

A. S. NORSK TELEGRAMBYRA

A typical meeting of the Nobel Peace Prize Committee (in 1974). All the decisions are made around this table in a room in the Nobel Institute in Oslo. The walls are lined with portraits of former Peace laureates. In addition to the committee of five which includes the chairman, Mrs. Aase Lionaes, is Tim Greve, the director of the institute, seated at the extreme right.

carefully. He suggested that the various governments should enter into agreements on the peaceful settlement of their disputes, but that the validity of these agreements should be strictly limited to one year. Even the most cynical of statesmen, Nobel believed, would have no objections to committing themselves over such a short period, and in time this might produce an atmosphere in which the overall term of the peace agreements could be extended.

In 1892 Nobel appointed an unemployed Turkish diplomat, Aristarchi Bey as adviser on the peace problem. Although they worked together only for a short period, there is evidence that the Turk's diplomatic skill was instrumental in clarifying Nobel's ideas on the subject. There is not much doubt that the plan for collective security which Nobel outlined in a letter to Bertha von Suttner in 1892 came originally from Aristarchi Bey: by mutually binding military agreements between nations, he argued, one might in time be able to create an international atmosphere of security, which in turn should facilitate general disarmament.

Nobel, as August Schou points out, was not unaware of the possibilities of the great social revolution: "A new tyranny, that of the dregs of the population, is lurking in the shadows, and one can almost hear its distant rumble."

As we have seen, he claimed to believe that the increased effectiveness of the weapons of war would in itself act as a deterrent. But the very fact that he included a Peace Prize among his awards is proof that he had no real faith in the validity of this argument. If he had, there would be no need to offer a prize for the champions of peace; for he had done more than any man until then to make war unimaginably terrible.

There is no evidence to explain why Nobel chose to bestow on the Norwegian Storting the privilege of choosing the annual champion of peace. It has been argued that Nobel felt that this might bring about some relaxation in the tension between Norway and Sweden at the time. However, there is no indication that Nobel was particularly concerned about this conflict; nor did his action do anything to allay it. On the contrary, several Swedish newspapers were highly indignant that the task of awarding the Peace Prize should have gone to the "Separatist Norwegians."

In addition to awarding the prizes, the Nobel Peace Institute has the task of disseminating information on international questions. Their reading room is open to the public and from 1923 onwards, the institute has arranged lectures by international scholars and experts. Later, in 1928, lectureships were established in international law, economics and political history, and from 1947 seminars have been held on international problems, primarily intended for journalists and teachers.

At the outset, to forestall criticism of its choice, the committee decided to give no detailed explanations of the reasons for its decisions; but this, in effect, increased criticism whenever the choice was controversial. As time passed, perhaps for this reason, the presentation addresses became longer and more explicit, sometimes almost defensively so.

On the controversial choices, August Schou writes: "Admittedly, if we follow the awards of the Peace Prize from year to year, we shall at first glance have some difficulty in tracing any line, let alone any development. But this may be partly due to the fact that the peace movement, taken all round, has not undergone any 'comprehensive development' which is the case with the various spheres of activity of the recipients of the science prizes, or the prizes for medicine. After all, this is characteristic of the fatal split in our culture. But if we try to arrange the prizewinners in groups, in botanical fashion, as it were, we shall nevertheless discover a clear continuity, and get the impression that the committee has sought to further certain *tendencies* of the age, which have in many cases without doubt resulted in a relaxation of international tension."

It is perhaps worth pointing out that a great deal of the initial objection to Nobel's Peace Prize bequest was based on a general impression that it was the Norwegian Storting which would choose the prizewinner. This is not so: the Norwegian Nobel Committee, although appointed by the Storting, is completely independent of it. It is true that the composition of the committee has to a large extent reflected the political climate in Norway at any given time, particularly in the early days of the award. If one could put a label on the early committees, they might be described as "bourgeois-liberal" in general tendency. It was not until 1913 that a socialist (la Fontaine) was awarded the Peace Prize. True, as early as 1903 it went to William Randal Cremer from Fareham in southern England who came from a working class background and was active in the trades union movement. Cremer, however, was far from being a socialist—he wanted a better deal for the workers *within* the existing social framework and was alarmed at the Marxist tendencies of his fellow trades unionists on the Continent—and he received his award for his activities in connection with a workers' organization dedicated to preventing Great Britain from becoming involved in any continental war.

On the other hand, none of the early prizewinners could be said to be anti-socialist either; they were mainly liberals opposed, as Schou points out, "to the former conception of the peace movement as being organically bound up with the principles of free competition."

Another objection which was constantly made, over the years, has been that the prizewinners were usually old people, and not bright young sparks with years of promising endeavor ahead of them. The Peace Prize undoubtedly has had, over the years, the highest average age of prizewinners—around sixty-five. In the early years—say from 1901 until the end of World War I—this was perhaps natural since it was not the practice then to give responsible positions to young people; most of the top military commanders in the 1914-18 war—for example, Kitchener, Gough, Pétain and Foch—were old men. Also, the initial Peace Prizes were awarded for contributions to the cause of peace dating back to the middle and late nineteenth century; the contribution by Dunant, the first prizewinner, for example, was made as early as 1863 when he arranged a conference in Geneva at which the Red Cross was founded.

In more recent years the prize has tended to go to younger men: Martin Luther King, Jr., at the age of thirty-five, was the youngest of all the laureates. Ralph Bunche, the first black Nobel laureate, was forty-six when he received the award; so was Carl von Ossietzky, the German pacifist who was in a hospital recovering from a term of imprisonment in a Nazi concentration camp when the award was announced. Henry Kissinger was fifty.

In the early days of the award, the committees seemed to be unable to think of champions of peace other than in terms of pure pacifists, organizers of peace conferences, advocates of international arbitrations, experts on international law and the like.

When, despite all of the laureates' efforts, World War I broke out, the committee very naturally decided to suspend all activities, apart from offering the prize in 1917 as a contribution to help the Red Cross in the magnificent work it was doing both on the battlefields and on behalf of prisoners of war.

After World War I, the focus shifted for a time to the League of Nations and its architects and functionaries, and to those responsible for getting Germany back on her feet and safely into the League.

When events proved this to be a catastrophic folly and the world again began to darken towards war, the committee once more suspended activities, only to transfer their enthusiasm immediately after the war to those principally concerned with the shaping of the United Nations. During the cold war, whenever the tension grew so unbearable that the award of a prize for peace was unthinkable, they withheld the Peace Prize altogether or awarded it to organizations like the UNHCR (the Office of the United Nations High Commissioner for Refugees) or the Quakers, or the Red Cross, or to men like Father Pire, who devoted his life to eliminating poverty and hopelessness in the emerging nations and to alleviating the sufferings of refugees, particularly old people, in the period immediately following World War II.

The choice of Albert John Luthuli in 1960 could be said to have marked the beginning of a new pattern of thinking on the part of the Nobel Committee. He was, for a start, the first black African to be awarded the Peace Prize, and his selection entailed a decisive expression of opinion, on the part of the committee, concerning a dispute between groups of people of different races. Luthuli, a Zulu tribal chieftain, was the leader of a great nonviolent protest against apartheid in South Africa, and against other repressive measures by the all-white South African government.

The whole question of human rights—stirred initially by the fate of the Jews in the Nazi concentration camps—increasingly preoccupied the committee as the wind of change howled through Africa and Asia, and colored people everywhere began to clamor for a fair deal. In 1964 the prize went to Martin Luther King, Jr., who led a nonviolent struggle for the equality of American blacks which began with a boycott of segregated buses in Montgomery, Alabama, in 1955, and culminated in August 1963 with a march on Washington, D.C., of 250,000 protestors, which was instrumental in achieving the Civil Rights Act of 1964.

In recent times the committee seems to have vacillated between awarding the prize for a specific effort to restore or preserve peace, like Dag Hammarskjöld's (disastrous, as it turned out) attempt to solve problems arising out of the abrupt termination of Belgian colonial rule in the Congo with the aid of a United Nations peace-keeping force, or Henry Kissinger's part in bringing about a cease-fire in Vietnam (unsuccessfully, and some believe insincerely); and, on the other hand, for general (or special) contributions to the well-being of underdeveloped and underfed nations on the broad general principle that the preservation of peace is not unconnected with economic prosperity and, above all, the securing of adequate food supplies. Such contributions have been made by John Boyd Orr, the 1949 laureate from Great Britain who founded the Food and Agricultural Organization (FAO), and Norman Borlaug, the 1970 laureate from the United States who developed in Mexico a new, high-yield dwarf wheat ideal for cultivation in the Third World.

By interpreting what they conceive to be the spirit, if not the letter of Nobel's will, the committee has given themselves considerable flexibility in deciding who, in any given year, can be regarded as the most outstanding of the world's champions of peace.

Champions of Peace

1901	Henri Dunant and Frédéric Passy
1902	Elie Ducommun and Charles Gobat
1903	William Cremer
1904	Institute of International Law
1905	Bertha von Suttner
1906	Theodore Roosevelt
1907	Ernesto Moneta and Louis Renault
1908	Klas Arnoldson and Frederik Bajer
1909	Auguste Beernaert and Paul d'Estournelles de Constant
1910	International Peace Bureau
1911	Tobias Asser and Albert Fried
1912	Elihu Root
1913	Henri de la Fontaine
1914-1916	Prizes not awarded
1917	International Committee of the Red Cross
1918	Prize not awarded
1919	Woodrow Wilson
1920	Léon Bourgeois
1921	Karl Branting and Christian Lange
1922	Fridtjof Nansen
1923-1924	Prizes not awarded
1925	Joseph Chamberlain and Charles Dawes
1926	Aristide Briand and Gustave Stresemann
1927	Ferdinand Buisson and Ludwig Quidde
1928	Prize not awarded
1929	Frank Kellogg
1930	Nathan Söderblom
1931	Jane Addams and Nicholas Butler
1932	Prize not awarded
1933	Norman Angell
1934	Arthur Henderson
1935	Carl von Ossietzky

1936	Carlos Saavedra Lamas
1937	Robert Cecil
1938	Nansen International Office for Refugees
1939-1943	Prizes not awarded
1944	International Committee of the Red Cross
1945	Cordell Hull
1946	Emily Balch and John Mott
1947	Friends Service Council and American Friends Service Committee
1948	Prize not awarded
1949	John Boyd Orr
1950	Ralph Bunche
1951	Léon Jouhaux
1952	Albert Schweitzer
1953	George Marshall
1954	Office of the United Nations High Commissioner for Refugees
1955-1956	Prizes not awarded
1957	Lester Pearson
1958	Georges Pire
1959	Philip Noel-Baker
1960	Albert Luthuli
1961	Dag Hammarskjöld
1962	Linus Pauling
1963	International Committee of the Red Cross and League of Red Cross Societies
1964	Martin Luther King, Jr.
1965	United Nations Children's Fund (UNICEF)
1966-1967	Prizes not awarded
1968	René-Samuel Cassin
1969	International Labor Organization
1970	Neil Borlaug
1971	Willy Brandt
1972	Prize not awarded
1973	Henry Kissinger and [declined by] Le Duc Tho
1974	Eisaku Sato and Sean MacBride
1975	Andrei Sakharov

The First Decade

Three-quarters of a century ago, when the first Nobel prize-awarding committees sat down to consider the nominations, it was in a world nearly as unstable as one of Nobel's early nitroglycerin mixtures.

Queen Victoria had died at long, long last, right at the beginning of the decade, but the cracks that were so soon to shatter the safe, solid world of the Victorians were already beginning to show.

In South Africa the British were fighting a guerrilla war to put the Boers—the descendants of the original Dutch settlers—firmly in their place. They succeeded, but at a cost of 5,774 killed in battle and 16,000 dead from disease, against a total of 4,000 Boers killed.

It was only a few years since the Americans had sent the battleship *Maine* to Cuba—then in revolt against Spain—and when the ship was blown up by a mine in Havana harbor, a war between Spain and America ensued which lasted for sixteen weeks of 1898.

At the turn of the century, however, public attention in America was firmly focused on economic growth. The real bosses of the country were the big iron and steel corporations, the oil monopolies and the railroad companies, represented by men like J. P. Morgan who set up US Steel, the world's first billion-dollar corporation and who at one stage had tried to get a monopoly on all transportation between the Great Lakes and the Pacific Coast.

Naval power was regarded as being of paramount importance in the early 1900s, and although Britain still ruled the waves it was now only by a narrow neck. The United States Navy was becoming more formidable with every passing year, and in Europe the Germans were busy building battleships for the power struggle that now seemed inevitable.

But these warlike events and portents, significant as they were, may in the long run have brought about less of a profound change in the everyday life of the ordinary citizen of this planet than many items which seemed trivial at the time and received only scant notice in the newspapers.

It is not likely that many people were unduly disturbed by the announcement in 1901 that a scientist called William Cooks had succeeded in separating uranium.

Or by the first Zeppelin flight trials the same year.

Nor could anybody have hazarded a guess at the effect that the publication of Sigmund Freud's book *The Interpretation of Dreams* would have on the world's mental health. He followed it with *Psychopathology of Everyday Life* and went touring the United States, lecturing vast numbers of people who made the shattering discovery that they too were neurotic.

On December 17, 1903, when the brothers Orville and Wilbur Wright staggered momentarily into the air in a flying machine near Kitty Hawk, North Carolina, nobody regarded it as anything more than a passing novelty. Even six years later, when Blériot succeeded in crossing the English Channel in a monoplane, flying was still considered as no more than a slightly bizarre sport. The previous year both the *Mauretania* and the *Lusitania* had been launched and all sensible men realized that for the forseeable future, transportation overland would be by railroad and overseas by liner.

Even the automobile was not yet considered a serious contender in the transportation stakes. There was still a 20 m.p.h. speed limit on motor cars in England, and although Henry Ford in 1903 had already introduced his famous Model T—the car that was to bring motoring within the reach of everyone—it was to take a few years to establish itself even in a small way.

When Marconi transmitted a message from Cornwall to Newfoundland in 1901 by means of wireless telegraphy, most people probably realized that this invention heralded a new era in rapid communications. But how many could have guessed that within a few short years it would blossom into radio, and then television, bringing about a fundamental change in our whole way of life?

Or who then could have charted the course of an industry which began with the offer in Pittsburgh, in 1905, of a new kind of entertainment: a short "moving picture" called *The Great Train Robbery*.

There were signs, all over the civilized world, of new forces to be reckoned with. Everywhere women were clamoring for equal rights, and labor was beginning to assert itself as a political force.

In February 1900 the British Labor party was founded and five years later a Trades Disputes Act legitimized peaceful picketing in England. There was a general strike in Italy and a coal strike in the United States which ended only when President Theodore Roosevelt threatened to bring in federal troops to work the mines.

In St. Petersburg, Russia, on January 22, 1905, workers staging a peaceful demonstration were fired on by the police; and in the same year a union of trades unions was formed in Russia which immediately began to agitate for parliamentary representation. In October of the same year there was a general strike there, twenty-six workers in St. Petersburg formed the first soviet, and the famous mutiny on board the battleship *Potemkin* took place.

This was the decade of the safety razor and the motor bicycle and the popular daily newspaper, pioneered by Hearst in the States and by Lords Northcliffe and Rothermere in Britain.

It was during the first decade of this century that Oscar Wilde and Verdi and Ibsen and Cézanne all died, and that Walt Disney and Graham Greene were born. Mahler wrote his fifth symphony, Puccini produced *Tosca* and *Madame Butterfly,* and Picasso changed the face of art with a painting called *Les Demoiselles d'Avignon.*

Books in the news included Joseph Conrad's *Lord Jim,* Colette's first Claudine novel, Rudyard Kipling's *Kim,* W. H. Hudson's *Green Mansions,* Henry James's *The Golden Bowl*, and H. G. Wells's *The War in the Air.*

Towards the end of the decade the United States began to restrict immigration; a Belgian industrial chemist named Leo Baekland invented bakelite, the first modern chemical plastic; Lenin left Russia under an assumed name; Albert Einstein worked out his first theory of relativity; Sergei Diaghilev brought his Russian ballet to Paris for the first time and D. W. Griffith, an obscure producer in the new motion picture industry, transformed a child actress called Gladys Smith into the world's first international film star—Mary Pickford.

THE NOBEL PEACE Prize Committee, faced for the first time with interpreting the terms of the will, tended throughout the decade to follow the then current conviction that the way to stop war was by international legislation, arbitration, interparliamentary cooperation, pacifist literature and peace conferences. Consequently, most of the prizes went to people who had been prominent in the many different peace societies that were fashionable around that time and to those responsible for establishing a firm basis for international law, an interparliamentary union and an international arbitration league. In contrast to more recent years, when the prize has often been awarded for a specific act that contributed to world peace—usually during the year immediately prior to the award—or for specific humanitarian work for refugees or civil rights, the early laureates were awarded the prize for work which they had done over the years, in some cases as far back as the Franco-Prussian War of 1870 and the Crimean War of 1853–56.

1901 Henri Dunant

1901 Frédéric Passy

1902 Elie Ducommun

1902 Charles Gobat

1903 William Cremer

1904
Institute
of
International Law

1905 Bertha von Suttner

1906 Theodore Roosevelt

1907 Louis Renault

1907 Ernesto Moneta

1908 Klas Arnoldson

1908 Frederik Bajer

1909 Auguste Beernaert

1909
Paul d'Estournelles de Constant

1910

International
Peace Bureau

1901

HENRI DUNANT (1828–1910), Switzerland: *Founder of the International Red Cross Society.*

FRÉDÉRIC PASSY (1822–1912), France: *Founder of the Ligue Internationale et Permanente de la Paix [International and Permanent Peace League] and a founder of the Interparliamentary Union.*

THE CHOICE OF Dunant as co-laureate with Passy for the first Peace Prize was a highly controversial one. A great many people felt that as all Dunant's efforts as founder of the Red Cross had been aimed at mitigating the effects of war, he was, in effect, accepting war as something inevitable instead of working to eliminate it altogether as a disease of mankind. It was probably the knowledge that their decision would produce exactly this reaction which prompted the Nobel Committee to divide the first prize between him and Passy, a pacifist who had energetically been promoting peace conferences for fifty years.

Dunant was born in Geneva into a religious household. At eighteen he became a child of the *Réveil,* a new evangelistic movement which had taken hold in Geneva in the wake of a visit from a Scottish revivalist preacher by the name of Haldane. Dunant became a worker for the Lord and joined the League of Alms, which entailed taking comfort, both material and spiritual, to the sick poor in Geneva and further afield.

While in Geneva he met Harriet Beecher Stowe and added the abolition of slavery to his list of missions to be accomplished.

Initially, Dunant worked full-time on his religious activities, among them the newly formed YMCA. As evangelism, however, could not provide him with a living, he entered the business world at the age of twenty-six, joining one of the big Geneva banking houses, Lullin et Sautter.

His work took him to Algeria, which France had captured and was now attempting to colonize using as agents, among others, the Geneva banking firm which Dunant represented. There he established outposts of the YMCA and furthered the work of the Lord at least as diligently as he attended to that of Messrs. Lullin et Sautter.

Financed by an unexpected legacy from an aunt, in 1858 he became involved in what can only be described as a madcap expedition to reach the Emperor Napoleon III and present him with a manifesto announcing the re-establishment of the empire of Charlemagne in his (the emperor's) person. The manifesto quoted ancient biblical and other prophecies in support of this theory and urged the emperor to grant him certain concessions for agricultural and colonial developments in Algeria. Dunant took himself to the European field of battle, where the emperor happened to be, dressed all in tropical white so that he could be easily discerned. He never succeeded in achieving an audience with Napoleon, but he did see Marshall MacMahon and became, willy-nilly, an eye-witness to the Battle of Solferino in northern Italy on June 24, 1859, in which the Allies (the Italians under Cavour and the French under Napoleon III) lost 14,000 men killed or wounded and 3,000 missing while the Austrians (under Franz Joseph) lost 13,000 killed or wounded and 9,000 missing, a frightening total of 39,000 casualties for one day's fighting. The sight of such suffering affected Dunant's thinking for the rest of his life.

"This was hand-to-hand fighting, indescribably hideous," he wrote. "Austrians and Allied troops trampled on one another, slaughtering one another over the bleeding corpses, felling their adversaries with rifle butts, smashing in their skulls, disemboweling them with saber or bayonet. There was no question of quarter; it was butchery, a battle of wild beasts, maddened with rage and drunk with blood. Even the wounded defended themselves as long as they had breath. . . . On all hands the same frenzied struggle, sometimes made more horrible by the approach of a squadron of cavalry at the gallop, the horses crushing under their hooves the dead and the dying. . . .

"Further on came the artillery in the wake of the cavalry: it ploughed its way through the dead and the wounded which lay together indistinguishable on the ground. Brains spurted out as the wheels went over, limbs were broken and mangled so that men's bodies were a shapeless, featureless conglomeration, unrecognizable as human creatures. . . ."

All this was written three years later. At the time Dunant, strictly a man of action, found five hundred wounded men who had been carried into the Chiesa Maggiore at Castiglione and were promptly forgotten about. Immediately he took over the church as his "command," organized the women of Castiglione as first-aid workers and enlisted a mixed collection of ex-officers, tourists, priests and journalists to help him.

Dunant then went back to Geneva and wrote a detailed account of what he had seen during the battle, and argued his case: "Could not the means be found in time of peace to organize relief societies whose aim would be to provide care for the wounded in time of war by volunteers of zeal and devotion, properly qualified for such work?"

Sixteen hundred copies of the book—*Un Souvenir de Solferino* [A Memory of Solferino] were issued and sent to various crowned heads and princes, ministers of war and foreign affairs, and to others whom Dunant regarded as influential.

The effect was electric. The book—which was never offered for sale through the trade—was instantly acclaimed in Paris, Berlin, Vienna, St. Petersburg, Munich, Turin and Milan. Within a month a second edition was being printed and soon it had been translated into several languages.

On February 7, 1863, the Société Genevoise d'Utilité Publique [Geneva Society for Public Welfare] appointed a committee of five, including Dunant, to examine the possibility of putting his plan into action. This committee called for an international conference and in effect founded the International Red Cross. The conference in October of the same year had thirty-nine delegates from sixteen nations and laid the groundwork for the Geneva Convention of the following year at which twelve nations guaranteed neutrality to medical personnel, agreed to expedite supplies for their use, and adopted the red cross on a white field as their emblem.

Dunant had been neglecting his business affairs for so long that he now went bankrupt. He left Geneva in 1867 to live most of the remainder of his life in obscurity and poverty, though he continued to fight to promote interest, by whatever means he could, in the treatment of prisoners of war, the abolition of slavery—still flourishing in parts of Africa —international arbitration, disarmament and the provision of a permanent homeland for the Jews. During the Franco-Prussian War he founded an association, originally known as l'Association de Prévoyance [Provident Society], with branches in France, England, Belgium, Bavaria and the United States; one of its aims was to work for the establishment of an international court of arbitration.

Before leaving Geneva in 1867 he had proposed at the general meeting there of the Red Cross that prisoners of war be treated with the same inviolability as the sick and wounded. The French and British branches of his Association de Prévoyance supported this idea and in 1874, on the initiative of Tsar Alexander II, a conference was held in Brussels to draw up a convention generally outlining the rules of war, including the treatment of prisoners.

Meanwhile, Dunant was living as an eccentric recluse in a series of *pensions* in Appenzell in Switzerland, often like a beggar. There were times, he says, when he dined on a crust of bread, blackened his coat with ink, whitened his collar with chalk and slept out of doors.

For twenty years he lived in solitude until, in 1859, he was "rediscovered" in a hospital in Heiden by a journalist from St. Gall. His rediscovery led to fresh participation in pacifist propaganda (from Room

12 in the Heiden hospital), notably contributions for the periodical *Die Waffen Nieder* [Lay Down Your Arms], edited by Bertha von Suttner.

He spent eighteen years in Room 12 at Heiden—he was there when awarded the first Nobel Peace Prize—and when he died in 1910, there was no funeral ceremony, no mourners, no cortège. In accordance with his own wishes he was carried to his grave "like a dog."

Dunant never spent any of the prize money. He bequeathed some legacies to those who had looked after him in the hospital, endowed a free bed that was to be made available to the sick poor of the village, and left the remainder to various philanthropic societies in Norway and Switzerland.

FRÉDÉRIC PASSY WAS born into a Parisian civil service family. Educated as a lawyer, he passed into the civil service at the age of twenty-two, but left after three years to study economics. Thereafter he devoted himself entirely to writing, lecturing and organizing. He was an ardent free trader of the school of British economists like Richard Cobden and John Bright, and firmly believed that free trade would draw nations together as partners in a common enterprise, thus resulting in the abandonment of war.

His work for peace began during the Crimean War (1853–56), and it was widely held that his eloquent pleas for peace in the journal *Le Temps* helped to avert war between France and Prussia over Luxembourg in 1867.

In the same year he founded La Ligue Internationale et Permanente de la Paix, which was broken up by the Franco-Prussian War of 1870–71 but re-emerged later as La Societé Française des Amis de la Paix [French Society of the Friends of Peace]. Passy became its secretary general and in 1871 published a famous appeal *Revanche ou Relèvement* [Revenge or Retreat], demanding a real peace settlement between France and Germany on the basis of voluntary arbitration and national sovereignty, with permanent neutrality for Alsace-Lorraine.

In 1881 he became a member of the French Chambre des Deputés, and successfully urged arbitration in a dispute between France and the Netherlands concerning French Guiana. He was also instrumental in realizing an ideal which had been first suggested by the British politician Randal Cremer, winner of the Peace Prize in 1903—the establishment of an Interparliamentary Union. The idea was to bring together at regular intervals interested members of the parliaments of all countries to discuss international issues and explore ways of improving collaboration between the nations via their parliamentary institutions. Above all, it was hoped that such a union would help to promote international arbitration on matters in dispute.

A start was made in 1888 with a meeting of French and British parliamentarians, and the next year, during the World Exhibition in Paris, a fully international interparliamentary meeting was held.

To the end of his long life—he was ninety when he died—Passy continued to write articles and pamphlets on the peace problem. "Though no one, it is true," he wrote in 1895, "wants to attack, and everybody protests his love of peace and his determination to maintain it, yet the whole world feels that it only requires some unforeseen incident, some unpreventable accident, for the sparks to fall in a flash . . . on those heaps of inflammable material which are being foolishly piled up in the fields and on the highways and blow all Europe sky-high."

1902

ELIE DUCOMMUN (1833–1906), Switzerland: *Head of the Bureau International Permanent de la Paix* [*International Peace Bureau*] *at Berne.*

CHARLES ALBERT GOBAT (1843–1914), Switzerland: *director of the Interparliamentary Bureau at Berne.*

IN HIS TOAST to the laureates, Jørgen Gunnarsson Løvland, chairman of the Nobel Peace Committee, made the point that it was quite natural that three of the first Nobel Peace Prize winners should be Swiss. Switzerland had, in difficult times not so long ago, been a place of refuge, an asylum not only for political refugees, persecuted freedom fighters and reformers, but also for misunderstood and persecuted ideas of freedom and progress.

Elie Ducommun was the son of a Neuchâtel clockmaker. Having completed his early studies at Geneva, he worked as tutor for a wealthy family in Saxony for three years and perfected his German. He then returned to Geneva and taught in public schools for a couple of years until 1855, when at twenty-two, his career as a journalist began with the editorship of a political newspaper, the *Revue de Genève.*

In 1865 he moved to Berne where he founded the radical journal *Der Fortschritt* [Progress], also published in French under the title *Progrès;*

next, between 1871 and 1872 he edited *Helvétie* [Switzerland]; and from 1868 he edited the news sheet *Les États-Unis d'Europe* [The United States of Europe] published by the International League for Peace and Freedom.

In 1891 when the Permanent Peace Bureau was set up in Berne—the idea was to establish a permanent central propaganda bureau for all peace work—Ducommun became its general secretary and then its director, refusing to take any remuneration for his work. He published the bureau's *Correspondence Bimensuelle* [Bi-monthly Correspondence] and edited and wrote a number of articles and pamphlets. In one of the most famous of these he refuted the popular idea that war, when it came, would necessarily be fearful but of very short duration. He argued that, on the contrary, a system of trenches and fortresses could lead to a long-drawn-out war of attrition with alternating advances and retreats, foretelling with awful accuracy the shape of things to come in Flanders and Champagne in World War I.

In his Nobel lecture Ducommun remarked: "One question often asked of pacifists is: Granted that war is an evil, what can you find to put in its place when an amicable solution becomes impossible? The treaties of arbitration concluded in the past few years provide an answer to this question. . . . The Convention for the Pacific Settlement of International Disputes signed at The Hague in 1899 by twenty-six nations offers a solution to international conflicts by a method unknown in the ancient world, in the Middle Ages, or even in modern history—a method of settling quarrels between nations without bloodshed."

CHARLES ALBERT GOBAT was the son of a Protestant pastor from Tramelan. He was a brilliant student, studying at Basel, Heidelberg, Berne and Paris, and taking his doctorate in law at Heidelberg in 1867.

For fifteen years Gobat concentrated on law; he had a practice in Berne and at the same time lectured on civil law at Berne University. After 1882 he became increasingly interested in cantonal and national politics and although he was appointed superintendant of public instruction for the canton of Berne, and continued to hold the post for thirty years, he was at the same time pursuing his political career. In 1882 he was elected to the Grand Council of Berne, and was president of the cantonal government from 1886 to 1887. From 1884 to 1890 he was a member of the Council of States of Switzerland, and from 1890 until his death a member of the National Council.

From its inception in 1888, Gobat worked enthusiastically for the Interparliamentary Union. In 1892 he was president of the union's fourth conference held at Berne, at which a permanent information office was established, called the Bureau Interparlementaire [Interparliamentary Bureau]. Similar to the International Peace Bureau, it was to be a permanent link between all the parliaments concerned.

Gobat was appointed general secretary and director of the bureau and like Ducommun, refused to take any payment for the task. After Ducommun died in 1906, Gobat suceeded him as director of the International Peace Bureau, itself subsequently a Nobel Peace Prize winner in 1910.

Among his many books on international affairs and history, the best known is *La Cauchemar de l'Europe* [The Nightmare of Europe], published in 1911.

Like Ducommun, Gobat was a firm believer in arbitration and had great hopes that The Hague Convention represented the first step towards world peace. "If we examine The Hague Convention carefully," he said in his Nobel lecture, "we see that it considers the offer of good services a duty of every nation. In other words, such offers should be made whenever a dispute becomes critical and threatens to explode into war. . . . At the beginning of the war between Russia and Japan, the president of the United States persisted in offering his good services to the Russians and Japanese. Neither party chose to condemn the offer as an unfriendly act. Exhausted by a terrible war, both accepted, and peace was concluded. . . . President Roosevelt was the first head of state to apply the rules of The Hague Convention concerning the preservation of general peace."

1903

WILLIAM RANDAL CREMER (1828–1908), Great Britain: *Founder of the Workmen's Peace Association, which later became the International Arbitration League. He was cofounder, with Frédéric Passy, of the Interparliamentary Union.*

UNTIL NOW THE winners had been staunchly middle-class: the 1903 laureate came from a working-class English background, the child of poverty-stricken parents.

Sir William Randal Cremer, born in 1828 in Fareham, Wiltshire, had to go to work at a very early age, first as a pitch boy in a local shipyard and then as a carpenter's boy working for a London builder. The building trade was active in the early trades union movement and Cremer soon became involved in union organization. When a campaign for a nine-hour day was started in 1858, Cremer was one of its leading lights both as a propagandist and as a fund raiser; he was also one of seven who directed labor during a lock-out of 70,000 men.

Around this time the idea of an international organization of workers was beginning to form; when a start was made in London, Cremer played a major part in the foundation of the First International Working Men's Association in 1864. He was a curious mixture: he had no desire to overturn the social structure, but hoped that some way could be found by which the workers could play a larger part in society as it then existed. In these circumstances he was strongly opposed to the revolutionary line advocated by Marx and many of the leaders from the continental countries, and withdrew his support from the association when it was taken over by more revolutionary thinkers.

Cremer was involved in agitation for an extension of the franchise (which then included qualifications of residence and occupation of business premises), and during the Franco-Prussian War of 1870–71 he founded the Workmen's Peace Association, later renamed the International Arbitration League. The principal aim of the organization was to prevent Britain from becoming involved in the war between France and Germany. Convinced that labor should be actively represented in Parliament, he stood for Warwick in 1868, but it was not until 1885 that he was elected as MP for Haggerston in London. Two years later he persuaded 234 members of the House of Commons to sign an appeal to the president and Congress of the United States urging them to conclude a treaty with Britain, stipulating that any disputes which arose between the two countries which defied settlement by diplomacy should be referred to arbitration. Cremer headed a delegation to the United States and presented this resolution to President Cleveland.

The idea was supported by President Cleveland and his successor McKinley, but although it received a majority vote in the Senate it was not a sufficient majority to secure its ratification. It was not until 1904 that the United States finally agreed to arbitration treaties with a number of European states. In the meantime, however, Cremer's resolution excited the interest of Passy and other French deputies, and they invited Cremer and his colleagues to a meeting in Paris in 1888 which resulted in the formation of the Interparliamentary Union the next year. Cremer was elected vice-president and secretary of the British section.

Although not a rich man by any means, Cremer, who was knighted in 1907, gave the Nobel Peace Prize money to the International Arbitration League.

1904

Institut de Droit International [Institute of International Law]:
Founded in Ghent, Belgium, in September 1873.

IN 1904, FOR the first time, the Peace Prize was awarded to an institution, the Institute of International Law. Initially a private association of politicians and international jurists, the man behind it was Dr. Rolin-Jaquemyns, editor of the *Revue de Droit International* [International Law Review], published in Ghent.

In a speech at the presentation, Johannes Irgens, the then Norwegian minister of foreign affairs, emphasized the private nature of the institute. It is, he said, a free association of individuals from nearly every civilized country in the world interested in two fields of international law: on the one hand, in public law, the institute strives to develop peaceful ties between nations and make the laws of war more humane; on the other hand, in private law, its aim is to minimize or eliminate difficulties arising from differences existing in the laws of different countries.

In the private sector, the sort of area on which their deliberations centered concerned such matters as the extradition of criminals, marriage, divorce, trusteeship, and questions regarding the rights of citizenship and the coming of age of foreign nationals.

At the annual session in Geneva in 1874 the general principles for international judicial proceedings were laid down. In the years following, the institute hammered out such details as the competency of the tribunals, the forms of procedure to be adopted and the rules for the execution of judgments.

In 1879 the institute published a *Handbook of the Rules and Observances of War,* which tacitly accepted war as an inevitable feature of mankind's history. The introduction to the handbook begins: "War occupies a considerable place in the pages of history, and it is not reasonable to suppose that man will be capable of breaking away from it so soon, despite the protests it arouses and the disgust it inspires. For it proves to be the only possible solution to the conflicts which jeopardize the existence, the freedom and the vital interests of nations. But the gradual raising of accepted standards and morals should be reflected in the way war is conducted." (Carry on fighting, in other words, but try to kill one another as humanely as possible.—T.G.)

One of the practical ways by which the horrors of war could, in the opinion of the institute, be restricted, was by neutralizing all vital areas of international communication. To this end, during the Russo-Turkish War it set up a commission to examine the situation of the Suez Canal in the event of a major European war, and at a meeting in Brussels in 1879 a resolution was adopted appealing to the powers to declare the canal zone neutral and place it under international protection. This proposal was accepted and a treaty was signed in Constantinople (now Istanbul) in 1885. The previous year a similar treaty had been signed, at the institute's instigation, with regard to all submarine cables.

Georg Francis Hagerup, then president of the institute, had no illusions about its instant success. "If our work has had some success, he told his Oslo audience at the Nobel Institute, "it is undoubtedly because of our efforts to 'calculate the limits of the possible,' as one great statesman put it; because of our patience in refusing to advocate premature solutions; and because of our belief in the necessity of developing *gradually* and *progressively* as our statutes bid us. . . . The goal, the undisputed and inviolable region of law in international relations, is most certainly still a long way off. . . ."

1905

BERTHA VON SUTTNER (1843–1914), Austria: *Pacifist, author of* Die Waffen Nieder [*Lay Down Your Arms*], *and editor of the most influential peace journal of its time, called after her novel.*

THE 1905 LAUREATE was the woman who claimed to have influenced Alfred Nobel's ideas on peace and who believed herself to be largely responsible for the very existence of the Peace Prize: Bertha von Suttner. She worked briefly as Nobel's secretary in 1876, just before her marriage. The first female peace worker of established international stature, she was so closely identified with the cause of world peace during the closing years of the nineteenth century that many people credit her with influencing not merely Nobel's will, but also Tsar Nicholas II's decision to convoke a Peace Conference at The Hague in 1899.

Born Countess von Kinsky in Prague, she was a member of a distinguished Austrian noble family. In 1876, against the express wishes of her fiancé's family, she married Baron Arthur Gundaccar von Suttner, seven years her junior. For eleven years the couple lived at Tiflis in the Caucasus, in comparative poverty, existing on the proceeds of their joint journalistic and literary output; then, in 1885, the family became reconciled to the marriage, and they were able to return to Vienna.

Her studies had convinced Bertha von Suttner that as part of the general process of evolution, a new set of social standards would emerge, which would result in greater solidarity between the nations. She embodied these ideas in a book called *Das Maschinenzeitaler* [The Machine Age] published anonymously in 1888; it took the form of a series of lectures on the period in which she was living, supposedly delivered by a professor around the year 3000 A.D. Demonstrating how ancestral notions of religion had persisted right into the "age of science," the professor attacks the respectably pious, the spiritualistically pious, the politically pious and the militarily pious.

She was bitterly opposed to the official attitude of hostility towards life which she felt permeated nineteenth-century society. "You praise death so highly," she wrote, "that you deem it worthy of being suffered by your God Himself—in agony, bleeding, lamenting—on the cross. The most honorable and enviable death is in your opinion the one found in "homicidal struggle," and to your love children you affix the label "illegitimate birth."

Her novel *Die Waffen Nieder* (1884) was a tremendous success and was translated into many languages; it was probably more widely read than any novel published in the nineteenth century, with the possible exception of Harriet Beecher Stowe's *Uncle Tom's Cabin*. The central character of the novel marries, in 1859, an officer who is killed in the war in Italy. Later she marries another officer who shares her hatred of war, but out of a sense of duty and patriotism goes to war in 1864 and again in 1866. Finally, he resigns his commission and is shot on suspicion of being a Prussian spy during the Franco-Prussian War, while the couple happen to be living in Paris.

After the book was published, Bertha von Suttner devoted all her energies to the peace movement. In 1891 she founded the Austrian Peace Organization and attended the International Peace Congress in Rome. The title of her world-famous novel was used for a peace propaganda periodical which she edited between 1892 and 1899, and she was instrumental in forming an interparliamentary group in Austria.

When the Boer War broke out she maintained that the imperialistic policy behind it was not the most dangerous thing; what was really dangerous was the fact that the leaders were prepared, in order to back an indefensible imperialistic policy, to mobilize some of man's noblest instincts—self-sacrifice and a firm belief in fighting for justice. If these instincts could be channeled into loftier causes, she believed, a new society would evolve in which war would be unthinkable.

After her husband's death in 1902, she continued to work fiercely for peace. She played a prominent part at the 1905 Peace Congress to further Anglo-German conciliation; she warned of the dangers of militarizing China and of using the rapidly developing airplane as a weapon of war; and she repeated again and again that "Europe is one" and that uniting it was the only way to prevent the world disaster which seemed to be imminent.

"If the Triple Alliance included every state instead of only three," she said, "then peace would be assured for centuries."

Bertha von Suttner died in Vienna on June 21, 1914, exactly a week before the assassination in Sarajevo of the Archduke Franz Ferdinand, heir to the Austro-Hungarian empire—the incident which set in motion a train of events that led, two months later, to the war she had so clearly foreseen and so deeply dreaded.

And in this war, thanks largely to the ingenuity of her pen-friend Alfred Nobel in developing the "perfect" explosive for war purposes, 9,700,000 men were slaughtered.

1906

THEODORE ROOSEVELT (1858–1919), United States: *26th president, and the man responsible for achieving a peace treaty between Russia and Japan at Portsmouth, New Hampshire, in September 1905.*

ROOSEVELT WAS PROBABLY the first really controversial laureate. Unlike all the others to date, he had no record of consistent work in the cause either of peace or even of making war more "palatable" and "civilized."

On the contrary, Roosevelt had initially been very much a man of war. The award in his case was made for one specific action: the part he played in bringing about a conciliation between Russia and Japan in 1905.

Born of an old Dutch family which had settled in America in the seventeenth century, he was educated at Harvard, then studied for a year in Germany before entering politics. In his youth he was a member of a Republican Reform Club and in the 1880s leader of a small group of "blue stocking" opponents of corruption and boss rule which had been a feature of both party machines.

An imperialist of the old school, he believed that peace could best be secured by domination by the Great Powers, and advanced the theory in his autobiography, *The Strenuous Life* (1902), that the growth of peacefulness between nations had been "confined strictly to those who are civilized." Talking about pacifists in that work, he wrote: "The trouble comes from the entire inability of these worthy people to understand that they are demanding things that are mutually incompatible when they demand peace at any price and also justice and righteousness."

As assistant secretary of the navy from 1897 to 1898, Roosevelt became the leader of a jingoist group within the Republican party. He called for a war with Spain and frequently embarrassed his superiors with precipitate and unauthorized moves to strengthen the navy.

When the Spanish-American War did break out in April 1898, he resigned his government post to join his friend Leonard Wood in organizing the First United States Voluntary Cavalry, known as "The Rough Riders." Before long he was their spectacular commander, with a penchant for ordering a charge even when the odds were heavily against him and a healthy disregard for red tape and officialdom.

In 1900 he was elected vice-president under McKinley, and when McKinley was assassinated at Buffalo the same year, he became president. In 1904 he was elected to a full term as president.

On the domestic front Roosevelt welcomed union leaders to the White House and launched a campaign to restore open competition in the business and financial world; he did this by trying to strengthen the Sherman Anti-Trust Act of 1880, which had largely been ignored, and use it to curb and control the industrial and financial monopolies. He also worked to improve conditions for immigrants.

In foreign policy his first concern was the settling of relations with former Spanish colonies, Cuba and the Philippines; the securing of the Panama Canal Zone from Colombia; the occupation of Hawaii; and the development of the United States as a genuine Pacific power with considerable interests in the Far East.

It is in this context, rather than as a champion of peace, that his action in bringing about a conciliation between Russia and Japan should probably be judged. Roosevelt was opposed to Russian expansion in China and felt that a peace treaty negotiated while Japan held the upper hand might more effectively further America's interests in that zone by creating a better balance of power.

Roosevelt was obsessed with the idea of the balance of power. In 1911 he put it in this way: "As long as England succeeds in keeping up the balance of power in Europe, not only in principle but in reality, well and good; should she, however, for some reason or other fail in doing so, the US would be obliged to step in, at least temporarily, in order to re-establish the balance of power in Europe, never mind against which country or group of countries our efforts may have to be directed. In fact, we ourselves are becoming, owing to our strength and geographical situation, more and more the balance of power of the whole globe."

He believed that strong and virile nations survived while the weak and placid ones were swept under. He also realized more keenly than most people of that period that their peaceful Victorian summer was drawing to a close. Germany, he believed, was the one nation whose international ambitions constituted a real threat to the United States.

With the acquisition of parts of Samoa, Hawaii, Guam, Midway and the Philippines, the United States had become a major power in the Pacific and it was in America's interests, he believed, that Japan's sphere of influence should be expanded in the Pacific, to offset and prevent increased Russian expansion in China.

Roosevelt used the prize money as a foundation to establish in Washington a permanent industrial peace committee, the object of which, he said, would be "to strive for better and more equitable relations among my countrymen who are engaged, whether as capitalists or as wage workers, in industrial and agricultural pursuits. This will carry out the purpose of the founder of the prize, for in modern life it is as important to work for the cause of just and righteous peace in the industrial world as in the world of nations."

In his Nobel lecture he recommended that statesmen of the world study what had been done in the United States by the Supreme Court. "I cannot help thinking," he said, "that the Constitution of the United States . . . offers certain valuable analogies to what should be striven for in order to secure, through The Hague courts and conferences, a species of world federation for international peace and justice."

He also made a strong call for naval disarmament by international agreement. "No one power could or should act by itself; for it is eminently undesirable, from the standpoint of the peace of righteousness, that a power which really does believe in peace should place itself at the mercy of some rival which may at bottom have no such belief and no intention of acting on it. But granted sincerity of purpose, the great powers of the world should find no insurmountable difficulty in reaching an agreement which would put an end to the present costly and growing extravagance of expenditure on naval armaments."

1907

Ernesto Teodoro Moneta (1833–1918), Italy: *Editor of* Il Secolo, *one of the most influential newspapers in Italy; publisher of the pacifist periodical* La Vita Internazionale [*International Life*] *and chief Italian representative on the Commission of the International Peace Bureau.*

Louis Renault (1843–1918), France: *Expert on international law, counsellor to the French Ministry of Foreign Affairs and France's representative at a large number of important international meetings between 1893 and 1907.*

Moneta was another curious and much criticized choice; he was a soldier and the first freedom-fighter to receive the Peace Prize, though he was awarded it not for that but rather for his subsequent work as editor of an influential pacifist newspaper. Never a believer in nonviolence, Moneta could see no basic incompatibility between a nation's right to fight for self-government and the work of promoting international peace—and neither, apparently, could the Nobel Peace Committee. A man of deep contrasts, he has been described both as a "militant pacifist" and as a "nationalistic internationalist."

Moneta participated as a boy of fifteen in the insurrection of the people of Milan against the Austrians. His father, then a man of sixty with eleven children, joined in the fighting, which broke out in 1848, and young Ernesto helped him to defend the family house.

After the Austrian victory in the resulting war against Piedmont in 1848–49, Moneta was compelled to leave home and moved to Piedmont where he attended the military academy at Ivrea.

In 1859 when war broke out against Piedmont and Austria, he enlisted with four of his brothers in a corps of mountain troops organized by Garibaldi. The following year he took part in the liberation of Southern Italy and fought at the battle of Volturno in 1860. After the proclamation of the Kingdom of Italy in 1861, he joined the regular army and fought at the battle of Custozza against the Austrians.

In 1867 he resigned from the army to become first a contributor and then editor of the Milan newspaper, *Il Secolo.* He remained with the paper until 1896, and under his editorship it became the most widely read newspaper in Italy. He wrote a good deal on military matters and was in favor of turning the army into a militia.

The suffering that Moneta had witnessed during his military life deeply impressed him and in 1887 he founded in Milan the Lombardy division of the Societa Internazionale per la Pace [International Society for Peace]. The society sponsored disarmament, the establishment of a league of nations and the settlement of all international disputes by arbitration. To disseminate these ideas, he founded in 1898 the periodical *La Vita Internazionale,* to which many Italian and foreign pacifists contributed.

He became the Italian representative on the Commission of the International Peace Bureau in 1895 and in 1906 presided at the International Peace Conference at Milan.

Even after he had received the Peace Prize, Moneta retained his own firm views about war and repeatedly argued that while he was opposed to warmongers, he was not willing to sacrifice his ideas of justice to the desire for peace. In 1911 he whole-heartedly supported the then-impending Italian occupation of Libya on the grounds that it would open up to civilization a territory that was being laid waste by Turkey's backward and corrupt rule, and in 1915 he advocated Italy's entry into the war to fight the aggressive and imperialistic designs of the Central Powers.

In his Nobel lecture, Moneta said: "Today, unfortunately, what many facts indicate only too well is that universal peace, as we conceive it, still lies in the far distant future, and in view of the growing greed for the lands of others, the weaker countries can no longer trust the stronger ones.

"Keep your powder dry and always be ready to defend yourself; this is for Italy, as well as for others, a hard necessity at the present time.

"I do not believe that there is at the moment a single government in Europe which is actually planning war, but the time could come when those who are thinking of it least might find themselves embroiled in war by force of circumstances."

LOUIS RENAULT WAS the son of a bookseller and was born in Autun, in the Saône-et-Loire district of France. He took a degree in literature at the University of Dijon and then spent seven years studying law in Paris.

From 1881 he was a professor of international law at the University of Paris. In 1890 he was appointed legal consultant to the French Foreign Office and soon became France's leading authority on international law.

For the next twenty years Renault was the key French representative at a number of international conferences on such matters as international private law, international transport, military aviation, submarine cables, naval affairs, the abolition of white slavery and the revision of the Red Cross Convention of 1864. For these services he was awarded the rank of minister plenipotentiary and envoy extraordinary in 1903.

A dominant figure at the second Hague Peace Conference in 1907, he was *rapporteur* to the conventions relating to the opening of hostilities, to the application of the Geneva Convention to naval warfare and to the defining of the rights and duties of neutral nations in naval war. He was later chosen to be president of the Academy of International Law created at The Hague in 1914.

Renault was an ardent advocate of the idea of arbitration. He was also against too rigid an interpretation of the principle of international democracy. For example, he believed that the idea of equality between the nations should not be allowed to let Luxembourg's vote on a matter of maritime law cancel out Britain's. This does not mean that he was unaware of the valuable part that small nations could play in the settlement of disputes between the Great Powers. "They most often represent justice," he said, "precisely because they themselves are not able to impose justice." He was also in favor of unanimity at international conferences as being preferable to a majority vote resulting in a state's being forced to accept something against its will— an issue that was later to plague the League of Nations and subsequently the United Nations.

Like so many of the laureates, he clearly realized that, for all their work, war remained a distinct possibility. "Anything that contributes to extending the domain of law in international relations contributes to peace," he said. "Since the possibility of a future war cannot be ignored, it is a far-sighted policy that takes into account difficulties created by war in the relations between belligerents and neutrals; and it is a humanitarian policy that strives to reduce the evils of war in the relations between the belligerents themselves and to safeguard as far as possible the interests of noncombatants and the sick and wounded. Whatever may be said by those who scoff at . . . peace conferences, wars will not become rarer by becoming more barbarous"—a sentiment, incidentally, diametrically opposed to Nobel's own expressed view.

1908

KLAS PONTUS ARNOLDSON (1844—1916), Sweden: *Journalist, pacifist and a member of the Swedish parliament. He was one of the founders of the Swedish Peace and Arbitration Association and was prominent among those responsible for the peaceful dissolution of the Swedish-Norwegian Union.*

FREDERIK BAJER (1837–1922), Denmark: *Journalist, pacifist and a member of the Danish parliament. He was responsible for the foundation of the Danish Peace Society and held a seat on the council controlling the Interparliamentary Union. He was involved in the formation of the International Peace Bureau in Berne in 1891 and was its president until 1907.*

FROM 1815 NORWAY and Sweden had been united under one monarchy, but it was an uneasy relationship which even in Nobel's time had been the cause of much bitterness and controversy. The peaceful dissolution of this union in 1905 was not an event likely to have a profound effect on world peace or indeed to excite much interest outside Scandinavia, but it is understandable that the Nobel Peace Committee, sitting in Oslo, should look on it in a rather different light.

The decision to award half the prize to Arnoldson was highly unpopular in Sweden, as he had tended to favor Norway's claims in the final constitutional crisis. The Swedish newspapers were highly critical, calling the award an "outrage against Sweden" and "a disgrace to every Swedish man who takes pride in his national honor," pointing out that to add insult to injury the prize was Swedish money.

Klas Arnoldson was the son of a Göteborg caretaker; his family was so poor that when his father died he was obliged to leave school at the age of sixteen and work as a railroad clerk. After eleven years he became stationmaster. In all, he spent twenty-one years working for the railroad, during which time he continued his studies, reading widely in history, religion and philosophy.

He held a liberal, essentially Unitarian outlook on religion. His views on tolerance, freedom of conscience and kindred subjects were published in the *Nordiska Dagbladet* [Northern Daily], which he edited for a short time in the early 1870s, in *Sanningssokaren* [The Truth Seeker], a monthly journal devoted to the exposition of "practical Christianity," and in the numerous books and pamphlets that he wrote.

Politically Arnoldson was a radical and a convinced pacifist though his horizons were never very wide; they were in fact limited to the Scandinavian frontiers. In 1881 he was elected to the Swedish Riksdag [Parliament] and in 1883 was among the founders of the Swedish Peace and Arbitration Association.

He sought a guarantee for the permanent neutrality of the Nordic countries and his greatest contribution to the cause of peace was probably the one he made to the peaceful dissolution of the Swedish-Norwegian Union in 1905.

In his Nobel lecture he came up with a novel notion: a world referendum on peace. "In all countries," he suggested, "an appeal should be issued for every adult man and woman to sign the following declaration: If other nations will abolish their armed forces and be content with a joint police force for the whole world, then I, the undersigned, wish my own nation to do the same."

Although he didn't say so, presumably he was thinking of confining this referendum to the so-called civilized countries; but even at that, the problems and the cost of holding such a referendum would have been staggering, and it is doubtful whether governments would have paid any more attention to the result than they do today to the wishes of the electorate. But Arnoldson was convinced that they would; such a referendum, with an overwhelming majority in its favor, would, he believed, give the world's leaders sufficient moral support to agree to an effective commencement of general disarmament.

As subsequent Nobel lectures were to show, however, not even the fact that many of the statesmen were convinced that their people did not want war was sufficient to persuade them to agree to disarmament lest they leave themselves vulnerable to another power less meticulous in its implementation of the agreement.

THE SON OF a clergyman, Frederik Bajer was born near Naestved in Denmark. He entered the Sorø Academy in 1848. After attending a military school, he joined the army as a lieutenant in the Dragoons but was discharged when it was reduced after the 1864 war with Prussia, despite his fine military record in the war.

Between 1865 and 1872, Bajer studied languages, established himself as a teacher and translator and became a freelance journalist to augment his earnings.

In 1872 he was elected to the Folketing [the Danish House of

Representatives] where he worked untiringly for the emancipation of women, international peace, Danish neutrality and Scandinavian unity. He was among the founders of the Dansk Kvindesamfund [Danish Women's Society] and of the Nordisk Fristats Samfund [Society of Nordic Free States] and for two years edited its journal.

As time passed Bajer became more and more interested in the international peace movement and offered to distribute the literature of the Ligue Internationale Permanente de la Paix [Permanent International Peace League]. Initially he saw neutrality as one road towards peace and when he founded the first Danish peace society in 1882 it was under the title Foreningen til Danmarks Neutralisering [Society for the Promotion of Danish Neutrality]. The society later became known simply as the Danish Peace Society.

As an ex-military man, he was fully aware of the danger Scandinavia would face in the event of a European war, because of the strategic importance of the water routes around her coastline, and he proposed Nordic neutrality on the same lines as Switzerland's traditional neutrality.

He soon moved closer to the general European peace movement. In 1884 he attended the Peace Conference at Berne and was instrumental in arranging the first Scandinavian Peace Conference in 1885. He attended the first World Peace Congress in Paris in 1889 and the same year attended the first meeting of the Interparliamentary Union, also held in Paris.

At the second World Peace Congress in London in 1890, he suggested the formation of a permanent propaganda bureau for the dissemination of pacifist literature, and when the proposal was accepted at the next congress in Rome in 1891 and the International Peace Bureau set up, Bajer was made president of its governing board.

He founded the Danish Interparliamentary Group in 1891, acting as its secretary for twenty-five years, and was closely involved in the creation of the Scandinavian Interparliamentary Union in 1908.

Bajer believed that pacifist literature was being read all right—but mainly by pacifists. He put up a money prize for the best article on the subject of peace to appear in a national newspaper.

"There are in most states one or two ministers of war . . . ," he told his Nobel lecture audience. "I would not wish on any account to abolish them; as long as the status of international law is no better than it is at present, we cannot very well do without them. But I feel convinced, and I venture even to prophesy in this regard, that the time will come when there will also be a minister of peace in the cabinet."

1909

AUGUSTE MARIE FRANÇOIS BEERNAERT (1829–1912), Belgium: *Finance minister and president of the Belgian Chamber of Representatives, he was chairman of the commission set up at the first Hague Conference to formulate proposals for the restriction of armaments. He was also a member of the Permanent Arbitration Commission and honorary president of the Societé de Droit International [International Law Association].*

PAUL HENRI BENJAMIN D'ESTOURNELLES DE CONSTANT (1852–1924), France: *Diplomat and ultimately senator, one-time counselor to the French Embassy in London with the title of minister plenipotentiary. In 1899 he was a French representative at the first Hague Conference and was largely responsible for the arbitration treaties between France and several other countries.*

AUGUSTE BEERNAERT WAS born in Ostend, into a middle-class Catholic Flemish family. Beernaert took a doctorate in law at the University of Louvain in 1851. He then spent two years in Paris, Heidelberg and Berlin.

Called to the bar in 1853, he set up an independent practice, specializing in fiscal law. He soon had a flourishing practice and in addition was a regular contributor to legal journals.

In 1873, however, he gave up his lucrative practice to become minister of public works. Over the next five years Beernaert improved Belgium's road, rail and canal system, established new port facilities at Ostend and Anvers, and attempted—though unsuccessfully— to end child labor in the mines.

For a time in 1884 he was minister of agriculture and in the same year became prime minister. Under his administration the state of the Congo was created in 1885 with Leopold as sovereign; military fortifications were constructed in the vain hope of protecting Belgium's neutrality; and the Belgian constitution was revised.

When his cabinet fell on the question of proportional representation, Beernaert became an active member of the Interparliamentary Union: he presided over several of its conferences and served initially as president of its Council, and, when it was formed in 1908, its Executive Committee. At the Peace Conference at The Hague he presided over the first Commission on Arms Limitation. He was member of the Permanent Court of Arbitration and on many occasions acted as arbiter of international quarrels.

One of the problems which he tried to resolve was the question of the treatment of enemy property in naval warfare. On this matter, Belgium voted in favor of an American proposal for full inviolability, except for war contraband. As he didn't see much prospect of this proposal's being accepted, Beernaert suggested that enemy property at sea should be put under the same rules as on land. It could then be confiscated and held until the termination of hostilities, and, if destroyed, full compensation could be made. He did not get sufficient support to pursue this matter further.

As advocate of the principle of compulsory arbitration, he found himself, as a Belgian, at a slight disadvantage at the second Hague Conference since King Leopold was of no mind to apply this principle to the current Congo dispute and Beernaert, for his own good, was obliged to soft-pedal the issue.

BEERNAERT'S CO-LAUREATE THAT year has the distinction of possessing the longest and most impressive title of all the prizewinners: Paul Henri Benjamin Balluet, Baron d'Estournelles de Constant de Rebecque. He was the son of a family that could trace its ancestry back to the Crusades.

Hailing from the Loire Valley, d'Estournelles de Constant was educated at the Lycée Louis le Grand in Paris and received a diploma from the School of Oriental Languages. He entered the diplomatic corps in 1876 and represented France in Montenegro, Turkey and the Netherlands before being sent to England as counselor to the French Embassy in London. While in London he managed to avert war between France and Britain over a blockade, to which the British objected, during the French-Siamese border disputes of 1893. This incident convinced him of the general impotence of the diplomatic service and he decided to abandon his diplomatic career in favor of a political one, where he thought his influence would have more effect.

In 1895 the baron was elected deputy for Sarthe in the Loire district and in 1904 became a senator for the same region, a seat he held until his death.

His long-range solution for Europe's problems was a political one—the formation of a European Union. The immediate need, he was convinced, was a Franco-German rapprochement: he agreed that the past could not be forgotten but insisted that both countries must realize that peace was imperative. "War," he said, "drives the republics into dictatorships, and the monarchies into the grip of revolution."

At both Hague conferences, he took part as a French delegate and tirelessly plugged the theme of compulsory arbitration at a time when the tribunal at The Hague was being constantly sabotaged by the Great Powers. He paid a visit to the United States in 1902, managed to persuade Theodore Roosevelt to refer a dispute with Mexico to The Hague Tribunal, and obtained from Andrew Carnegie a considerable sum of money for the building of a "Peace Palace."

In 1903 he formed a Franco-German association in Munich and the following year was instrumental in achieving a Franco-British entente, but he was insistent that it should not be used against Germany. In 1909 he lectured the Prussian House of Peers on the need for a Franco-German rapprochement.

It was not his fault that his words were lost in the thunder of armaments then pouring off the European assembly lines.

The decade was over. The champions had had their say. And for all their well-intentioned efforts, the prospect of peace in Europe was further away than ever.

A World at War

Although the years from 1910 to 1919 were dominated by the Great War, as it was then called, it was a decade in which many of the new developments which had gone almost unnoticed in the first ten years of the century made tremendous strides, some stimulated by the war situation, some despite it.

Flying, motoring, wireless telegraphy, films—all advanced at an almost alarming rate, and the determination of working people everywhere to exercise more control over their own destinies became an overwhelming and irrestible fact of life.

Just as the previous decade had opened with the death of Queen Victoria, the Edwardian age came to an end in 1910, when Edward VII was succeeded by George V. Theodore Roosevelt was still president of the United States, where Mount Wilson's 100-inch reflecting telescope had just been completed and the Manhattan Bridge in New York City opened.

It was an age of exploration and discovery. Peary had reached the North Pole in 1909; in 1911 Amundsen narrowly beat Scott in a race to the South Pole from which Scott never returned. In London members of the Alpine Club were urging the secretary of state for India to give them permission to make an attempt on Everest.

But to most British people, India was still the jewel in the crown of the King-Emperor George V. The Delhi Durbar of 1911—the most massive and impressive demonstration of the power of the British Raj ever staged in India—turned out to be a fitting piece of pageantry for what was, in effect, a final curtain scene. Two years later Mahatma Gandhi, leader of the Indian Passive Resistance Movement, was arrested for the first time.

There were signs of impending trouble all over the world: a revolution in Portugal; another in China where the Manchu dynasty abdicated after three centuries, to be replaced by a provisional republic; and, in the Balkans, an endless succession of ententes and alliances and guarantees which could only lead to an immediate and widespread conflagration as soon as someone, somewhere, fired the first shot.

More and more money was being voted for warships; more and more submarines were being launched to lurk under the surface of the world's waters and prey on shipping; more and more countries were introducing conscription or calling up their reservists. The kaiser was now talking openly about the "place in the sun" which his new navy would secure for Germany.

Woodrow Wilson was elected president in November 1912 of a United States that was fast outstripping the world in technical innovation. Henry Ford had just pioneered the assembly-line system of automobile manufacture and before the end of the decade the motor traffic in New York was dense enough to demand the world's first three-color traffic lights. Arizona became a state in 1912, and in 1914 President Wilson sent the American fleet to Tampico, Mexico, and to Vera Cruz, where they occupied the customs house. Throughout the early part of the decade there had been constant tension between the United States and Mexico; the US Cavalry had already been sent to preserve the neutrality of the Rio Grande in the Mexican Civil War in January 1911.

In Ireland, as early as January 1912, the Ulster Unionists had resolved to repudiate the authority of any Irish government set up under the then imminent Home Rule Act, using catch-cries very similar to those which they are still chanting today, over sixty years later. And when the inevitable European war did break out, in August 1914, and Home Rule was shelved, the southern Irish Sinn Fein republicans immediately began to plan a rebellion which came at Easter 1916 and could be said to have marked the real beginning of the end of the British Empire.

When war broke out and spread right across Europe, America remained resolutely neutral at first; but in 1917, exasperated at Germany's arrogant refusal to stop using submarines to attack neutral shipping, Wilson declared war on Germany. The first of the doughboys arrived in France on June 26, 1917.

This was the year of the Russian collapse, when riots forced the tsar to abdicate. Lenin later led the Bolsheviks in the October Revolution, and the Soviets made a separate peace with Germany and Austria before the end of the year. In America, Buffalo Bill died at the age of 71, and John Fitzgerald Kennedy was born.

In January 1918 Woodrow Wilson presented Congress with his famous "Fourteen Points" to guarantee world peace: the most important of these was the setting up of a League of Nations—not a new idea by any means, but now pressed with a new urgency and by a man who was determined to wage war effectively only in order to secure a lasting peace.

In October, after the failure of their last desperate push and faced with starvation in the cities, the Germans appealed to Wilson both for an armistice and for terms on which peace could be negotiated. He offered them his Fourteen Points, and the Germans agreed. There was a brief revolution in Berlin, followed by the abdication of the kaiser and the formation of a Council of People's Delegates.

But it was the military commanders, Marshal Foch of France in particular, who dictated the terms of the armistice, and when Wilson arrived towards the end of the year for the Versailles Peace Conference, much of the damage had already been done. His ambitious ideas of self-determination for all small nations soon became bogged down in a welter of conflicting and irreconcilable demands—and the world now knows that the Versailles Peace Conference merely laid the foundations for World War II.

Throughout the decade women continued their struggle for a bigger say in things. In 1915 the US House of Representatives had thrown out a proposal for women's suffrage, and in England the Suffragettes were chaining themselves to railings, trying to starve themselves to death in prisons and damaging works of art in museums. They suspended activities for the duration of the war.

On June 14, 1919, J. W. Alcock and A. W. Brown flew the Atlantic in 16 hours and 27 minutes, landing in a field in Galway, Ireland, where the second round of the still-continuing fight for self-determination was just about to break out.

Observations of a total eclipse of the sun on May 29 had completely borne out Albert Einstein's theory of relativity; a new form of music called jazz had swept the United States and subsequently seeped over to Europe. The foxtrot and bobbed hair (which was safer for women working in factories than long hair) were all the rage, and the word "surrealism" was heard for the first time. By now 5,000,000 Americans were visiting the cinema daily. The popular star of the silver screen was a newcomer called Charlie Chaplin, but it was above all a decade of great silent cinema epics: *Queen Elizabeth* with Sarah Bernhardt, *Quo Vadis, Anna Karenina, The Fall of Troy, Spartacus* and D. W. Griffith's *Birth of a Nation.*

The books of the decade included Henry James's *The Golden Bowl,* James Joyce's *Dubliners* and *A Portrait of the Artist as a Young Man,* John Buchan's *Thirty-nine Steps* and *Greenmantle* and a popular novel about Gauguin by Somerset Maugham, *The Moon and Sixpence.* H. L. Mencken was writing about the American language, and intellectuals were reading D. H. Lawrence, Marcel Proust and Thomas Mann. At the other end of the scale, the popular songs of the period were "Pack Up Your Troubles in Your Old Kit Bag," "It's a Long Way to Tipperary" and "Keep the Home Fires Burning."

At the end of the decade Charlie Chaplin was still top favorite in the cinema, Dixieland had taken over from jazz, Lady Astor had become the first woman MP to take her seat at Westminster and Suzanne Lenglen was dominating the Wimbledon tennis championships. Herbert Hoover became director general of the International Organization for Relief in a Europe which was not only in ruins, but had changed, changed utterly.

The Bolsheviks were rapidly gaining control of Russia, the National Socialist party had been founded in Germany and in Italy Benito Mussolini had already founded a Fascist party.

In 1914 there had been five emperors; now there was only one, the king of England, and he was emperor only of India. The kaiser of Germany had been defeated. For centuries the Habsburgs had been Holy Roman Emperors and represented a kind of continuity with Charlemagne. The Ottoman emperors had kept alive, at Constantinople, some of the ancient spirit of Byzantium, while in Russia the Romanoff crest had still carried the double-headed eagle emblem of the Roman Empire of the East. Now all these links with Europe's past were severed.

The entry of the United States into the European war had another and very profound effect, as A. J. P. Taylor points out in his book *From Sarajevo to Potsdam.* "Ever since the Turks had been halted at the gates of Vienna more than two hundred years before, the traffic between Europe and the rest of the world had been all one way. Europeans everywhere were the invaders and the conquerors. Now the New World bounced back. Henceforth, European events were to be influenced, sometimes to be shaped, from outside. The Americans were Europeans with a difference: Europeans in origin and largely in culture, but without the Europeans' traditions of political behavior. . . . They disliked the European monarchies and, still more, the extension of European empires overseas. They wanted all Europeans to become peaceful, prosperous and sensible, like themselves. They could not understand why Europeans failed to abandon their parochial loyalties. European civilization, once apparently so superior and complacent, was now under challenge. Thus questioned by the Americans, Europeans began to doubt themselves. Morally, their age of supremacy was over."

It was in this context that the Nobel Peace Prize Committee had to bend their thoughts when considering the nominations in the immediate aftermath of the war.

But at the beginning of the decade, all hope had not yet been abandoned and the committee continued to award the prize to people (and an institution) still dedicated to the cause of preserving the fragile, visibly crumbling peace.

1911 Tobias Asser

1911 Albert Fried

1912 Elihu Root

1913 Henri de la Fontaine

**1914-1916
Prizes not awarded**

**1917
International Committee
of the
Red Cross**

**1918
Prize not awarded**

1919 Woodrow Wilson

1910

THE INTERNATIONAL PEACE BUREAU: *Founded in Berne in 1891 as a result of discussions at the third Universal Peace Congress in Rome that year. Frederik Bajer was one of its chief protagonists and its first president.*

BASICALLY AN INFORMATION office for the dissemination of literature of all kinds on peace matters, the International Peace Bureau was set up, at the suggestion of Frederik Bajer, the 1908 Peace laureate, to collect and codify data about all the various institutions, associations and individuals working towards world peace. Also active in the early days of the bureau were Gobat and Ducommun, the 1902 co-laureates, both of whom had worked as honorary secretary generals of the bureau. The Nobel Peace Committee officially acknowledged that it regarded the bureau in its early years "as virtually synonymous with the popular peace movement of the time—that is to say, with all the peace organizations affiliated with it and with their then homogenous ideology and program."

The bureau was established at Berne as the central office and executive organ of the International Union of Peace Societies "to coordinate the activities of the peace societies and promote the concept of peaceful settlement of international disputes." Figuring in its program were such matters as arbitration procedures, bilateral peace treaties, the creation of a permanent court of justice and some kind of intergovernmental or even supranational body for fostering cooperation and negotiation between nations. To disseminate these ideas, it became the bureau's function to arrange the annual peace congresses, prepare material for discussion and keep a watch on the resolutions which were passed at the congresses, to see as far as possible that they were implemented.

To carry out this work, the bureau badly needed financial support; until it received the Nobel Peace Prize, its income had varied from 8,000 to 9,000 Swiss francs a year (worth about $8,300 to $9,400 today), from various sources.

To the extent that the bureau was short of funds and needed a fair bit of money to carry out its formidable task—a task which was probably very necessary at a time when communications were not nearly as good as they now are, and when a great many diverse elements were working in often quite disparate ways towards the cause of peace—the award of the prize was probably a sound and practical decision. At this particular period, it was widely believed that a solution to the problem of peace was most likely to come from peace congresses and international arbitration, and people and institutions who were prepared to work industriously and unostentatiously to this end were regarded as at least as useful to the cause of peace as the brilliant if somewhat erratic individualists who became laureates in later years.

The outbreak of the war in 1914 brought the International Union of Peace Societies to an abrupt end, and to a large extent robbed the International Peace Bureau of the reason for its existence. It continued, after the war, to try to communicate ideas and proposals on peace and humanitarian welfare from nongovernmental organizations and place them before those responsible for governmental decisions. To facilitate this endeavor it moved its headquarters to Geneva, to be near the League of Nations.

The bureau is still in existence as a clearing house for communications between different national and international peace organizations, and between those organizations and national governments. It still organizes peace congresses, but more on the lines of seminars on specific projects such as UN peace-keeping operations.

1911

TOBIAS MICHAEL CAREL ASSER (1838–1913), the Netherlands: *Authority on international law, Dutch delegate at the two peace conferences at The Hague, arbiter in the Bering Straits dispute between Russia and the United States. Asser was responsible for persuading the Dutch government to summon the four conferences at The Hague in 1893, 1894, 1900 and 1904 on international private law, over which he presided, and was one of the founders of the Institute of International Law.*

ALBERT HERMANN FRIED (1864–1921), Austria: *Founder of the Deutsche Friedengesellschaft [German Peace Society] and editor of* Die Friedenswarte [The Peace Watch], *regarded by the Nobel Committee as "the best journal in the peace movement" at that time.*

RIGHT UP UNTIL the moment war broke out, the peacemakers—and along with them the Nobel Peace Committee—continued to pin their faith in international arbitration, pacifist societies and propaganda, and this ill-founded faith was reflected in the choice of the two men they chose to share the Peace Prize in 1911.

Tobias Michael Carel Asser was born in Amsterdam into a family with a long tradition of service to the law; both his father and his grandfather had been lawyers and his uncle was for a time Dutch minister of justice. He studied law at the Athenaeum in Amsterdam, receiving a doctor's degree in 1860 at the age of twenty-two.

He practiced law briefly but devoted his life mainly to teaching, scholarship and politics. In 1862 he became professor of private law at the Athenaeum, and when in 1876 the latter became the University of Amsterdam, he was appointed professor of international and commercial law. He believed that legal conflicts between nations could best be solved by international conferences, and in 1891 he persuaded the Dutch government to call a conference at The Hague to establish a uniform international procedure for conducting trials. This later became a permanent institution responsible, among other things, for international treaties, family law and bills of exchange as well as matters relating to marriage, divorce, legal separation and the guardianship of minors.

He collaborated with Dr. Rolin-Jaquemyns and John Westlake in starting the *Revue de Droit International et de Legislation Comparée* [the Journal of International Law and Comparative Legislation] in 1869 and four years later was one of a group which founded the Institute of International Law at Ghent, which he later headed.

In the field of international law, his biggest achievement was during the negotiations connected with the neutralization of the Suez Canal. He succeeded in getting Spain and Holland elected to the Suez Canal Commission as representatives of the smaller nations, alongside the Great Powers and Turkey.

In 1893 he resigned his professorship and retired from the bar to become a member of the Dutch Privy Council. He was the Netherlands delegate to The Hague Peace Conferences of 1899 and 1907; at the former, his great success was to organize the Permanent Court of Arbitration.

He sat later as a member of the Permanent Court when it heard its first case—the dispute between the United States and Mexico over the "Pious Fund" in 1902. This was a dispute over a fund set up in the eighteenth century to finance the Catholic Church in California; after the Mexican War (1845–48), when Mexico ceded Upper California to the United States, she refused to pay the Californian bishops moneys due to them from the fund. The United States won the case.

His view on the subject of private international law, expressed in a thesis he wrote in 1880, was that the most practical method would be for nations at international conferences to agree as far as possible on common solutions to legal conflicts. In this way the legislation in the various countries could gradually be brought to conform; and this, in practice, is how it has worked out.

ALFRED HERMANN FRIED left school at the age of fifteen to work as a bookseller in his native Vienna, but moved, after a few years, to Berlin where he established his own publishing company.

A dedicated pacifist and disciple of Bertha von Suttner, he founded the Deutsche Friedengesellschaft [German Peace Society] and edited its major publication, *Monatliche Friedenskorrespondenz* [Monthly Peace Correspondence] between 1894 and 1899. He also founded, in 1891, the pacifist journal *Die Waffen Nieder* [Lay Down Your Arms], edited by Bertha von Suttner and named after her book. In 1899 it became *Die Friedenswarte* [The Peace Watch], which under his editorship became the most influential pacifist journal in the world. Fried's aim was to treat the peace question in a way that would arouse interest in intellectual circles. A humanitarian, he was an advocate of what he called "casual pacifism." He believed that international tension would be alleviated not only by legislation, but also by increased international understanding. Too much concentration on disarmament was wrong he felt, because armaments and wars were only symptoms of the unhealthy international relations which existed and they would disappear automatically as soon as the underlying international anarchy had been removed. This could best be achieved, in his view, by a "Pan-European Bureau" (taking an example from the Pan-American pattern) which could contribute to European unity and international understanding by acting as a center of information on various cultural, economic and political matters.

When World War I broke out, Fried emigrated to Switzerland in protest against Germany's official war policy and continued his work for international peace as editor of a periodical with the highly indigestible title *Blätter für internationale Verständigung und zwischenstaatliche Organisation* [Papers for International Understanding and Interstate Organization]. He continued to edit *The Peace Watch,* a rallying point for international peace efforts, until his death. He was also a member of the Berne Peace Bureau, secretary of the International Conciliation for Central Europe and secretary general of the Union Internationale de la Presse pour la Paix [International Union of the Press for Peace].

After the war Fried organized a journalistic campaign against the Versailles Treaty and repeatedly pressed the point that the war had been proof of the pacifist analysis of world politics. An idealist and an intellectual, he despaired of the cynical attitude of newspaper editors and commentators to what he called the "dreamers" and even more of the utter lack of interest shown by the general public in matters which he regarded as being of fundamental importance. "The events of an international bicycle race," he wrote in one article, "are described in great detail and are eagerly swallowed up by the readers, just as the least significant comedian on the local stage is better known to the public than the people who make world history or the great events of historical importance."

Fried would not find things greatly changed in the world today, except that "the people who make world history" are at least known from their television appearances, though less well-appreciated, perhaps, than the comedians who mimic them.

1912

ELIHU ROOT (1845–1937), United States: *Secretary of war and secretary of state. He was responsible for organizing affairs in Cuba and the Philippines after the Spanish-American War and for bringing about a better understanding between the countries of North and South America. Founder of the Pan-American Bureau (1908) and later president of the Carnegie Peace Foundation, he was an energetic champion for an unconditional arbitration treaty between the United States and Great Britain.*

ELIHU ROOT BELIEVED that war was the natural reaction of human nature in the savage state. "The law of the survival of the fittest led inevitably to the survival and predominance of the men who were effective in war and who loved it because they were effective," he said. "War was the avenue to all that man desired. Food, wives, a place in the sun, freedom from restraint and oppression, wealth of comfort, wealth of luxury, respect, honor, power, control over others, were sought and attained by fighting. . . ." Believing all this, he was nevertheless convinced that nations could learn to live in peace.

Root was born in Clinton, New York, and graduated from Hamilton College, where his father was a professor of mathematics. He took a degree in law at New York University Law School in 1867, was called to the bar and founded a law firm with John H. Strahan. The company became concerned with corporate litigation involving banking, railroads and municipal government, a field of activity which drew him into close contact with the conservative Republicans, though he himself was more closely associated with the reform element in the party.

He became a close friend of Theodore Roosevelt and was his legal adviser during the time Roosevelt was mayor and later police commissioner of New York City. After Roosevelt became governor of New York City, he continued to consult Root, who served on two conventions to revise the New York State Constitution.

When McKinley was elected president in 1900, with Roosevelt as his vice-president, Root was asked to join the cabinet as secretary of war. McKinley explained this somewhat unusual appointment by saying that he wanted a lawyer, not a military man, in the post.

In the Philippines, Root dealt summarily with Aguinaldo's revolt by tripling the American armed forces stationed there and writing what was in effect a constitution for the administration of the islands under an American commission headed by William Taft. He also reorganized the American army, enlarged West Point, founded the Army War College and created a general staff.

He left the cabinet in 1903 and returned, as secretary of state, when Roosevelt succeeded McKinley. In 1906 he made an extended tour of Latin America and did a good deal to alleviate South America's mistrust of the United States, suggesting, among other things, that the next Pan-American Conference should take place in Rio de Janeiro. He cooperated with Mexico in mediating troubles in Central America and founded the Pan-American Bureau in New York in 1908.

He succeeded, too, in persuading the US Senate to forego their objections to treaties of arbitration with European countries and in 1908–9 managed to achieve a total of twenty-three treaties of arbitration with various Latin American and European countries as well as with Japan.

His success in the case of Japan was particularly important because at that period there had been a great wave of Japanese immigration all along the Pacific coast, which had led to violent racial discrimination in which, among other things, Japanese children were being refused admission to Californian schools. Root solved the problem by negotiating a "Gentleman's Agreement" with the Japanese government to control emigration to the United States. He then persuaded the Californian authorities to waive their objections to Japanese children attending the schools.

Later, as chief counsel for the United States at The Hague Tribunal, he settled the long drawn-out controversy with the British over the North Atlantic fisheries. He also improved relations between the United States and Canada.

Root worked on the Permanent Court of Arbitration and was president of the Carnegie Endowment for International Peace. His ideas on diplomacy were firmly based on the realization that isolationism could no longer be the guiding spirit in American foreign policy. For that reason he was opposed to Wilson's policy of neutrality when the war broke out, but later supported him as a wartime leader. He was head of an American mission which was sent to Russia in 1917 in a futile effort to persuade the Russians to carry on the war against Germany.

He was the leading Republican supporter of the League of Nations and was a member of the League's commission of jurists who framed the Statute for the Permanent Court of International Justice. One of the four American delegates to attend the International Conference on the Limitation of Armaments which met in Washington in 1921, he sponsored a treaty to restrict the use of submarines and poison gas in warfare.

He was, above all, a realist. Referring to pacifist propaganda in his Nobel lecture, he made the very valid point that "the mere repetition of the obvious by good people of average intelligence, while not without utility and not by any means to be despised as an agency for peace, nevertheless is subject to the drawback that the unregenerate world grows weary of iteration and reacts in the wrong direction. . . .

"The attractive idea that we can now have a parliament of men with authority to control the conduct of nations by legislation or an international police force with power to enforce national conformity to rules of right conduct is a counsel of perfection. The world is not ready for any such thing, and it cannot be made ready except by the practical surrender of the independence of nations, which lies at the basis of the present social organization of the civilized world. . . . Human nature must come much nearer perfection than it is now, or will be in many generations, to exclude from such control prejudice, selfishness, ambition and injustice. An attempt to prevent war in this way would breed war, for it would destroy local self-government and drive nations to war for liberty."

1913

HENRI MARIE DE LA FONTAINE (1854–1943), Belgium: *President of the International Peace Bureau in Berne from 1907 until his death and a prominent member of the Interparliamentary Union.*

DESCRIBED IN THE Nobel presentation address as "the true leader of the popular peace movement in Europe," Henri Marie de la Fontaine was the archetype of what might be described as the first wave of Peace Prize winners.

He studied law at Brussels University, was called to the bar in 1877 and became an authority on international law. He was appointed professor of international law at the Université Nouvelle in Brussels in 1893, and two years later was elected to the Belgian Senate as a representative of the Socialist party. He was a senator for thirty-six years and the senate's vice-president for fourteen of those years.

After he succeeded Frederick Bajer as head of the Peace Bureau at Berne in 1907, he became one of Europe's leading pacifists. He played an active part in bringing about The Hague Conferences of 1899 and 1907 and on several occasions acted as *rapporteur* for the ratification of international agreements.

He was a member of the Belgian delegation to the Paris Peace Conference in 1919 and to the League of Nations Assembly in 1920. One of his ideas for promoting international understanding was the Centre Intellectuel Mondiale [World Intellectual Center], which he founded in Brussels. The center later became part of the League of Nations Institute for Intellectual Cooperation. He had far more grandiose ideas, including a world school and university, a universal library, an international auxiliary language, a central monetary office, an international parliament, and international offices for labor, trade, statistics, immigration and emigration.

As early as 1912 la Fontaine saw the dangerous possibilities of war in the air, and at the Peace Congress in Geneva that year managed to get a resolution passed outlawing aerial warfare. A socialist, he made great efforts to interest the workers' organizations in the peace movement, though without any marked success. He regarded the Interparliamentary Union as an embryo world parliament, the precursor to world government, and was an enthusiastic delegate to the union's various conferences.

He was secretary general of the Société Belge de l'Arbitrage et de la Paix [Belgian Society of Arbitration and Peace] from 1889 on, and participated actively in virtually all peace congresses held over the following twenty-five years. In addition, he founded the review *La Vie Internationale* [International Life], which was dedicated to promoting international understanding. His prodigious literary output included a manual on the laws of peace and the code of arbitration, a source book of 368 documents on arbitration including all the agreements, rules of procedure and case decisions printed in their original languages and covering all treaties made from 1794 to 1900, and a bibliography of international arbitration containing 2,222 entries. His best known literary work is *The Great Solution* (1916), in which he sketched a constitution for a world state, which he then considered many years away; his ideas envisaged the setting up of certain institutions straight away, which would eventually be incorporated in the world state, and in the meantime could be used to prevent wars.

On the outbreak of war, when in 1914 Belgium was invaded, he escaped to the United States and settled in Washington, D.C. In a letter to a friend he wrote: "The peoples are not awake. . . . [There are dangers] which will render a world organization impossible. I forsee the renewal of . . . the secret bargaining behind closed doors. People will be as before, sheep sent to the slaughterhouses or to the meadows as it pleases the shepherds. International institutions ought to be, as the national ones are in democratic countries, established by the peoples for the peoples."

1914–1916

Prizes not awarded.

1917

THE INTERNATIONAL COMMITTEE OF THE RED CROSS: *Founded in Geneva, Switzerland, in 1864.*

WHEN THE WAR broke out in 1914, the Nobel Peace Committee understandably decided to suspend its activities and make no further awards to those engaged in promoting the cause of world peace. On the other hand, right from the beginning of the war, it was quite clear to everybody what magnificent work the Red Cross was doing both on the battlefields and in the matter of establishing lines of communications between prisoners of war and their relatives. All this cost a great deal of money. The Nobel Committee thus decided to give the 1917 Peace Prize to the International Committee of the Red Cross, acknowledging once again, as they had done by awarding a half-share of the very first Peace Prize in 1901 to Henri Dunant, founder of the Red Cross, that they regarded the work of succoring the war wounded as a contribution to peace.

The International Committee was the successor to the original five-person committee of the Société Genevoise d'Utilité Publique [Geneva Public Welfare Society], which met in 1863 to consider the possibility of implementing Dunant's idea of establishing a society to look after the wounded in time of war. Dunant was a member of the original committee, whose objectives were: the creation in all countries of societies to aid the sick and wounded in time of war; the establishment of an international convention for the reciprocal protection of soldiers wounded on the battlefield; and the proclamation of the neutrality and inviolability of ambulances and hospitals.

The original meeting called by the Geneva Committee and held in October 1863 was attended by fourteen countries, and it was here that the basic principles of the Red Cross were formulated. The first Red Cross Convention, drawn up at Geneva the following year, committed the governments which signed it to care for the wounded in time of war, whether friend or foe. In later years this convention was revised and expanded and new conventions were adopted to protect the victims of warfare at sea (1907); the care of prisoners of war (1915); and, in more recent years, the care of civilians in wartime (1949), and the prevention and relief of human suffering in the time of peace as well as war.

The first national Red Cross societies to come into existence were in France, Belgium, Italy and Spain; they were all formed in 1864 in the wake of the Geneva Conference of 1863. The American National Red Cross was formed in 1881 with Clara Barton, a volunteer worker on the Civil War battlefields, as its first president. Altogether, thirty societies were formed in the nineteenth century and another seven nations had joined the group before the outbreak of the war in 1914.

When the International Committee succeeded the original committee of five, it retained its private, almost ad hoc nature, and even today consists of a council of twenty-five ordinary Swiss citizens who meet regularly in

Geneva. One of its main functions is to accord recognition to new national Red Cross societies which must meet certain requirements before they become part of the organization.

The governments of the countries concerned must have adhered to the Geneva Convention, and each society—only one is allowed per country—must use the Red Cross emblem and be open to all citizens regardless of race, sex, politics or religion. (The emblem in Muslim countries is a red crescent; in Iran it is a red lion and sun.)

Immediately after the outbreak of World War I the International Committee of the Red Cross in neutral Geneva became the center for the many efforts which were made to ensure that all humanitarian principles were not immediately thrown overboard in the fervor of battle. It became, in effect, the moral guardian of the provisions of the Geneva Convention, reminding the belligerent governments of their obligations under the Convention and making protests in cases of flagrant violation of these principles.

It collected funds necessary for the development of Red Cross facilities in warring countries and sent delegations to the various fronts to investigate and where possible improve on the situation of the wounded. The Committee itself took the initiative in attempting to protect Red Cross organizations in the various warring countries. In particular, it succeeded in getting the Turkish medical organization, the *Croissant Rouge Ottoman,* recognized by the signatory powers as being on the same footing as the other Red Cross societies; it also managed to see that the Serbian Red Cross was granted recognition, officially at any rate, even after Serbia had been conquered.

Another issue fought by the Geneva Committee was the right of medical personnel to be repatriated immediately upon becoming prisoners of war; this right was recognized by England, France and Germany. As well as arranging for the exchange of correspondence from prisoners of war, the Committee succeeded in enforcing the rule that seriously wounded soldiers be exchanged via Switzerland. The warring countries were not willing to exchange badly wounded officers (because they might have information which could be used effectively against them), but did agree to their internment in Switzerland.

The Committee also protested, though to little avail, against particularly inhuman acts of war such as the sinking of hospital ships by German submarines and the Turkish massacre of the Armenians. In addition, it concerned itself with the care of prisoners of war in the only way it could—by acting as a bureau for the exchange of information. Through the Red Cross, thousands of families all over the world were able to trace their menfolk who had become prisoners of war, and in some cases they were able to communicate with them through the Red Cross. The Committee in Geneva looked after the Western Front while the Danish Red Cross undertook the care of the Eastern Front; these organizations were supported by the Red Cross societies in Petrograd (Leningrad), Vienna, Budapest, Rome and Constantinople (Istanbul).

The Nobel Peace Prize, coming as it did, when the war had reached its most desperate stage, gave the International Committee of the Red Cross an extremely welcome and badly needed contribution to the vast funds that were needed to carry out all these activities.

1918

Prize not awarded.

1919

THOMAS WOODROW WILSON (1856–1924), United States: *28th president, who in his celebrated "Fourteen Points" speech to Congress in January 1918 outlined his concept of a League of Nations and laid the foundations for the Paris Peace Conference and the Treaty of Versailles which ended World War I.*

WHEN THE FIGHTING stopped with the armistice of November 11, 1918, and a peace conference was convened in Paris the following year, the Nobel Committee resumed their search for champions of peace: and in 1919 there was no doubt about the choice. At the presentation of the prize, Woodrow Wilson was praised by the president of the Norwegian Storting for his success in establishing "a design for a fundamental law of humanity" in present-day international politics. "The basic concept of justice on which it is founded will never die," he went on, "but will steadily grow in strength, keeping the name of Wilson fresh in the minds of future generations."

Indeed, it was not Wilson's fault that the permanent peace he envisaged when he said that the proposed League of Nations would "bring peace and safety to all nations and make the world itself free at last" turned out to be a mere twenty-year interruption in hostilities.

Born in Staunton, Virginia, of Ulster and Scottish Calvinist stock, Wilson was the son of a stern Presbyterian minister. He was deeply affected by his memories of the Civil War; he was nine when it ended and spent his youth among defeated, dispirited and disinherited Southerners.

Wilson graduated from Princeton in 1879 and then studied law for a time at the University of Virginia. When ill health interrupted his course, he switched to government and history at John Hopkins University, Baltimore, where in 1886 he received his Ph.D. for a thesis attacking the control exercised by congressional committees in the legislative process of the United States.

He began his teaching career at Bryn Mawr College as associate professor of history and political economy. In 1888 he became a professor at Wesleyan University in Connecticut and two years later joined the faculty of Princeton as professor of jurisprudence and political economy. In 1902 he became president of the university.

The addresses he gave and the articles he wrote in this capacity soon drew wide political attention, and in 1910 the Democrats nominated him as their candidate for the governorship of New Jersey. He was elected in November of that year and proceeded to carry out a program of reform designed to clean up corruption and protect the public from exploitation by the big trusts—a program which shocked and horrified the very politicians who put him in power. He was a huge popular success and in a matter of months was brought into the wider arena of national politics. At the Democratic Convention of June 1912, he was nominated as presidential candidate and—largely because Theodore Roosevelt split the Republican vote—found himself president of the United States within two years of leaving Princeton.

Although his foreign policy was theoretically dominated by a strong respect for the rights of small nations, he was forced by the disturbed conditions in the Caribbean to take actions not exactly in full accord with his theories. At one stage during his stewardship, the United States assumed a virtual protectorate over Haiti: precautionary visits by US warships to Santo Domingo were followed in 1915 by the landing of US Marines and the proclamation of martial law. Throughout his two terms as president, he was constantly plagued by Mexican anarchy, which at one period assumed the proportions of a small war.

However, as soon as World War I started, US foreign affairs were dominated by its effects, and by Wilson's efforts to protect America's rights as a neutral nation. By careful and patient negotiation he managed to avoid an open breach with the Germans for almost three years—even after the sinking of the liner *Lusitania,* with the loss of 1,000 lives, including 128 Americans. To many, Wilson was "the man who kept

America out of the war," and it was largely on this pacifist sentiment that he was re-elected in 1916.

Shortly thereafter, he approached the British, indicating that he was ready "if Britain and France considered the moment opportune" to propose a conference to end the war. Britain and France did not seem to be in any great hurry to take him up on his offer, but in September 1916 the kaiser himself drafted an invitation to Wilson, asking him to take the initiative in a peace move.

In the US Senate on January 22, 1917, Wilson outlined his ideas on what would form a sound basis for continuing peace. Peace must be arranged by the major force of mankind organized under the protection of a League of Nations. No nation should extend its power over another, and no one power should be allowed to dominate the land or the ocean. There would have to be a limit on armaments and as a guarantee of future peace and justice, the existing war must not result in the violation of the rights of one side or the other. As he put it, it must be a "peace without victory."

Wilson's first attempts to achieve peace were frustrated by Germany's renewal of unrestricted submarine warfare which led to America's declaration of war on Germany on April 6, 1917.

Wilson, an intolerant Calvinist with a good deal of Ulster intransigence in his soul, refused to deviate from the path which he believed himself appointed by Providence to tread, wherever it happened to lead; he had no difficulty at all in switching from the policy of neutrality and pacifism to total war, which he now saw not as aggression but as a crusade against freedom. He rallied the nation, managed to produce an efficient fighting force which towards the end of the war numbered two million, and told the nation that it was "a war for freedom and justice and self-government amongst all the nations of the world . . . the German people themselves included." By putting it this way and implying that the Germans were to be liberated from a war which was not really of their making, he managed to assuage his conscience for what might otherwise have looked like a pretty abrupt change of front.

He reiterated his principles for peace on January 8, 1918, in his famous "Fourteen Points" speech,* which the Germans accepted in principle in another appeal to Wilson to end the war. Unfortunately, in the congressional elections of November 1918, his party lost control of the Senate and of the vital Senate Foreign Relations Committee, a loss which greatly weakened his position in the peace negotiations.

*Eight of the points involved more or less specific territorial and political problems and six dealt with general principles of international relations: open covenants, freedom of navigation, removal of economic barriers, the reduction of armaments, the adjustment of colonial claims and the establishment of a League of Nations.

He achieved an early triumph with the acceptance of the principle that the League of Nations should be an integral part of the peace treaties, and a preliminary draft of a covenant for the League was unanimously accepted in Paris on February 14, 1919. The United States asked for certain amendments and restrictions which in turn entailed corresponding European concessions, but agreement on a final draft was reached by April 28. However, his success in getting the League idea through was obscured by the concessions he was forced to make on almost every other point.

His "peace without victory" plan had to be abandoned as the victors insisted, point by point, on making the Germans pay for the war. The unilateral disarmament program imposed on Germany made nonsense of the basic idea behind his Fourteen Points; so, too, did the savage reparation demands. But at least the settlement recognized the rights of the small nations to a degree which had never before been approached. On June 28, 1919, the Versailles Treaty was signed and the following day Wilson returned to the States convinced that what he had done was good and right.

Ratification of the treaty in the States was opposed by the Senate Foreign Relations Committee—they wanted to make certain reservations on the collective security provisions which membership in the League would entail and which Wilson found, in his intransigent way, unacceptable. In bad health, Wilson set out on a mission to convert the American people to his own way of thinking. After thirty-four major addresses and innumerable interviews, he collapsed with a thrombosis.

Strenuous efforts were made to effect some sort of a compromise but Wilson was adamant and now talked about submitting the issue to some form of national referendum. On March 19, 1920, the final Senate vote was taken, and the reservations on collective security were strong enough to provoke Wilson's condemnation. He appealed to his followers to vote against ratification on these terms. They did, and as a result the United States was excluded from the League of Nations by the man who had done more than any other to create it.

In a telegram accepting the Nobel Peace Prize, Wilson expressed his respect for "the far-sighted wisdom of the founder in arranging for a continuing system of awards.

"If there were but one such prize," he went on, "or if this were to be the last, I could not of course accept it. For mankind has not yet been rid of the unspeakable horror of war. I am convinced that our generation has, despite its wounds, made notable progress. But it is the better part of our wisdom to consider our work as only begun. It will be a continuing labor. . . ."

The Terrible Twenties

When we think about the twenties today, it is almost always in terms of the lighter side of life—the Scott Fitzgeralds, the Charleston, the Black Bottom, Lindbergh flying the Atlantic, Noel Coward's first plays, bobs and shingles, the Astaires and Coco Chanel, Babe Ruth, and Irving Berlin and George Gershwin.

True, there was prohibition in America for almost all of the time, with gang fights in the streets of Chicago and other American cities, and a general strike in England. There was the collapse of the mark and economic confusion in Germany. And right at the end of the decade, there was the Wall Street crash, which triggered off a worldwide depression. But the overall impression remains of a rip-roaring era when people (those who could afford it anyway) cast away all inhibitions and concentrated on celebrating the fact that the war was over and the world was a place for "having fun."

For the peacemakers, however, it was a highly disturbing decade, deeply concerned as they were with tidying up so many of the loose ends which the war had left behind—like who was to pay for it and how—and with trying to assess the possible effects on world peace of the emergence of totally new forces like Russian communism, German national socialism and Italian fascism.

Stalin, Hitler and Mussolini all emerged from obscurity during this decade and it was in these years that the finally irresistible rumblings of revolution could be heard from the enormous Indian subcontinent and from tiny Ireland.

The decade began hopefully enough: the League of Nations came into being on January 10, 1920, and moved to its permanent headquarters in Geneva in October. The Hague was selected as the seat of the International Court of Justice and the Supreme Allied Council agreed that Germany should make forty-two annual reparation payments, largely to France, Britain, Italy and Belgium; the amount was later fixed at over $74 billion in today's terms.

But there were signs in plenty, for those who had ears to hear them above the chatter in the speakeasies and the din of the jazz bands, that the war to end all wars had saddled the world with a host of almost insurmountable problems.

Prohibition had come into force in the United States on January 16, and in March the US finally rejected the Versailles Treaty.

The Bolsheviks were gaining ground everywhere in Russia and there was a lot of grabbing of territory. Britain annexed the German East African Protectorate, which is now Kenya; France occupied Damascus; and the Greeks under King Alexander occupied Adrianople, now Ederne, in that part of the Greek peninsula on the side of the Dardanelles opposite Constantinople.

In April 1920 the Supreme Allied Council assigned the mandates of Mesopotamia and Palestine to Britain; halfway through the decade Cyprus was declared a British crown colony, and Lebanon was proclaimed a republic by France. Towards the end of the decade Italy signed a twenty-year treaty of friendship with Abyssinia.

In August, in the United States, the 19th Amendment gave women the same voting rights as men. A few months later, in November, the first US public broadcasting station was opened in East Pittsburgh to give the results of the Harding-Cox presidential election. Within a couple of years America would have more than a million receiving sets.

The Empress Eugénie died, Douglas Fairbanks married Mary Pickford, a man called J. T. Thompson invented the submachine gun, and people were reading Sinclair Lewis's *Main Street,* Colette's *Chéri* and H. G. Wells's *Outline of History.*

In 1921 the first Indian parliament met, and the first parliament of Northern Ireland opened at Stormont. The fascists were returned in the Italian elections, and French troops were mobilized to occupy the Ruhr in protest against Germany's failure to pay the first installment of the reparations. Through the early part of the decade, this battle over war reparations and Germany's obvious inability to pay them was a constant headache, as indeed was Britain's inability to repay her wartime borrowings from the United States.

In 1922 a civil war broke out in Ireland as soon as the British troops left, and Mahatma Gandhi was arrested in India and sentenced to six years' imprisonment for civil disobedience; an anti-lynching bill was passed in the House of Representatives.

In January 1923 the USSR—a confederation of the Ukraine, White Russia and Transcaucasia—was formed, and the German economy began to slow towards a standstill. In Italy all nonfascist parties were dissolved, and in the United States, President Harding died and was succeeded by

Calvin Coolidge. As the months passed, Germany went from bad to worse. Rioting became more and more severe; the bank rate soared to 90 percent; martial law was introduced; and in October the value of the mark dropped to the rate of about 50,000,000 to the US dollar. A coup led by Adolph Hitler in Munich in November failed; Hitler was sent to jail for five years but was released within a year, during which he had usefully employed himself by writing the first volume of *Mein Kampf*. E. N. da C. Andrade published a study on *The Structure of the Atom*, and in January 1924 Ramsey MacDonald formed the first but short-lived Labor government in England.

Also in 1924: Britain and France recognized the USSR; there was rioting between Hindus and Moslems in India; and the Germans stated the terms on which they would join the League of Nations. The books of the year included E. M. Forster's *A Passage to India* and Thomas Mann's *The Magic Mountain;* the plays were Marc Connelly's *Green Pastures,* G. B. Shaw's *Saint Joan* and Noel Coward's *The Vortex.* There was a big Empire Exhibition at Wembley and the Olympic Games were held in Paris. But a lot of people stayed home in the evenings, listening to music on the gramophone.

Woodrow Wilson, Marie Corelli, Eleanore Duse, Giaccomo Puccini, Lenin, and Joseph Conrad died; so did Gimpy O'Banion, riddled with bullets by three members of Al Capone's gang, in his own flower shop in Chicago at the height of the bootleg war. Earlier casualties of the decade had included Saccho and Vanzetti, who may or may not have shot a bodyguard in an armed robbery at South Braintree, Mass, but who were certainly card-carrying Communists; they were executed in Charleston, near Boston.

In 1925 Mrs. Ross of Wyoming became the first woman governor in the United States and Frank B. Kellogg was appointed US secretary of state. Paul von Hindenburg was elected president of Germany and Cyprus became a British crown colony.

There was also a conference at Locarno to guarantee Germany's frontiers, to provide for arbitration in the case of a dispute and to give assurances against future sanctions such as the occupation of the Ruhr by Belgium and France; the way was now open for Germany to join the League of Nations.

Scott Fitzgerald's *The Great Gatsby* was published and a man called Clarence Birdseye extended the deep-freezing process to precooked foods, little realizing just how profoundly his invention was going to change our world. In the United States both *Time* magazine (1923) and the *New Yorker* (1925) were growing in popularity and Chaplin's *The Gold Rush* was a big hit. Anita Loos's *Gentlemen Prefer Blondes* was published.

In April 1926 came the first of many attempts to assassinate Mussolini, and in May a general strike in Britain, which lasted for nine days. In May, too, the League of Nations held a preparatory disarmament conference which was attended by the United States but not by the USSR. Later in the year there was a Belgian financial crisis, followed by a French one, with the devaluation of the French franc. Germany was admitted to the League of Nations in September, and in Russia Josef Stalin made his mark on the Russian political scene for the first time.

In Soho, London, J. L. Baird demonstrated half-tone television for the first time (both Baird and C. F. Jenkins in America had already shown that a moving silhouette could be transmitted by radio); two years later he was to give a transatlantic television transmission—from Britain to the *Berengaria,* in mid-ocean—and demonstrate color television in Britain. Unaware of the shadow that these developments were casting over its future, the film industry went from strength to strength with black-and-white epics like *The Last Days of Pompeii, Ben Hur* with Ramon Novarro and *Don Juan* with John Barrymore, while behind the scenes the technicians were working on the talking picture and new and constantly improving forms of color film. Rudolf Valentino died and the future Queen Elizabeth II of England was born. Le Corbusier published a paper called "The Coming Architecture" and a young sculptor named Henry Moore exhibited a "reclining figure." Books in the news were Theodore Dreiser's *An American Tragedy* and T. E. Lawrence's *The Seven Pillars of Wisdom.*

In January 1927 the interallied military control of Germany ended and on May 13, Black Friday, Germany's economic system finally crashed.

In September 1926 there had been an international convention on slavery, which most people even then could hardly believe still existed; yet it was not until September 1927 that slavery was finally abolished in Sierra Leone.

Towards the end of the year Frank B. Kellogg, US secretary of state, suggested a pact for the renunciation of war, and in Russia Trotsky was expelled from the Communist party as a deviationist.

Important as these events were, people were more interested, probably, in Lindbergh's 37-hour solo flight across the Atlantic from New York to Paris on May 20-21; and in the fact that with *The Jazz Singer,* starring Al Jolson, the talking picture had finally arrived.

In May 1928 women of twenty-one were given the vote in Britain; and in fascist Italy a new electoral law reduced the electorate from ten million to three million.

The Kellogg-Briand Pact outlawing war was signed in Paris in August and in September was adopted by the League of Nations. In October a plebiscite in Germany failed to condemn the building of new battleships. Chiang Kai-shek was elected president of China, and the following month, on November 7, Herbert Hoover was elected president of the United States.

It was the year in which Benito Mussolini published a book entitled *My Autobiography* (a little prematurely, as it turned out—by far the most interesting period of his life still lay ahead); two scientists, H. Geiger and W. Muller, invented a device known as the geiger counter; Alexander Fleming discovered penicillin; the Graf Zeppelin flew from Friederichshafen in Germany to New Jersey in 4 days and $15\frac{1}{2}$ hours and later flew around the world; and in Yankee Stadium in New York City a baseball player named Babe Ruth was earning as much, they said, as the president of the United States.

It was the year of *The Three-Penny Opera* by Kurt Weill and Bertolt Brecht, of *Lady Chatterley's Lover* by D. H. Lawrence and of Walt Disney's first all-color Mickey Mouse cartoon.

In January 1929 an inter-American treaty of arbitration along the lines of the Kellogg-Briand Pact was signed in Washington and Trotsky was expelled from the USSR.

Germany accepted the Kellogg-Briand Pact in February of 1929. The following month the fascists won—if that's the word—a one-party election in Italy, and Arabs attacked Jews in Jerusalem following disputes over the use of the Wailing Wall.

In September Aristide Briand suggested a European Federal Union—along the lines of today's European Economic Community—and on October 28 came the Wall Street crash. In a country with 11,000 millionaires, twice as many as there had been in 1914, and over 26,000,000 motor cars, where continuing and increasing prosperity had been taken for granted, the effect was shattering. Thousands were ruined; there were so many suicides that it soon became a black joke. "You had to stand in line," one went, "to get a window to jump out of."

Now, suddenly, the first of the novels and plays about the Great War caught the public's attention. They included Ernest Hemingway's *A Farewell to Arms*, Erich Maria Remarque's *All Quiet on the Western Front* and R. C. Sheriff's *Journey's End.*

The publication of these books made a tremendous impact, drawing the attention of thousands of ordinary people to horrors they had never even suspected and making the peacemakers more than ever determined to ensure that it would never happen again. They genuinely believed that they now possessed the instrument which could prevent it: the League of Nations.

1920 Léon Bourgeois

1921 Karl Branting

1921 Christian Lange

1922 Fridtjof Nansen

1923-1924

Prizes
not
awarded

1925 Joseph Chamberlain

1925 Charles Dawes

1926 Aristide Briand

1926 Gustave Stresemann

1927 Ferdinand Buisson

1927 Ludwig Quidde

1928
Prize not awarded

1929 Frank Kellogg

1920

LÉON VICTOR AUGUSTE BOURGEOIS (1851–1925), France: *Politician and statesman, president of the French Senate (1920–23). Chairman to the first Hague Peace Conference (1899) and a member of the Permanent Court of Arbitration (1907), he was highly instrumental in laying the groundwork for the League of Nations.*

THE FAITH THAT the peace-loving nations of the world had put in the League of Nations was reflected in the Nobel Committee's choice of Peace Prize winners during the decade; almost without exception the laureates were men associated with one or another aspect of the League's activities. Bourgeois, the 1920 winner, had been one of the first to suggest a League of Nations and was chairman of a commission set up in 1917 to study the possibilities of founding such an organization.

Léon Victor Auguste Bourgeois was the son of a clockmaker from the Jura in France, but he lived most of his life in Paris. He was educated at the Lycée Charlemagne and, after fighting in an artillery regiment in the Franco-Prussian War of 1870–71, studied law at the University of Paris. In 1876, after having practiced law for several years, he went into the public service and then into politics. He was that rare animal, a politician without ambition who twice refused to run for the presidency of the republic, although it was fairly certain that he would have been elected.

Bourgeois's first public office was as deputy head of the Claims Department in the Ministry of Public Works. In rapid succession he became secretary general of the Préfecture of the Marne in 1877; underprefect of Rheims in 1880; prefect of the Tarn in 1885; director of personnel in the Ministry of the Interior in 1886; and, at the age of thirty-six, chief commissioner of the Paris police.

In 1888 he was elected deputy for the Marne. He was a member of several governments in the years following, and was prime minister for a brief period between November 1895 and April 1896 when his government fell after a constitutional fight over finances. He served as minister of foreign affairs in Ferdinand Sarrien's government from March to October 1906. He was minister of foreign affairs again in Alexandre Ribot's two-day government in 1914, and was then without portfolio until he became minister of labor in Aristide Briand's government of 1916–17. He had been elected to the senate in 1905 and was its president from 1920 to 1923.

Bourgeois had previously distinguished himself at the first Hague Peace Conference in 1899 and was made a member of the Permanent Court of Arbitration there in 1907.

But by far the most important work he performed was on the commission set up to study the possibilities of a League of Nations and the conditions under which it could be made to work. The principles laid down by this commission were submitted to the Paris Peace Conference by Bourgeois in January 1919.

Bougeois saw the League as a juridical military organization whose sole purpose was to preserve peace, if necessary by sanctions; and he saw it as being called into existence only when the need arose. He believed that international cooperation could be best achieved on the basis of The Hague conferences of 1899 and 1907; the League should be used only to reinforce the two areas that had been left unresolved by these conferences: arbitration, which had not yet been made obligatory; and the enforcement of international justice, for which there was as yet no machinery. He was convinced that international justice could only be enforced by sanctions, whether diplomatic, economic or military.

As his plans were turned down by the United States and Great Britain as impracticable, it could be said that to a large extent he had failed. Nevertheless, Bourgeois had done much of his outstanding work for the League, not immediately before it came into existence, but as early as the beginning of the century. As leader of the French delegation at the two Hague conferences, he had stoutly argued the case for a League and the duty of nations to submit to arbitration. As early as 1908 he announced: "The League of Nations is created. It is very much alive."

Bourgeois retained his belief in the League idea right through the war and did not allow patriotism to obscure his judgment. Very early in the war he realized that materially France had been outstripped by her enemies, and that ultimate world security could not rest on the balance of power alone.

"We must see things as they are," he wrote in 1916. "We in France are not, from the point of view of birth rate and material strength, at the same stage of development as, for example, our enemies. Now the balance of power, however skillful diplomats may be, results in the triumph of the greatest number and the most brutal, and not in the triumph of the noblest, the proudest, the worthiest. It is another policy, therefore, the policy of justice, which alone can give peace and security to France and the nations which do not seek to establish themselves by violence. There will be no policy of justice if the League of Nations is not set up."

When the League was formally inaugurated, Bourgeois became France's principal representative at Geneva, both in the Council and in the

Assembly, but approaching blindness soon forced him to retire. His publications include a book on the 1919 Treaty of Versailles and the League of Nations, and a history of the work of the League of Nations between 1920 and 1923.

In a communication to the Nobel Peace Prize Committee in 1922, he said that the victory [in the war] had been, above all, a victory for law and order.

"The collapse of the three great monarchies based largely upon military power has given birth to a number of young nations, each representing the right of people to govern themselves, as well as to enjoy the benefits of democratic institutions which, by making peace dependent on the will of the citizens themselves, has infinitely reduced the risk of future conflict.

"Out of the horror of four years of war has emerged, like a supreme protest, a new idea which was implanting itself in the minds of all people: that of the necessity for civilized nations to join together for the defense of law and order and the maintenance of peace. The League of Nations, heralded in 1899 and 1907 by The Hague Peace Conferences, became, through the Covenant of June 28, 1919, a living reality.

"But, can it furnish us at last with a stable instrument of peace? Or shall we again encounter, at the very moment when we think we are reaching our goal, the same obstacles which for centuries have blocked the way of those pilgrims of every race, creed and civilization who have struggled in vain towards the ideal of peace? . . . We are far from being blindly confident about the future. . . . Certain powers that were defeated in the Great War have not been whole-hearted in their acceptance of the moral disarmament which is the primary condition for any peace.

"Now and henceforth there exists an international law whose doctrine is firm and whose jurisprudence is not contested by a single civilized nation. . . . If this law was all too obviously violated in 1914 and during the war years, the victory has righted the wrong done. Should such violations ever happen again, then indeed we must despair for the future of mankind."

1921

KARL HJALMAR BRANTING (1860–1925), Sweden: *The "father" of socialism in Sweden, and closely involved in achieving the peaceful dissolution of the union between Sweden and Norway in 1905. He led the successful movement to bring Sweden into the League of Nations.*

CHRISTIAN LOUS LANGE (1869–1938), Norway: *Secretary general of the Interparliamentary Union from 1909, first secretary general of the Interparliamentary Bureau. From the opening of the League of Nations until his death, he was standing adviser to the Norwegian delegation as well as either a delegate or an alternate delegate himself.*

BELIEVING AS FIRMLY as they did in the League of Nations, it was perhaps only natural that the members of the Nobel Peace Committee would want to reward the two men primarily responsible for the admission of Sweden and Norway respectively to the League. Branting had the added appeal that, like Klas Arnoldson, the 1908 Peace laureate, he had been among those responsible to the peaceful separation of Norway and Sweden, though he was distinctly unpopular, because—again like Arnoldson—he took the Norwegian side.

Karl Hjalmar Branting was born in Stockholm, the only child of Professor Lars Branting, one of the innovators of the Swedish school of gymnastics. He was educated at the Beskow School in Stockholm and then studied mathematics and astronomy at the University of Uppsala. In 1882 he became an assistant to the director of the Stockholm Observatory.

He gave up his scientific career in 1884 and switched to journalism, working first for the radical paper *Tiden* [The Times] and becoming its editor in a very short time. In 1886 he was made editor of the newspaper *Socialdemokraten* [Social Democrat], and was among the founders of the Social Democratic Labor party, formed in Sweden in 1889. In 1907 he became its president, a post he held until his death.

Branting was elected to the lower chamber of the Riksdag (the Swedish parliament) in 1896, and until 1902 was its only Social Democrat. He was energetic in supporting his party's plans to mobilize working-class support for equal and direct suffrage for adults, but was careful not to alienate the progressive middle class, ultimately working towards the Liberal-Socialist coalition government which came about in 1917, in which he was minister of finance. This government achieved a reform of the constitution in 1918 which helped to spread social democracy throughout Sweden.

Branting became prime minister in 1919, depending on Liberal support as he didn't have a majority in parliament. He dissolved this parliament in October 1920—women received the vote under his government in 1921—and the elections went against him. At another election, he became prime minister again in October 1921, retaining the foreign affairs portfolio, and departed in April 1923, when the Liberals and the Conservatives combined to vote him out. When the elections of 1924 gave the Social Democrats a majority over the other two parties, Branting became prime minister for the third time, resigning in January 1925, when his health failed.

So far as foreign policy was concerned, Branting was opposed to appropriating unduly large sums of money for defense at the expense of social services; at the same time, however, he was against what he called "defense nihilism."

During the negotiations for the separation of Norway and Sweden Branting insisted that Sweden should grant Norway its own foreign service; he made a speech so bitterly opposed to the use of force against Norway that he was sentenced to three years' imprisonment, though this was later commuted to a fine.

He led the successful movement to bring Sweden into the League of Nations and was the League's first Swedish representative in Geneva. He became a member of the Council of the League in 1923. His principal concern was disarmament and, ironically, one of his bitterest opponents on this score was a fellow Peace laureate, Léon Bourgeois, who won the prize in 1920. As we have seen, Bourgeois believed that the League should have the power to impose sanctions by military force if necessary. He didn't think that there was any need for a permanent international army or navy, but he believed that a sort of supranational general staff would be needed, ready at all times for immediate military action. This plan—which in any event was rejected as impracticable by Great Britain and the United States—ran directly counter to Branting's conviction that the League should go all-out for total disarmament.

"As a result of the World War and of a peace whose imperfections and risks are no longer denied by anyone, are we not even further away from the great aspirations and hopes for peace and fraternity than we were one or two decades ago?" he asked in his Nobel lecture.

"In spite of the unique extent of the devastation, we should not forget that this hard labor constituted the birthpangs of a new Europe . . . the beginning development of a League of Nations in which disputes between members are solved by legal methods and not by the military superiority of the stronger. . . . The annual meetings of the League's Assembly are in effect official peace congresses binding on the participating states to an extent that most statesmen a quarter of a century ago would have regarded as utopian. . . . Nobel's basic idea has been realized. The whole collective force of the League is to be turned against the aggressor, with more or less pressure according to the need. . . . [But] the League of Nations [must] become universal in order truly to fulfill its task."

CHRISTIAN LOUS LANGE is unusual among the Peace laureates in that he had been connected with the Nobel organization right from the beginning. He was working as secretary to the organizing committee of the Interparliamentary Conference, held in Oslo in 1899, when the Norwegian Storting agreed to appoint a committee to adjudicate on the Peace Prize; and in 1900 he was appointed first secretary of that committee. Among his achievements was the organization of the library of the Norwegian Nobel Institute which was founded in 1904. He left the committee in 1909, but continued to act as an adviser.

Lange was born in Stavanger, West Norway; his father was an engineer in the armed services. He studied history and languages at the University of Christiania (now Oslo) and graduated in 1893. For some years he taught in secondary schools in Oslo.

The Norwegian government chose him as one of its technical delegates at the second peace congress at The Hague in 1907. Two years later he became secretary general of the Interparliamentary Union and it was largely as a result of his efforts that the organization survived the war. Its secretariat was situated in Brussels and when Germany invaded Belgium in 1914, Lange had to leave. Returning to Oslo, he took the union with him, as it were, and began to conduct its business as best he could from his home there, keeping in touch with members abroad and holding meetings of the Scandinavian Interparliamentarians to plan the revival of international cooperation as soon as the war ended.

It was not until 1921 that the first postwar conference of the Interparliamentary Union could be held; this took place in Geneva which has been the headquarters of the organization ever since.

Lange was also active in the League of Nations, which he attended regularly as a Norwegian delegate. Like Branting, he was primarily interested in disarmament, or at least in the limitation of arms.

During the war he had worked on a history of the development of internationalism from the earliest days: *l'Histoire de l'Internationalisme.* He always preferred the word "internationalism" to "pacifism," and explained why in his Nobel lecture: "[Pacifism] . . . leads one to think merely of the negative side of the peace movement, the struggle against war; and for this side of our efforts 'antimilitarism' is a more fitting name. . . . A pacifist will usually—at any rate in our day—be an internationalist, and vice versa. But history shows us examples which prove that the pacifist need not think internationally. Jesus of Nazareth was a pacifist; yet all his sayings, in so far as they are preserved, prove that internationalism was quite foreign to him, for the very good reason that he did not think politically at all; he was apolitical. If we were to place him in one of the categories of our age, we should have to call him an antimilitarist or an individual anarchist. Internationalism is a *social* and a *political* theory a definite conception of how society should be organized especially a conception as to how the nations should settle their mutual relations.

"Today we stand on a bridge leading from the territorial state to the world community," he continued. "Politically we are still governed by the concept of the territorial state; economically and technically we live under the auspices of worldwide communications and worldwide markets. . . . Modern techniques have torn down state frontiers, both economic and intellectual. The growth of means of transport has created a world market and an opportunity for the division of labor embracing all the developed and most of the undeveloped states. . . .

"If the territorial state is to continue as the last word in the development of society, then war is inevitable. For the state by its nature claims sovereignty, the right to an unlimited development of power, determined only by self-interest. It is by nature anarchistic. . . . Therefore all hope of a better future for mankind rests on the promotion of a higher form of development for world civilization, an all-embracing human community. . . . The sovereign state has in our times become a lethal danger to human civilization because technical developments enable it to employ an infinite number of means of destruction.

"The idea of eternity lives in all of us," he continued. "We thirst to live in a belief which raises our small personality to a higher coherence—a coherence which is human and yet superhuman, absolute and yet steadily growing and developing, ideal and yet real. Can this desire ever be fulfilled? It seems to be a contradiction in terms.

"And yet there is a belief which satisfies this desire and resolves the contradiction.

"It is the belief in the unity of mankind."

1922

Fridtjof Nansen (1861–1930), Norway: Scientist and explorer, cited for "his work in the repatriation of prisoners of war, his work for the Russian refugees, his work in aiding the millions in Russia struggling against famine and . . . his work for the refugees in Asia Minor and Thrace." Nansen was the League of Nations' first high commissioner for refugees from 1921 until his death.

Arctic explorer, ocean voyager, artist and writer, Fridtjof Nansen was far and away the most romantic of all the Nobel laureates.

Born in Store-Froën on the outskirts of Christiania (Oslo), the son of a prosperous lawyer, he went to school in Christiania and in 1888 attended the university there to study zoology, perhaps because he thought the fieldwork involved would enable him to live a largely outdoor life as well as to utilize fully his artistic talents. He was keen on skating, skiing, hunting and fishing; and even as early as this, he had set his heart on a career of exploration.

In 1882 he joined the sealing ship *Viking* for a voyage into Greenland waters. On this voyage he saw the Greenland ice cap and became determined to cross it someday. Instead of starting from the inhabited west coast, he decided to start from the east coast: with no possible means of escape he would thus be forced to keep going. With five others he left Norway in May 1888, reached Greenland in a sealing ship and crossed the cap on foot, reaching the highest point (8,920 feet) in September. About twenty days later, through storms and intense cold, they struggled to Ameralik fjord where they were forced to winter in an Eskimo settlement at Godthaab. Here Nansen gathered material for a book on Eskimo life. They returned home in May 1889.

Five years before this, in 1884, Nansen had read an article describing how the wreck of the *Jeannette*—the ill-fated ship of de Long, the American explorer—had been caught in the pack ice off the Bering Strait and had drifted slowly, tortuously, in a northwesterly direction for nearly a year before sinking. Nansen immediately thought of using that slow drift of the ice as a means of exploring the polar regions; he began to plan a ship that would ride up on the ice as soon as the pressure caught the hull, and drift with the currents from Siberia across the Arctic Ocean towards the Greenland Sea. Such a voyage would, he thought, settle the question of whether, at the Pole, there was another continent or only open polar sea; and whether there was any animal life in the Arctic Ocean.

On his return from the Greenland expedition, with the experience and reputation he had gained from that adventure, he decided to put his idea to drift with the ice floes across the Pole before the Norwegian Geographical Society and in 1892 tried the Royal Geographical Society in London. His plan met with a good deal of criticism from contemporary explorers, but the Norwegian parliament gave him two-thirds of his estimated expenses and the rest was raised by subscription, some from King Oscar II and the remainder from private sources; the Royal Geographical Society contributed £300 (or $8,375 in today's terms).

On June 24, 1893, nine years after he had first read the article which gave him the idea, he set sail with twelve others on board the *Fram,* a stout ship built to his own design.

The *Fram* behaved perfectly, rising above ice floes that would have crushed any other ship and drifting, as Nansen had predicted, across the Polar Basin. By March 1894 it was clear that the *Fram* would not drift right over the Pole but would by-pass it, so Nansen set out with F. H. Johansen to make a dash across the ice floes with two sleds, two kayaks and twenty-eight dogs, leaving the others on board the *Fram,* which he now knew was perfectly safe. On April 8 Nansen turned back at 86 degrees, 13.6 minutes N, the highest latitude so far reached by man and, since they had no way of knowing where the *Fram* was by then, headed towards Franz Josef Land. He and Johansen wintered there in a hut of stone covered with walrus hides, living on polar bear and walrus meat and using blubber as fuel.

On their way to Spitzbergen in May 1896, they met up with Frederick Jackson and the British Jackson-Harmsworth arctic expedition, and returned to Norway on his ship *Windward.*

At Tromsø, in August 1896, Nansen and the *Fram* were reunited. Nansen's two-volume account of the voyage, *Farthest North,* appeared in 1897.

On his return Nansen was offered a professorship of zoology at Oslo University (the chair was created in his honor), but by now his interest had switched to oceanography; so the university created a chair of oceanography instead and changed his status to professor of oceanography.

Nansen was largely responsible for the establishment of the International Council for the Exploration of the Sea and for a time directed the council's central laboratories at Oslo. He took part in a number of deep sea voyages both with other explorers and in his own yacht *Veslemoy* in the Norwegian Sea, through the northeastern Atlantic, in Spitzbergen waters, to the Azores, through the Barents Sea and the Kara Sea and back through Siberia.

As he grew older, he became more and more interested in the relationship between individuals and nations. "Any union in which one people is restrained in exercising its freedom is and will remain a danger," he wrote. He was involved in the peaceful dissolution of Norway and Sweden in 1905, and upon the establishment of the Norwegian monarchy he became its first minister to London (1906–8).

In 1917 he was appointed head of a Norwegian commission to the United States to negotiate a trade agreement for the supply of essentials to Norway. During the war years he worked energetically to achieve an international organization which could bring about a secure and lasting peace settlement. He was an ardent believer in the idea of the League of Nations and spent the early part of 1919 in Paris trying to bring his influence to bear on the statesmen meeting there.

The Norwegian delegation to the first assembly of the League was headed by Nansen and he remained a well-known and popular member until his death. Tall and bony, with a craggy frame, snow-white hair, a flowing moustache and a broad-brimmed hat which he wore at a rakish angle, he was a familiar figure in Geneva.

His first big humanitarian task came in April 1920 when the League appointed him high commissioner responsible for the repatriation from Russia of about 500,000 German and Austro-Hungarian prisoners of war. The Soviet government would not recognize the League but was prepared to deal with Nansen on a personal basis, and by September 22 he was able to report that 427,886 of the prisoners had been repatriated, with aid from the Red Cross. He was able to do this largely because of the high opinion the Russians held of him as a man.

In August the following year there was a famine in Russia as a result of drought in the Volga Valley and Maxim Gorki appealed to Nansen for help. Although opposed to Bolshevism, Nansen immediately secured several hundred tons of salt fish for Leningrad and then set about organizing international aid on a large scale. On August 15 thirteen governments and eighteen Red Cross organizations appointed him commissioner to direct efforts to bring relief to Russia. At the League assembly in September he made an urgent appeal for about £15 million (about £81 million—$155 million—in today's terms). "We are running a race against the Russian winter," he said. "Make haste to act before it is too late to repent."

There was no shortage of grain in the world; in the United States wheat lay rotting for lack of buyers and in Argentina there was so much maize that it was being used as fuel for railway engines. Nor was the shipment of the grain any problem: whole fleets of ships were lying idle. To solve the problem it was necessary to arrange a loan to Russia of £10 million, since it was felt that the scheme should not be financed by charity alone. However, as other governments neither recognized the Soviet government nor approved of the political system which it represented, Nansen could not raise the loan. "I do not believe that we are supporting the Soviets simply because we are showing the Russian people that there is compassion in Europe," he argued. "But suppose that such aid should support the Soviets. Is there any man who dares come forward and say: It is better to allow twenty million people to die of starvation than to support the Soviet government?"

Nansen's appeal to the League was turned down, but he then repeated it to the world at large and with the money that came in, including $20 million from the US government, particularly from the Food Administration and the War Relief Bureau directed at this time by Herbert Hoover, at least ten million lives were saved; some estimates put it as high as twenty-two million.

In 1922, at the request of the Greek government and with the approval of the League of Nations, Nansen tried to solve the problem of the Greek refugees who had poured into their native land from Asia Minor when the Greek army had been defeated by the Turks. Nansen arranged for the exchange of over one million Greeks living on Turkish soil for about 500,000 Turks living in Greece.

On July 5, 1922, on Nansen's initiative, an international agreement was signed in Geneva recognizing an identification card for displaced persons, known as the "Nansen passport." This was introduced very largely to help the vast numbers of White Russians who had emigrated at the time of the revolution. Many of them had been caught in Constantinople (now Istanbul) where, without papers or money, they were in a very difficult situation. As League of Nations commissioner for refugees, Nansen took on the problem of resettling them in new countries, where they could earn a decent living, and the "Nansen passport" that they were all issued was eventually recognized by fifty-two governments.

His next great humanitarian effort, again at the invitation of the League was to save the remaining Armenian people from extinction. He drew up a political, industrial and financial plan for creating a national home for Armenians in Erivan. The League failed to implement the plan, but the Nansen International Office for Refugees, created in 1930, later settled some 10,000 in Erivan and 40,000 in Syria and the Lebanon.

Nansen had scant respect for politicians and diplomats. "The golden produce of the earth has been trampled under iron feet," he said in the course of his Nobel lecture, "the land lies in ruins everywhere, and the foundations of its communities are crumbling. . . . Where is the remedy to be sought? At the hands of politicians? They may mean well enough, many of them at any rate, but politics and new political programs are no longer of service to the world—the world has had only too many of them. . . . The diplomats perhaps? Their intentions may also be good enough, but they are once and for all a sterile race which has brought mankind more harm than good over the years. . . . We can no longer look to traditional leadership for any hope of salvation.

"In my opinion the only avenue to salvation lies in cooperation between all nations on a basis of honest endeavor. I believe that the only road to this goal lies through the League of Nations."

Nansen used the Nobel Peace Prize money for the furtherance of his international relief work. Of him, a Danish journalist wrote: "The Nobel Peace Prize has in the course of the years been given to all sorts of men. It has surely never been awarded to anyone who in such a short time has carried out such far-reaching *practical* peace work as Nansen."

1923-1924

Prizes not awarded.

1925

JOSEPH AUSTEN CHAMBERLAIN (1863–1937), Great Britain: *Statesman and, as foreign secretary, British signatory to the Locarno agreements of October 1925.*

CHARLES GATES DAWES (1865–1951), United States: *Financier, vice-president under Calvin Coolidge, and chairman of the committee set up by the League of Nations to investigate Germany's capacity to pay war reparations. He was the man behind the Dawes Plan (1924), which restored confidence in the economy—and, in effect, the future—of Europe; the plan marked the beginning of the policy of reconciliation and peace which led to the Locarno agreements.*

IF THE FIRST half of the decade was dominated by the early assemblies of the League of Nations, the second half was very much concerned with the problem of getting Germany back on her feet and integrated into the new Europe. The two men chosen as laureates for 1925 were intimately involved in the latter endeavor: Chamberlain in arranging the Locarno Agreements which guaranteed Germany's frontiers and opened the way for her entry into the League of Nations and Dawes with his plan to solve the reparations problem and get the German economy going again. In the light of events to come, these were, unfortunately, extremely short-lived contributions to the cause of world peace, to say the least of it.

Sir Joseph Austen Chamberlain, British statesman and foreign secretary from 1924 to 1929, was the eldest son of the "Empire Builder" Joseph Chamberlain, champion of imperial unity and tariff reform. Born in Birmingham in October 1863, Chamberlain was educated at Rugby school, Trinity College, Cambridge, and afterwards in Paris and Berlin. He served initially as secretary to his father, at a time when the latter was preoccupied with Parnell, the Irish Home Rule question and the Land War in Ireland.

Chamberlain entered Parliament in 1899 and remained an MP all his life. He was civil lord of the admiralty (1900), financial secretary to the Treasury (1900–02) and postmaster general (1902) in the governments of Lord Salisbury and A. J. Balfour during his father's term as colonial secretary.

When his father resigned his post to concentrate on tariff reform, Austen Chamberlain, himself a life-long supporter of protective tariffs, remained on in the government as chancellor of the Exchequer (1903–05).

He was secretary of state for India in Asquith's coalition government of 1915, and remained in the post when Lloyd George became premier. He resigned in July 1917 when his department came under criticism—though he was not held personally responsible—but rejoined the government in April 1918 as a member of the War Cabinet. From 1919 to 1921 he served as chancellor of the Exchequer in Lloyd George's Peacetime Coalition.

In March 1921, when Bonar Law retired temporarily because of ill health, he became leader of the Conservative party, lord privy seal and leader of the House of Commons. He was a loyal supporter of Lloyd George, particularly on the matter of the Anglo-Irish Treaty of 1921, and took part in the treaty negotiations. When the Conservatives withdrew their support from the coalition in October 1922, bringing it down, Chamberlain resigned his leadership and did not return to office until Baldwin's second government (1924–29) when he became foreign secretary.

His great achievement in that capacity was the Locarno Pact of October

1925—usually referred to in the singular as the Locarno Pact or Treaty, though in fact it consisted of a number of separate agreements, by which Germany's western frontiers were mutually agreed upon by Great Britain, France, Italy, Belgium and Germany. What was known as "the Locarno spirit," kept alive by frequent, friendly discussions at League meetings between Chamberlain, Aristide Briand and Gustav Stresemann (the British, French and German foreign ministers respectively), seemed to augur well for the future and led to Chamberlain's receiving not only the Nobel Prize but also a knighthood.

The proposal for such a pact had come, in the first instance, from Germany. At the end of 1922 Dr. Wilhelm Cuno, the German chancellor, had proposed that the powers with interests along the Rhine should, under a guarantee from the United States, agree not to make war on one another for a period of thirty years, unless a declaration of war was decided upon as a result of a plebiscite. This was rejected by the French government, and in May 1923 the Germans came up with another proposition, this time based on a treaty of arbitration—again without results.

In February 1925 the German government, now with Luther as chancellor and Stresemann as foreign minister, tried a third time, stating that Germany was willing to accept a pact which expressly guaranteed the Rhine frontiers by means of a collective and individual pledge.

This approach was coolly received in Paris by the Herriot government but warmly welcomed by Chamberlain; however, when Herriot was succeeded by Painlevé and Briand became France's foreign minister, it was immediately arranged that after the sixth assembly of the League of Nations in September, the leading statesmen would meet at Locarno.

The agreements concluded there between Germany, Belgium, France and Great Britain laid down that the parties would guarantee, individually and collectively, the boundaries between Germany and France. Another clause bound Germany, Belgium and France not to make war on one another except in the cases specifically mentioned in the pact itself (the right to defend themselves if the Rhine frontier was violated or if other flagrant breaches of the Versailles Treaty were committed).

After the Locarno Pact Austen Chamberlain's star seemed to wane. In 1931 he became first lord of the admiralty in the national government of Ramsey MacDonald, but during his tenure of office the navy mutinied at Invergordon against economy cuts, and again, although he was not in any way to blame, he resigned. He held no office after the general elections of 1931, though he remained an MP until his death in 1937.

His books include memoirs, *Down the Years* (1935) and *Politics from Inside* (1936).

CHARLES GATES DAWES was born in Marietta, Ohio, the son of a Civil War brigadier, and a descendant of one of the first Puritan families to come to America. Dawes's father owned and managed a lumber company in Marietta; his uncle was a successful banker.

Dawes graduated from Marietta College in 1884 and studied law at Cincinatti Law School before entering the legal profession and taking up practice in Lincoln, Nebraska, in 1887. Before long he controlled a city block of business offices and a meat-packaging company, acted as a bank director, and invested in land and bank stock. In 1894 he bought control of a plant manufacturing artificial gas in Wisconsin and another to the north of Chicago.

In 1902 he turned over the management of these enterprises to his brothers and went into banking, becoming president of the Central Trust Company of Illinois, often referred to as the Dawes Bank; he worked full-time as its manager until he enlisted in the army when the United States entered the war in 1917. He was commissioned as a major and put in charge of supplies for the American Expeditionary Force. He conceived the idea of a coordinated supply center for the Allied Forces and became the American member on Foch's Board of Allied Supply. After the war he stayed on in Europe to direct the disposal of war surplus materials, and had reached the rank of brigadier general when he retired in 1919, with a reputation as a tough but efficient administrator.

Dawes was then appointed first director of the US Bureau of the Budget, and in 1923 the Allied Reparations Committee appointed him chairman of a board of financial experts whose task it was to find some solution to the problem of Germany's inability to meet her reparations payments without endangering European financial stability. The idea had been suggested by US Secretary of State Hughes as early as 1922.

The Dawes Plan, prepared with Owen Young and submitted in 1924, provided for a reorganization of Germany's finances with the assistance of loans from Allied and US investors. Repayments were to be guaranteed by mortgages on the German railways and on German industries. Dawes was against the repeated occupation and evacuation of the Ruhr by France and Belgium; he believed that the Ruhr represented an integral part of Germany's economy and that Germany could not recover until it was stabilized. The plan saved Europe from immediate economic collapse, but it was only a partial and temporary solution to the basic problem and was, to say the least, a debatable contribution to the cause of peace. However, it could be said that it gave Germany a breathing space in which to collect her shattered finances and recover from the deep rancor which survived the war, and which would not disappear as long as the French and Belgian armies continued to occupy part of her territory. In this respect, the plan could be said to have paved the way for the Locarno Pact, which guaranteed Germany's western frontier and opened the way for her to join the League of Nations.

Dawes was nominated for the vice-presidency by the 1924 Republican committee, and after fighting an active campaign the Coolidge-Dawes team was elected with a large majority. After completing his term as vice-president, he represented the United States as ambassador to Britain between 1929 and 1932; and while in this post he served as US delegate to the London Five-Power Naval Conference of 1930, at which a pact was signed by the United States, Great Britain, France, Italy and Japan.

He served briefly as chairman of the US delegation to the Geneva Conference of 1931 but resigned both that post and the ambassadorship to return to the United States during the worst days of the depression to direct the Reconstruction Finance Corporation, which made loans to banks, railroads and other key enterprises in an effort to get the American economy moving again.

Dawes donated his Nobel Prize money to the endowment of the then newly established Walter Hines Page School of International Relations at John Hopkins University.

1926

ARISTIDE PIERRE HENRI BRIAND (1862–1932), France: *Foreign minister and ten times premier of France, cited for his part in bringing about the Locarno agreements in October 1925. He was also responsible, with US Secretary of State F. B. Kellogg, for the 1928 Kellogg-Briand Pact.*

GUSTAVE STRESEMANN (1878–1929), Germany: *Founder of the German People's Party, chancellor of a coalition government and secretary of foreign affairs. He took the initiative for Germany in arriving at a rapprochement with the Western Allies over the boundaries established at Versailles; his efforts paved the way for the Locarno Conference and Germany's admission into the League of Nations in September 1926.*

OF THE THREE statesmen who between them achieved the Locarno Pact,

Briand was the most constructive. France, after all, had more to lose than the others: she had only recently been invaded by Germany, not for the first time, and the French were very naturally reluctant to relinquish their control over their common frontier with Germany. But Briand had already tried in Cannes, in 1922, to establish an agreement with England, and as England was clearly sympathetic towards Germany at this juncture, he saw in the Locarno Pact a means of ensuring English support and a hope, however faint, that with the principal grievances removed, a new, democratic Germany might emerge. In a speech at the prize distribution, Nansen, cynical as ever, said: "What inspires our confidence is the fact that it was neither idealism nor altruism which compelled men to make this attempt; it was a feeling of necessity."

Aristide Pierre Henri Briand, ten times premier of France (a record for those days), was born in Brittany, the son of an innkeeper. He studied law in Paris and entered politics as a violently anticlerical syndicalist in favor of a general strike. At socialist meetings, in cafés and in articles, he preached the syndicalist doctrine of revolution by strike which, in a phrase of the period, would allow the proletariat to pass from words to actions; he also advocated the armed insubordination of soldiers called out to suppress strikes or to fight for their country.

His violent speeches and writings brought him to the attention of socialists like René Viviani and Jean Jaurès and with them he founded the French Socialist party in opposition to the uncompromisingly Marxist French Socialist party under Jules Guesde. In 1904 they founded *L'Humanité* as a Socialist newspaper (it became a Communist newspaper fifteen years later).

In 1902 Briand defended the French antimilitarist Gustav Herré (who had publicly announced that he thought the dung heap was the best place for the French flag), and the case brought him such nationwide fame that he was elected to the Chambre des Deputés at the age of forty. His bitterly anticlerical outlook, combined with his knowledge of law, proved useful in getting the legislation which separated church and state through the French parliamentary system. Once in the Chambre des Deputés he seemed to drift steadily towards the Right. He became minister of education and religion in Sarrien's government of 1906; the fact that he was prepared to accept a portfolio in a bourgeois ministry caused the final breach with the Socialist party, and he was dismissed.

He remained on as minister of education and religion in Clemenceau's government formed the same year, and when that fell in 1909, Briand formed his first cabinet, taking Home Affairs and Religion and announcing that he would adopt a policy of "national understanding and tranquillity."

By now he had strayed so far from his original syndicalist line of thinking that when in October 1910 there was a threat of a general railway strike, he mobilized all the railwaymen who were still subject to military service, dismissed those who disobeyed, and had the strike committee arrested.

Between 1911 and 1921 he was in and out of favor. From 1914, first as vice-premier and then as premier, he pressed energetically for a Balkan front and for closer cooperation with the Allies, particularly Britain. But France was a country desperately searching for scapegoats for the disasters at the front: Briand was eventually accused of inadequacy and forced out of office. In 1921, on the fall of Georges Leygue's ministry, he formed a government yet again and took charge of foreign affairs. He was particularly concerned with the way in which the Treaty of Versailles would be implemented, especially with regard to the reparation payments. In the autumn he went to Washington D.C. as French delegate to the Conference on Naval Disarmament. He then went to Cannes to discuss an Anglo-French mutual defense treaty with Lloyd George; on his return he was bitterly accused of failing to safeguard the interests of his own country and had to resign again in 1922.

In April 1925, after another period in the wilderness, he was offered the portfolio of foreign affairs in the cabinet of Paul Painlevé. He played a major part in the negotiations over the Locarno Pact in October 1925, and when Painlevé resigned he became premier yet again.

For over five years—through continuing crises, including a second devaluation of the franc and a world depression—he continued to direct foreign policy on the basis of European consolidation and reconstruction, and exercised great influence in the League of Nations. He was a firm supporter of the idea of the renunciation of war as an instrument of national policy and his ideas, combined with those of the US secretary of state, F. B. Kellogg, led to the signing of a treaty in Paris known as the Kellogg-Briand Pact. The actual idea of abolishing war as an instrument of policy by means of treaties had been an American one suggested by a Chicago lawyer, S. O. Levinson, taken up by the president of Columbia University, Nicholas Murray Butler (a Peace Prize winner in 1931), and discussed with Briand in June 1926. The aim of the movement started by Levinson and preached by Butler was that war should be abolished in the same way as dueling and slavery had been abolished. They made no distinction between wars of aggression and defensive wars; and they believed that disarmament would never be achieved until war as an institution had been abolished.

The French view was that France and the United States should conclude a bipartite agreement which would serve as a pattern and an example for other countries to follow; the American view, which prevailed, was that the pact should embrace as many countries as possible right from the start. It was signed in Paris in 1928 and finally adhered to by over sixty countries, including all the major powers.

Briand's last major proposal was a sweeping concept of a European Union, which was proposed at the League of Nations in May 1930—but got nowhere.

AT FIRST SIGHT, Gustave Stresemann was a curious choice for a Nobel Peace Prize: a fire-eating, aggressive Prussian who, during the war was a firm believer in unrestricted submarine warfare and the annexation of as much land as Germany could lay her hands on, and a rabid supporter of the kaiser. He was, nevertheless, a realist and was very quick to come to terms with the postwar situation, and although in retrospect we may consider that his motives were suspect, at the time it seemed as if he was as genuinely concerned as Chamberlain and Briand with integrating Germany into a new, peaceful European League.

Curiously enough, like Briand, he was the son of an innkeeper and the only member of his family to attend high school. He studied literature and history at Berlin University and economics at Leipzig, and was awarded a Ph.D. in 1902 for a thesis on the Berlin bottled-beer trade (a subject on which he had some expert knowledge since his father did a small trade in bottled beer). He grew up as a Prussian Protestant, utterly convinced of the political, spiritual and military superiority of Germany.

Stresemann had an unusually successful commercial career and married the daughter of a Berlin industrialist. He was legal adviser to the Saxon Industrialists Union, which he formed, and in 1903 he joined the National Liberal party.

As editor of an industrial paper, the Dresden *Sachsische Industrie* [Saxon Industry], and as Dresden town councillor, Stresemann acquired a thorough working knowledge of municipal affairs, and in 1907 he was elected to the Reichstag.

He believed in force, discipline and authority, and argued as early as 1907 for a strong navy, seeing it as essential for the extension and protection of German overseas trade.

He was an uncritical supporter of Kaiser Wilhelm II and made no secret of his hatred for Germany's enemies; he repeatedly attacked Chancellor Theobald von Bethmann-Hollweg's administration and demanded a more vigorous prosecution of the war. Bethman-Hollweg's downfall in July 1917 was largely Stresemann's doing.

In 1918, seeing the way that things were going, and like a true businessman, cutting his cloth according to his needs, he reformed his following as the German People's party, still monarchist in general tendency, but prepared to support the republic in the interests of peace, national unity and good business. At the Weimar Assembly of 1919 he voted against the acceptance of the Versailles Peace Treaty.

In August 1923 he succeeded Wilhelm Cuno as chancellor of a coalition government. It was a most difficult time. Germany was seething with internal disorders, the mark was rapidly falling and the Belgian-French occupation of the Ruhr was creating additional problems. Within fifteen months his government fell and he was replaced by Wilhelm Marx, though he retained his portfolio as foreign minister and in fact kept it in all subsequent cabinets until his death.

Stresemann, above all, was a realist. "As every reasonable person would have to admit," he said, "it would simply be madness to toy with the idea of a war with France today." He discontinued the policy of passive resistance against the French and Belgians in the Ruhr and was instrumental in having the Dawes Plan adopted, with its resultant evacuation of the Ruhr and Allied and US investment in Germany.

He took a leading part in the negotiations over the Locarno agreements—which he made acceptable to the German people by stressing that the agreements did not imply final recognition of the western frontiers, but was merely a guarantee that force would not be used against Germany. He negotiated a treaty with Russia the following year and worked to achieve Germany's admission to the League of Nations. He was also responsible for Germany's adherence to the Kellogg-Briand Pact and secured a promise from the Allies that the Rhineland would soon be evacuated. He put down Communist attempts at insurrection in Saxony and Thuringia by sending in troops and, in Bavaria, restored order after Hitler's attempted putsch had failed.

He lived to see the first zone of the Rhine evacuated, and the Inter-Allied Military Commission recalled from Germany.

Though he could hardly be regarded as a man of peace in the ordinary sense (there is little doubt that if Germany had been successful he would have remained as implacable and as rapacious for annexed territory as he was early on in the war), Stresemann's principal concern after the war was to consolidate the peace, though perhaps more as a preliminary to the restoration of Germany as a world power than from a deep desire for world peace for its own sake. He saw clearly how Germany's central position offered the possibility of alliance either with the Western powers or with the USSR and he exploited this to the utmost. Nevertheless, with Briand and Austen Chamberlain, he created an atmosphere in which a great deal of the old war bitterness could be dissipated, and it was largely due to his efforts that Germany reached some sort of an understanding with the Western powers.

"The purpose of the Nobel Foundation is the furthering of peace," he said in his Nobel lecture. "The intention of the man who created it was to counter the natural forces which his own genius had released with the restraining powers of the human spirit. Is the recent development of the German people such as to justify the award being given for a policy aimed at peace? One may well say that the question is answered by the very existence of the German policy of reconciliation and peace, for this policy would have been impossible had it not been in accord with the deepest desire of the German people, the desire for peaceful international cooperation in justice and freedom."

1927

FERDINAND EDOUARD BUISSON (1841–1932), France: *A progressive educator and statesman, who participated in the 1866 Geneva Conference which formed the Ligue Internationale de la Paix et de la Liberté [International League of Peace and Liberty]. He campaigned to reverse the Dreyfus decision and helped to found the Ligue des Droits des Hommes [League of the Rights of Man] in 1898, of which he became president in 1913. At the age of eighty-three he toured Germany, lecturing on the need for a détente between France and Germany.*

LUDWIG QUIDDE (1858–1941), Germany: *Professional historian and politician, he was on the Council of the International Peace Bureau at Berne and leader of the World Peace Congress at Glasgow in 1901. In 1905 he joined Frédéric Passy at the Congress at Lucerne to achieve a rapprochement between Germany and France and two years later supervised the World Peace Congress in Munich. He was the president of the German Peace Society for fifteen years.*

BUISSON WAS THE oldest of all the Peace Prize laureates—eighty-three when he was awarded the prize—a noble representative of French radical humanism and a man who, according to Auguste Schou, "by word and by deed had fought against the regime of Napoleon III."

Buisson was born in Paris and was educated at the Lycée Bonaparte. He left school at sixteen to help support the family when his father died. For a time he worked in Paris as a tutor and then took the state teachers' examination in philosophy. However, as he refused to take the oath of allegiance to the emperor, he was forced into political exile in 1866. From 1866 to 1870 he held the chair of philosophy at the Academy of Neuchâtel, Switzerland, and in 1867 took part in the first Geneva peace conference at which he advocated a United States of Europe.

After the fall of Paris in 1870, he organized an asylum for war orphans. He was made secretary of the statistical commission on primary education in 1870 and a school inspector in 1871 and during this period he published his *Dictionnaire de Pédagogie* and made a number of reforms in the French primary system of education. In 1896 he became a professor of education at the Sorbonne.

He was a member of the Chambre des Deputés for the Radical Socialist party from 1902 to 1914 and from 1913 to 1926 was president of the Ligue des Droits de l'Homme, which he had helped to found in the wake of the Dreyfus trial.

Although fundamentally opposed to war, Buisson was not anti-militarist; he firmly believed in France's right to defend herself in the war, because he believed that Germany was in the wrong and only an Allied victory could ensure justice for Europe. He disapproved of the Treaty of Versailles and was convinced that the only way to neutralize its dangers was by working towards a closer Franco-German understanding.

At the age of eighty-three he went on an extended tour of Germany, preaching the urgent need for a reconciliation between the two countries. He donated the proceeds of his Nobel Peace Prize to various pacifist organizations.

"From the day war conquered the skies," he said in his Nobel lecture, "nothing could check its progress. It is now possible to drop, from unmeasurable heights which defy any defense, tons of chemical products, some capable of destroying the largest cities in the world in a matter of hours, others of spreading terrible diseases over vast areas, making resistance totally impossible. Thus, war has put an end to itself."

LUDWIG QUIDDE MADE no spectacular contribution to the cause of world peace; but the very fact that there were a few persevering pacifists in a country so resolutely war-oriented as Germany must have seemed very encouraging to the Nobel Committee and it is natural perhaps that they should have seized on Quidde, like Ossietzky a few years later (in 1935), as a symbol.

Quidde, the oldest son of a wealthy Bremen merchant, studied at the universities of Strasbourg and Göttingen, where he specialized in historical research. He was asked to serve on a board of editors responsible for the publication of the medieval German Reichstag documents, a post he held until he was removed in 1933 for political reasons. In 1889 he founded the *Deutsche Zeitschrift für Geschichtswissenschaft* [German Review of Historical Sciences], which he edited until 1896; and from 1890 to 1892 he was on the staff of the Prussian Historical Institute in Rome.

He achieved prominence (anonymously) with the publication in 1893 of a violent attack on German militarism. He followed this with *Caligula* (1894), ostensibly a historical study but in fact a thinly disguised attack on Kaiser Wilhelm II and his policies. In the same year he started a pacifist organization in Munich and became active at the various international peace congresses. He was elected a member of the Bavarian Diet in 1907 and thereafter attended all Interparliamentary Conferences.

Quidde entered politics in Munich. In 1895 he helped to reorganize the German People's Party which was anti-Prussian and anti-militarist. In 1902 he won a seat on the Munich City Council and in 1919 was elected to the Weimar National Assembly.

After delivering a political speech in January 1896, Quidde was accused of *lèse majesté* and sentenced to three months in prison. In 1924 he was arrested for writing an article protesting against secret military training and spent another term in jail.

He was on the Council of the International Peace Bureau in Berne, was leader of the World Peace Congress in Glasgow in 1901 and joined with Frédéric Passy at Lucerne in 1905 in an attempt to achieve a détente between France and Germany. He supervised the organization of the World Peace Congress of 1907 in Munich, and was president of the German Peace Society for fifteen years beginning in 1914.

When war broke out, he went to The Hague and tried to maintain contact with the English and French peace associations. The attempt failed and when he returned to Germany he was accused of treason, though the charges were later dropped. Nevertheless, he was kept under close observation for months, his mail was censored and his pamphlets confiscated. At the end of the war he tried to revive the German peace movement, heading the German Peace Cartel; but when Hitler came to power, he fled to Geneva where he lived until his death. He worked on a book entitled *German Pacifism during the War,* which he never finished, and continued to attend World Peace conferences. He also formed a society to care for fellow political exiles from Nazi Germany.

Quidde did not believe that disarmament was the answer to the peace question. "Lightly armed nations can move towards war as easily as those who are armed to the teeth," he said in his Nobel lecture, "and they will do so if the usual causes of war are not removed. Even a total and universal disarmament does not guarantee the maintenance of peace. Should the occasion arise, flails and scythes would again come into their own as weapons. Disarmed nations embroiled in war would obtain modern weapons as quickly as possible by converting peacetime industry."

On the other hand, he did believe in the limitation of armaments. "The increase in armaments, the endless arms race—this in itself is a potential cause of war. Influential military men want to demonstrate that their profession has some use. Many people who are disturbed by the terrible growth of armaments become accustomed and resigned to the belief that war is inevitable. They say 'Better a terrible end than an endless terror.' That is the greatest cause of war. . . ."

1928

Prize not awarded.

1929

FRANK BILLINGS KELLOGG (1865–1937), United States: *Coauthor of the Kellogg-Briand Pact of August 1928. American lawyer and secretary of state under Coolidge, he was one-time ambassador to London and partly responsible for the London Reparations Conference convened to accept the Dawes Committee Report.*

FRANK BILLINGS KELLOGG was born in Potsdam, New York, and spent his early childhood there before moving, at the age of nine, to Minnesota where his family settled. He had no formal education beyond grade school and studied law in an attorney's office in Rochester, Minnesota. He specialized in corporate law, working for many of the big mining and manufacturing corporations, and established himself as one of the country's most successful lawyers in this field.

He was appointed special assistant to the attorney general during Theodore Roosevelt's administration and was prominent among the lawyers whom Roosevelt employed in his fight against the monopolies; he was primarily responsible for the prosecution of the Standard Oil Company in 1910–11 and several other big government law suits under the antitrust laws. In 1912 he became president of the American Bar Association.

A Republican, Kellogg was elected to the Senate in 1916, became a member of the Foreign Relations Committee and voted against the ratification of the Treaty of Versailles.

When he was defeated in 1922, he returned to practicing law until he was appointed ambassador to the Court of St. James in London in 1924. The most important diplomatic affair during his period of office was the London Reparations Conference called to accept the Dawes Committee report.

In 1925 he became secretary of state in Coolidge's cabinet, holding the position until 1929. He managed to solve America's problems with Mexico over oil and land expropriation by legal rather than military means and his policy towards the Caribbean and South American countries was described as a "retreat from imperialism." In general his policy towards Europe was one of isolationism.

Kellogg arranged for the signing of bilateral treaties with nineteen foreign nations, but his greatest achievement was the Kellogg-Briand Pact of 1928. Negotiations for this pact began with Aristide Briand, the French foreign minister, who envisaged it as a bilateral Franco-American treaty of perpetual friendship, outlawing war between the two nations. Kellogg saw it in a wider context as a multilateral treaty renouncing war as an instrument of national policy. The pact was signed on August 27, 1928, and proclaimed on July 24, 1929, with sixty-four signatories.

Kellogg served as a judge of the Permanent Court of International Justice at The Hague from 1930 to 1935.

In his speech of acceptance, Kellogg referred to the rumors of war, which as early as 1930 were again troubling Europe.

"I regret very much to hear so many people, many of my own countrymen, predicting war, stating that Europe is preparing and arming for such a conflict. I rather share the opinion of those of broader vision, who see in the signs of the time the hope of humanity for peace. Have we so soon forgotten those four years of terrible carnage, the greatest war of all time; forgotten the millions of men who gave their lives . . . and who today, beneath the soil of France and Belgium, sleep the eternal sleep? Their supreme sacrifice should inspire a pledge never again to inflict humanity with such a crime. I have said before and I wish to repeat today . . . that Western civilization would not survive another such conflict, but would disappear in the universal chaos."

The Threatened Thirties

DURING THE OPENING years of the thirties, Europe's statesmen were still preoccupied with problems left over from World War I. But before the decade was far advanced, they had a whole new set of problems to cope with, including the rise of fascism and naziism, and before it ended World War II had broken out.

In January 1930 Wilhelm Frick, a Nazi, became minister in Thuringia and an Austro-Italian treaty of friendship was concluded.

In March Gandhi initiated a civil disobedience campaign in India to protest against British rule; Constantinople became Istanbul; a revolt took place in Abyssinia (Ethiopia), where the following month Ras Tafari became the emperor Haile Selassie.

Also in April, Britain, the United States, France, Italy and Japan signed a treaty on naval disarmament, regulating submarine warfare and limiting aircraft carriers, while Italy started to build up her navy and Mussolini urged a revision of the Treaty of Versailles.

In June the last of the Allied troops left the Rhineland.

In September the National Socialist (Nazi) party gained 107 seats from the moderates in the German Reichstag, and in October the Passfield White Paper stressed Arab land hunger and suggested a halt to Jewish immigration to Palestine as long as Arab unemployment remained at a high rate; this white paper undermined Jewish confidence in Britain.

On December 12 the last Allied troops left the Saar and France started to construct the Maginot Line.

In a world still in the grip of a terrible depression, Perspex and the photographic flash bulb were invented; the planet Pluto was discovered and Amy Johnson flew solo from London to Australia in $19\frac{1}{2}$ days, arriving on May 24.

In October the era of the airships came to an end, so far as Britain was concerned, with the crash of Britain's R101 on her maiden voyage to India. The tragedy occurred in Beauvais, France, on October 7; forty-five people died, and only eight survived. Later in the decade, in May 1937, the

Hindenburg disaster in Lakehurst, New Jersey, finally put an end to the airship as a viable form of transportation

The Norwegian explorer Nansen died that year; and so did Arthur Conan Doyle and Alfred von Tirpitz, the German admiral.

In January 1931 the Allied Military Control in Europe was dissolved. Gandhi and other political prisoners were released for discussions on the future of India.

In May the Credit-Anstalt in Austria went bankrupt; in July the German Danatbank followed suit, leading to the closure of all German banks for several weeks. Herbert Hoover suggested a one-year moratorium on all war debts; the Bank of England offered to advance money to Austria to stave off the financial collapse of central Europe but France refused to support this move.

In September an Austrian fascist coup d'état failed and Britain abandoned the gold standard. In Brazil the National Coffee Department was established in December and, for the first time, official policy condoned the destruction of surplus stocks to keep the price high.

A scientist named Cockcroft developed the high-voltage apparatus that was needed for atomic transmutations and another, called Lawrence, devised the cyclotron for "smashing" atoms. Imperial Chemical Industries (ICI) succeeded in producing petrol from coal, and neoprene (synthetic rubber) was invented.

The year 1932 opened with more trouble in India: the government was granted emergency powers for six months, the National Congress was declared illegal and Gandhi was arrested again.

In February sixty nations, including the United States and the USSR, attended a disarmament conference at Geneva at which Germany opposed a French proposal for an international police force. There was a fascist coup in Memal, Lithuania, and a Nazi revolt in Finland; in Ireland the Republicans won an election and de Valera became president in March.

In the same month in Germany, Paul von Hindenburg received 18 million votes in the presidential election, against Adolf Hitler's 11 million. A new election was ordered as the majority was regarded as insufficient. In the second attempt Hindenburg became president with 19 million votes against Hitler's 13, but the Nazis had overwhelming majorities in Prussia, Bavaria, Würtemburg and Hamburg.

In June an Anglo-French pact was signed at Lausanne under which Germany agreed to a final conditional payment of three trillion marks in settlement of all war debts. A ban on storm troopers in Germany was lifted.

In July Salazar was elected premier of Portugal and established a fascist regime. Austria was awarded a loan by Geneva protocol on condition that she renounced *Anschluss* [union with Germany] until 1952.

On July 31 the Nazis won 230 seats in the Reichstag, against 133 Socialists, 97 Center and 89 Communists. The result was a stalemate, as neither the Nazis nor the Socialists would agree to form a coalition. The following month Hitler refused Hindenburg's request to serve as vice-chancellor under von Papen, and in September Germany walked out of a League Disarmament Conference.

In November fresh German elections produced another deadlock and in the United States Franklin D. Roosevelt won the presidential elections with a Democratic landslide: 472 electoral votes to Hoover's 59.

In Germany von Papen resigned and Hitler rejected the chancellorship. Kurt von Schleicher tried to form a ministry attempting to conciliate the center and the left.

On December 11 a "No Force" declaration against resorting to force to settle differences was signed by Great Britain, France, Germany and Italy, and Germany returned to the Disarmament Conference.

The first autobahn in Europe was opened between Cologne and Bonn, and in the United States Charles Lindbergh's baby son was kidnapped and later found dead.

On January 30, 1933, Adolf Hitler was appointed chancellor with a cabinet of Nazis including Hermann Goering and Wilhelm Frick. Edouard Daladier became premier of France.

On February 27 the Nazis engineered a fire in the Reichstag, which Hitler denounced as a Communist plot. As a result, he suspended all civil liberties and the freedom of the press.

FDR opened the New Deal with his "Good Neighbor Policy" speech in March.

The same month the Nazis gained 288 seats in the elections against 120 Socialists, 81 Communists, 74 Center and 52 Nationalists. Dollfuss suspended parliamentary government in Austria, and Britain's disarmament plan for a reduction in the size of standing armies failed because Germany insisted that storm troopers should not be included in the overall total. On March 23 Hitler was given dictatorial powers until April 1937 and the persecution of Jews began with a national boycott of all Jewish businesses and professions. German trade unions were suppressed in May and in July all German political parties except the Nazis were suppressed. In October Germany left the Disarmament Conference and the League, and in November the Nazis dominated the German elections with 92 percent of the electorate voting for Nazi candidates.

In the United States prohibition was repealed, and in Britain the Oxford Union debating society voted that in no circumstances would the house fight for king and country.

The first commercially produced detergent in the world was put on the market by ICI and Wiley Post flew around the world in 7 days, 18 hours and 49 minutes.

In January 1934 Germany signed a ten-year nonaggression pact with Poland; in June Hitler had the first of many meetings with Mussolini and a Nazi purge in Germany eliminated von Schleicher, Roehm and other party leaders after an alleged plot on Hitler's life. In July Dollfuss was murdered in an attempted Nazi coup in Austria, and in Britain Premier Stanley Baldwin announced a strengthening of the Royal Air Force.

In August von Hindenburg died, aged eighty-seven, and a German plebiscite vested sole executive power in Hitler as führer of Germany.

In December there were clashes between Italian and Abyssinian troops on the Abyssinian border.

The *Queen Mary* was launched in September, a regular air mail service was announced between London and Australia in December, and F. Joliot and I. Curie-Joliot discovered radioactivity.

The year 1935 began with a Saar plebiscite which restored the Saar to Germany and marked the beginning of the German postwar program of expansion. Italy sent troops to East Africa, and Germany repudiated the disarmament clauses in the Versailles Treaty.

In April Britain, France and Italy conferred at Stresa, Italy, to establish a common front against Germany, and in June there was an Anglo-German naval agreement by which Germany undertook to keep her navy under one-third the tonnage of that of the Royal Navy.

In September the Jews were outlawed in Germany and the swastika became the official German flag; in October Italy invaded Abyssinia and the now almost helpless League Council had to content itself with declaring Italy "the aggressor."

Germany reintroduced compulsory military service, Robert Watson-Watt built the first radar equipment for detecting aircraft and at Daytona Beach, Malcolm Campbell drove his Bluebird motor car at a record speed of 276.8 miles per hour. The *Normandie* crossed the Atlantic in 107 hours and 33 minutes and Pan-American Airways started a trans-Pacific service from California, using flying boats.

In January 1936 George V died and was succeeded by Edward VIII. In March the British defense budget jumped from £122 million to £158 million to augment the Fleet Air Arm, add 250 aircraft for home defense and enlist four new infantry battalions.

The same month the Germans violated the Treaty of Versailles by occupying the demilitarized zone of the Rhineland. Italy, Austria and Hungary signed the Rhone pact; Britain, the United States and France signed the London Naval Convention; the Nazis had a 99 percent vote in the German elections; and the first British civil defense anti-gas school opened, teaching people how to cope with poison gas attacks.

Austria reintroduced conscription in April and on May 5 the Italians occupied Addis Ababa, ending the war; on May 9 Italy annexed Abyssinia.

An army revolt in Spain under Emilio Mola and Francisco Franco started the Spanish Civil War on July 18.

In August the British military occupation of Egypt—apart from the canal zone—ended, and France signed a treaty of friendship with Syria and the Lebanon. Goebbels accused Czechoslovakia of harboring USSR aircraft and France, Switzerland and Holland all abandoned the gold standard.

Count Ciano, Italian foreign minister, visited Berlin in November and Mussolini announced the Rome-Berlin Axis. Two days later FDR was re-elected president of the United States.

In December Edward VIII abdicated and was succeeded by George VI. Germany and Italy recognized Franco's government in Spain and Chiang Kai-shek declared war on Japan.

The Olympic Games were held in Berlin, and in London a BBC television service started at Alexandra Palace and Allen Lane started the paperback revolution with the introduction of Penguin books. During the year Rudyard Kipling, Clara Butt, G. K. Chesterton, Maxim Gorki and Houdini all died.

In February 1937 the French decided to extend the Maginot Line and nationalize the Schneider-Creusot arms factory. The All-India Congress party carried the Indian elections but abstained from forming a government, demanding complete independence from Britain.

In May Roosevelt signed a neutrality act, and on Stanley Baldwin's retirement Neville Chamberlain formed a national government. In June the Duke of Windsor (formerly Edward VIII) married Wallis Simpson in France.

In July a royal commission recommended the end of the mandate in Palestine and the establishment of separate Arab and Jewish states, and in September the Arabs murdered the British district commissioner of Galilee.

The Germans guaranteed Belgian neutrality in October; a fascist group in Hungary formed a National Socialist party and there were riots in the Sudetan area of Czechoslovakia.

The following month an air raid precautions bill was introduced in the Commons and Lord Halifax visited Adolf Hitler to discuss the Sudetan situation and open the appeasement program.

In December Italy withdrew from the now rapidly failing League of Nations.

It was the year of the Paris World's Fair, the year that Whittle invented the jet engine and Carothers produced the first pair of nylon stockings. Marconi, Ravel, J. M. Barrie, F. B. Kellogg, Austen Chamberlain and Elihu Root all died; and a book of statistics recorded that the United States had 2,000,000 domestic refrigerators, Britain only 3,000.

In January 1938 Britain postponed partition of Palestine and appointed a commission to study the boundaries; it was boycotted by the Arabs.

In February, Adolf Hitler took office as war minister and appointed Ribbentrop as foreign minister. The British foreign secretary Anthony Eden resigned in protest against Chamberlain's determination to consult Italy before settling the question of recognition of the Franco regime, and Churchill led a censure motion against Chamberlain for his conduct of foreign affairs.

In March German troops entered Austria and on March 13 Austria was declared a part of the Reich.

The first Czechoslovak crisis came in May, and Britain and France stood firm against Hitler's demands. On August 12 Germany mobilized, and on September 7 the Sudetan Germans broke off all relations with the Czech government and France called up her reservists. On September 15 Neville Chamberlain visited Hitler at Berchtesgaden and Hitler stated his determination to annex Sudetanland on the general principle of self-determination.

The Royal Navy was mobilized on September 27, and on September 29 at a conference in Munich, Chamberlain, Daladier, Hitler and Mussolini agreed to the transfer of Sudetanland to Germany.

On October 10 the Germans occupied Sudetanland. The Japanese withdrew from the League of Nations, Eduard Beneš resigned in Czechoslovakia, Hungary annexed southern Czechoslovakia, and there were anti-Jewish pogroms in Germany, antisemitic legislation in Italy, and speeches in the Italian chamber claiming Nice and Corsica from France. The British drew up a national register for war service and Italy denounced her 1935 agreement with France.

The Wages and Hours Act in the United States made provision for the first time for a minimum wage and a maximum working week, prohibiting child labor.

A British Ministry of Labor committee recommended one week's holiday with pay as a national standard. Two characters called Ladisla and Biro invented the ball-point pen and Howard Hughes flew around the world in 3 days, 19 hours and 17 minutes in his monoplane *New York World's Fair*. The *Queen Elizabeth* was launched and there was a World's Fair in New York and an Empire Exhibition in Glasgow.

In January 1939 FDR asked Congress for $552 million for defense, and

Neville Chamberlain and Lord Halifax visited Rome for conversations with Mussolini.

Britain and France recognized Franco's Spain in February, while a month later German troops occupied Bohemia and Moravia, and Slovakia was put under German protection.

The Spanish Civil War ended on March 28 with Madrid's surrender to Franco; in the same month Hitler denounced Germany's nonaggression pact with Poland, and Britain and France promised to support Poland.

Italy invaded Albania in April, and Spain joined Germany, Italy and France in the Anti-Comintern Pact (Comintern is short for Communist International, an association of Communist countries founded in 1919 with the stated purpose of world revolution and the practical effect of achieving Soviet control over the whole Communist movement).

In the same month Hungary withdrew from the League. Britain and France guaranteed independence for Rumania and Greece. FDR asked Hitler and Mussolini for assurances that they would not attack thirty-one named countries and the USSR proposed a defensive alliance with Britain.

In May Molotov was appointed commissar of foreign affairs in Russia, Spain left the League of Nations, and Hitler and Mussolini signed a ten-year political and military alliance.

In August came the USSR-Germany nonaggression pact. The Anti-Comintern Pact collapsed and Chamberlain warned Hitler that Britain would stand by Poland.

By the end of the month attempts by Daladier and Chamberlain to negotiate with Hitler had failed and the evacuation of women and children from London had begun.

On September 1 Germany invaded Poland and annexed Danzig. The following day, in Britain, men aged between 18 and 41 were called up, Winston Churchill became first lord of the admiralty and the Germans sank the *Athenia* off Ireland. Britain and France declared war on Germany on September 3.

By September 7 the Germans controlled western Poland and by the 17th, the Russians had invaded Poland from the east. By the end of the month a British Expeditionary Force of 158,000 men had left for France.

As early as October 6 Hitler was putting out peace feelers which were rejected by Britain and France, and two days later Germany had incorporated western Poland into the Reich and had begun the deportation of Polish Jews.

In the United States FDR signed a bill enabling Britain and France to buy arms on a "cash and carry" basis, amending the Neutrality Act of May 1937, and magnetic mines laid by U-boats sank 60,000 tons of shipping off the English coast in one week.

On December 14 the USSR was expelled from the League of Nations.

Joliot demonstrated the possibility of splitting the atom of uranium isotope 235; Paul Muller invented DDT; polythene was developed; and John Cobb at Bonneville Salt Flats, Utah, reached 368.85 miles per hour, while Malcolm Campbell in England set a world's record by reaching a water speed of 141.77 miles per hour.

Films of the decade included *Journey's End*, *Hell's Angels*, Marlene Dietrich in *The Blue Angel*, Hitchcock's *Murder*, Chaplin's *City Lights*, Boris Karloff in *Frankenstein*, Katherine Hepburn in *Morning Glory*, Alexander Korda's *The Private Lives of Henry VIII*, Greta Garbo in *Queen Christina* and *Anna Karenina*, David O. Selznick's *David Copperfield*, Eisenstein's *Alexander Nevsky*, *Gone With the Wind* and Walt Disney's *Snow White and the Seven Dwarfs*.

Plays included Noel Coward's *Private Lives*, Elmer Rice's *Street Scene*, Eugene O'Neill's *Mourning Becomes Electra*, Robert Sherwood's *The Petrified Forest*, Emlyn Williams's *Night Must Fall* and T. S. Eliot's *Murder in the Cathedral*.

Among the books that caught the public's attention were Evelyn Waugh's *Vile Bodies*, Pearl Buck's *The Good Earth*, Antoine de St. Exupéry's *Vol de Nuit* [Night Flight], Hemingway's *Death in the Afternoon*, Gertrude Stein's *The Autobiography of Alice B. Toklas*, Scott Fitzgerald's *Tender is the Night*, Christopher Isherwood's *Goodbye to Berlin*, James Joyce's *Finnegans Wake*—he'd been writing it since 1922—and John Steinbeck's *The Grapes of Wrath*.

T. E. Lawrence (Lawrence of Arabia) was killed in a motor cycle accident.

1930 Nathan Söderblom

1931 Jane Addams

1931 Nicholas Butler

1932

Prize not awarded

1933 Norman Angell

1934 Arthur Henderson

1935 Carl von Ossietzky

1936 Carlos Saavedra Lamas

1937 Robert Cecil

1938

Nansen International
Office for Refugees

1939

Prize not awarded

1930

NATHAN SÖDERBLOM (1866–1931), Sweden: *Lutheran churchman and theologian, ultimately archbishop of Uppsala. A champion of world peace through church unity, he laid the foundations for the twentieth-century ecumenical movement at a church conference in Stockholm in 1925.*

SÖDERBLOM WAS THE first churchman to be awarded the Peace Prize, and it is probably only a coincidence that he also happened to be the clergyman called to San Remo at the time of Alfred Nobel's death to conduct the memorial service at his bedside. Nobel had been a member of Söderblom's congregation when the latter was pastor of the Swedish church in Paris.

The son of a Pietistic pastor, Söderblom was born at Trönö, in Sweden. He took his bachelor's degree in 1886 at Uppsala University, where he studied Greek, Hebrew, Arabic and Latin. He was ordained a priest in 1893 and became pastor of the Swedish Church in Paris.

He continued his studies in Paris and became the first foreigner ever to earn a doctor of theology degree at the Protestant faculty of the Sorbonne. His experience in France gave him an international outlook and convinced him of the importance of what he described as a "free unity" among the Christian churches.

From 1901 to 1914 he occupied a chair in the School of Theology at Uppsala and simultaneously, from 1912 to 1914, a chair at Leipzig University. He led a theological revival in Sweden and wrote a series of books on comparative religion and religious philosophy.

In 1914 Söderblom became archbishop of Uppsala and primate of the Church of Sweden, an unexpected appointment since he had never been a bishop. For the remainder of his life, he worked for the ecumenical movement; he believed that unity in the Christian church could be a powerful factor in achieving world peace. As early as 1909 he had made a move towards intercommunion between the Swedish Church and the Church of England, but his efforts to extend the ecumenical movement were hampered for various reasons: the French, German and American church officials were dubious about the idea; the archbishop of Canterbury was extremely cautious; and the Roman Catholic Church firmly opposed.

At a conference in Stockholm in 1925 he succeeded in bringing together Anglican, Protestant and Orthodox Christians; Rome was not represented.

In his Nobel lecture, Söderblom said: "The Christian mission is by its very nature supranational, a spiritual entity that addresses people as human beings and not as speakers of given languages and members of given races and nationalities. . . . The church must, therefore, uphold the sanctity of law and promote its development in the name of Christ, both inside and outside national boundaries. She must, therefore, fight against all glorification of violence and against any force contrary to the rule of law, and she must preach that all nations and communities, like individuals, must act according to ethical principles, basing their hopes for coexistence on the principles of truth, justice and love. . . . The intention is to extend the legal system in such a way as to preclude the desperate course of war between nations, in the same manner in which blood feuds have been abolished and tribal fighting stopped in law-abiding communities. . . . What we are recommending is not a breach of loyalty; on the contrary, it is obedience to a higher obligation. A supranational judicial system is being built. Binding treaties between nations who are committed to conciliation or arbitration when disputes arise rather than to war represent the foundations of a larger edifice of the rule of law. . . ."

1931

LAURA JANE ADDAMS (1860–1935), United States: *Social reformer and founder of Hull House in Chicago. She was chairman of the American Women's Peace Party and the Women's International League for Peace and Freedom at The Hague.*

NICHOLAS MURRAY BUTLER (1862–1947), United States: *President of Columbia University in New York, president from 1907 of the American branch of the Conciliation Internationale and the man largely responsible for Carnegie's endowment for international peace in 1910. He was also responsible for rallying public support in America for the Kellogg-Briand pact.*

ALTHOUGH JANE ADDAMS was principally famous for her social work, her choice does not indicate that the Nobel Committee had yet started to think of Peace Prize winners in terms of social reformers. Her social work was certainly mentioned in the presentation speech, but merely as a prelude to her work for international peace, for which the prize was obviously awarded.

The daughter of a prosperous miller and local political leader who had fought as an officer in the Civil War, Jane Addams was born in Cedarville, Illinois, graduated from Rockford College, Illinois, in 1881 and entered the medical college at Philadelphia University. But her health failed and after two years as an invalid, suffering from a spinal defect, she traveled extensively in Europe.

While in London she visited the Toynbee Hall settlement, a pioneer university and social experiment in East London founded in 1884 by Canon S. A. Barnett and named after Arnold Toynbee, the English social reformer and economist who worked for the poor in the Whitechapel district of London's East End. With money collected mainly at Oxford, Barnett had bought and reconstructed premises in Whitechapel for the study of the development of adult education, the collection of social data and the improvement of social conditions. Above all, he wanted to give university students an opportunity to live in a poor industrial area and contribute both to its life and their own education.

On her return from Europe, Jane Addams, much impressed by the Toynbee Hall settlement, founded Hull House in 1889, a pioneer United States social settlement in the old Hull Mansion on Chicago's West Side, where well-known social reformers lived as residents. In this large settlement she worked with Labor and other reform groups for many pioneer welfare laws such as the first juvenile court law, the first "mother's pension" law, tenement house regulations, an eight-hour working day for women, factory inspection and workers' compensation. She was also a keen supporter of women's suffrage.

By its second year, Hull House was host to two thousand people a week. Kindergarten classes were held in the mornings, meetings for older children in the afternoons, and a night school for adults in the evenings. Before long she had added to the facilities an art gallery, a public kitchen, a coffee house, a gymnasium, a swimming pool, a drama group, a library and an employment bureau.

Jane Addams was the first woman president of the National Conference of Social Work (1910) and took an active part in Theodore Roosevelt's presidential campaign in 1912. She spoke for peace at a ceremony in 1913 commemorating the building of the Peace Palace at The Hague, and in the next two years, as a lecturer sponsored by the Carnegie Foundation, spoke against America's entry into World War I.

In 1915 she accepted chairmanship of both the Women's Peace Party, an American organization, and the International Congress of Women at

The Hague. When the latter group founded the Women's International League for Peace and Freedom, she became its first president, serving until 1929, and then as honorary president for the rest of her life.

In 1917 she was expelled from the Daughters of the American Revolution for opposing America's entry into the war, and worked as an assistant to Herbert Hoover in providing relief supplies of food to the women and children of enemy nations. Her books include *Democracy and Social Ethics* (1902), *Newer Ideas of Peace* (1907) and two books on Hull House.

"The first days there," she wrote in *Twenty Years at Hull House*, "laid the simple human foundations which are certainly necessary for continuous living among the poor—first, genuine preference for residence in an industrial quarter than in any other part of a city because it is interesting and makes the human appeal; second, the conviction . . . that the things which make men alike are finer and better than the things which keep them apart, and that these basic likenesses, if they are properly accentuated, easily transcend the less essential differences of race, language, creed and tradition."

NICHOLAS MURRAY BUTLER was, according to the *Nobel Peace Lectures 1926–1950,* "an educator and university president; an adviser to seven presidents and friend of statesmen in foreign nations; a recipient of decorations from fifteen foreign governments and of honorary degrees from thirty-seven colleges and universities; a member of more than fifty learned societies and twenty clubs; the author of a small library of books, pamphlets, reports and speeches; an international traveler who crossed the Atlantic at least a hundred times; a national leader of the Republican Party; an advocate of peace and the embodiment of the 'international mind' that he frequently spoke about. He was called Nicholas Miraculous Butler by his good friend Theodore Roosevelt; the epithet was so perfect that, once uttered, it could not be forgotten."

Born in New Jersey, the son of an industrialist, he attended Columbia College in New York, where he received his doctorate in 1884; he then studied in Paris and Berlin, where he began a life-long friendship with Elihu Root, the 1912 Nobel Peace laureate. In 1885 Butler accepted an appointment to the staff of the Department of Philosophy at his alma mater, which in 1896 became Columbia University. He established an institute which later, affiliated with Columbia, became known as Teachers' College. He founded the *Educational Review* and edited it for thirty years, wrote reports on state and local educational systems, and served as a member of the New Jersey Board of Education. He was made acting president of Columbia University in 1901 and president in 1902, a position which he retained until his retirement.

His career embraced every phase of Columbia's transformation from a college with an old-fashioned classical curriculum to a modern university complex.

Butler was a delegate to the Republican Convention in 1888 and in the early years of the century, he, Root, Taft and Roosevelt constituted a powerful political quartet. Breaking with the others in 1912, Roosevelt ran for president as candidate of the Progressive party and in so doing split the national vote and allowed Woodrow Wilson, a Democrat, to win the election.

Butler was chairman on the Lake Mohonk Conferences on International Arbitration which met periodically between 1907 and 1912, and was president of the American branch of Conciliation Internationale founded by d'Estournelles de Constant, the 1909 Nobel Peace laureate. In 1910 Butler had been instrumental in persuading Andrew Carnegie to establish the Carnegie Endowment for International Peace with a gift of $10 million. During his thirty-five-year association with the endowment, he served as head of its section on international education and communication, founded the European branch of the endowment, and was its president from 1925 to 1945.

His books include *Education in the United States* (1910), *Across the Busy Years* (two volumes: 1939 and 1940) and *The World Today* (1946).

In a radio address accepting the award, he said: "The great hope is of a world that has learned the supreme lesson that civilization has to teach—that might does not make right and that war between nations is now as much out of date as the torture chamber and the scalping knife."

1932

No prize awarded.

1933

RALPH NORMAN ANGELL LANE (1872–1967), Great Britain: *Economist, author and well-known worker for world peace. His highly successful* The Great Illusion *(1910) took a new line in pacifist literature in arguing that war was an unsatisfactory method of settling international disputes, even if only judged from a purely economic viewpoint. He was a member of the Royal Institute of International Affairs and an active member of the League of Nations.*

APART FROM HIS writings, there doesn't really seem to have been any sound reason for the choice of Ralph Norman Angell for the 1933 prize, a fact which Christian Lous Lange, a member of the Nobel Committee and the man who made the presentation award, seems to have realized. He spoke of his achievements in very vague terms: "Norman Angell towers as high as Swift or Cobden . . . [he] speaks to the intellect. He is cool and clear. He is convinced that at long last reason will prevail when we succeed in sweeping away the mists of illusion and intellectual error. . . . It is this belief which supported him through the Great War, through the reparations tragedy and through the bitter postwar disappointments."

Angell was born in Holbeach, Lincolnshire, and was greatly influenced by the work of such writers as Spencer, Huxley, Voltaire and Darwin.

He was educated at elementary schools in England, in the Lycée at St. Omer in France, and in Geneva. He was convinced that Europe was hopelessly entangled in insoluble international problems and at seventeen decided to emigrate to America. In California he worked as a vine planter, a homesteader, a prospector, and eventually as a journalist, reporting for the St. Louis *Globe-Democrat* and the San Francisco *Chronicle.*

In 1898 he returned to Europe, working in Paris as a sub-editor on the English-language *Daily Messenger* and as a contributor to *Éclair*. At the same time he acted as correspondent for several American newspapers and his dispatches on the Dreyfus case made him famous.

His first book, *Patriotism under Three Flags: A Plea for Rationalism in Politics* (1903), was an immediate success, and in 1905 he became editor of the Paris edition of Lord Northcliffe's *Daily Mail.*

By 1912, when he had established himself as a writer, Angell resigned to concentrate on writing and lecturing. In 1909 he had published a small book, *Europe's Optical Illusion*, and in 1910 expanded the work considerably, retitling it *The Great Illusion*. The new edition sold over two million copies and was translated into twenty-five languages. In it he propounded a theory which came to be known as "Norman Angellism." This theory, as set out in the book's preface, holds that "military and political power give a nation no commercial advantage, that it is an economic impossibility for one nation to seize or destroy the wealth of another, or for one nation to enrich itself by subjugating another."

He argued that if war—a victorious war—were economically advantageous, then the citizens of those big powers which have built their world empires through victorious wars would necessarily be better off than the citizens of small, pacific nations. Yet statistics of capital and revenues in these two categories of nations prove that this is not so: Dutch stocks and Swedish, Swiss and Norwegian stocks stand higher on the world's exchanges, he claimed, than those of Great Britain, France and Germany.

In the next forty-one years he published forty-one books; invented a card game, "The Money Game," which was designed to illustrate visually the general misunderstanding of the nature of money; wrote regularly for newspapers and journals; and from 1928 to 1931 he edited *Foreign Affairs*. From 1929 to 1931 he was also a Labor MP but declined to stand for re-election because he felt that he was "better fitted to present the case for internationalism to the public direct, free from any party ties." He was knighted for his public services in 1931.

He was a member of the Royal Institute for International Affairs, an executive of the Comité Mondial contre la Guerre et le Fascisme [World Committee against War and Fascism], an active member of the League of Nations Union and president of the Abyssinia Association.

At the age of ninety he went on a two-month lecture tour of the United States.

"If we recognize that the will to peace is genuine," he said in his Nobel lecture, "it leads us to recognize a further truth related to it: war does not continue because men are selfish, evil, avaricious. It could not continue at all if millions on both sides were not prepared to make sacrifices which no other activity calls out in a similar degree. . . .

"The force which makes war does not derive its strength from the interested motives of evil men; it derives its strength from the disinterested motives of good men . . . it is made, not usually by evil men knowing themselves to be wrong, but is the outcome of policies pursued by good men usually passionately convinced that they are right. . . .

"The real case for the organization of the nations in some collective system is that so long as arms are retained, they can only become a means of effective security by putting them behind a law or rule which protects all parties. So long as an individual, whether person or state, has only his own arms to depend upon in order to defend his rights by arms, then he must be stronger than anyone likely to challenge those rights. Which means that the other is deprived of similar defense. . . . Defense must be a communal, a collective function or it cannot exist effectively at all.

"The obstacles to peace are not obstacles in matter, in inanimate nature, in the mountains which we pierce, on the seas across which we fly. The obstacles to peace are in the hearts and minds of men."

1934

ARTHUR HENDERSON (1863–1935), Great Britain. *Home secretary in Ramsay MacDonald's first cabinet (1924–25), delegate to the Assembly of the League of Nations, a member of the Committee of Security and Disarmament and of the Committee of Twelve. As the man largely responsible for prodding the Council of the League into arranging the Disarmament Conference in 1932, he presided over its opening sessions.*

IT WOULD PERHAPS be invidious to single out Arthur Henderson as a "failure" among the Nobel Peace laureates; to the extent that wars have continued to be fought since the prize was established, all the laureates were failures. But Henderson is in one way unique, inasmuch as the Disarmament Conference which he arranged, and for which he was awarded the prize, had for all practical purposes collapsed by the time he received the prize.

He was born in Glasgow, the son of a manual laborer. His father died in 1872, when he was nine, and he worked for a time in a photographer's shop to help support his poverty-stricken family. On his mother's remarriage, the family moved to Newcastle-upon-Tyne where he returned to school for three years before becoming an apprentice in an iron foundry. He joined the Ironfounders' Union at the age of eighteen, when he became a journeyman, and was soon elected secretary of the Newcastle lodge. For the rest of his life he held office continuously in the union at local, district or national level.

Henderson's political career began with his election as town councillor in 1892. In 1896 he moved to Darlington and in 1903 became the first

Labor mayor of Darlington. He attended the London conference which set up a Labor Representation Committee in 1900 and was elected to Parliament in 1903 under the sponsorship of that committee. In 1906 he chaired the conference which formed the Labor party and acted as its secretary from 1911 to 1934. In 1918 he was instrumental in altering the party's constitution to open its membership to those who by conviction, though not necessarily vocation, wished to become members.

Henderson was a member of Parliament almost continuously from 1903, chairman of the parliamentary Labor party, chief whip on three occasions, president of the Board of Education (1915–16), and paymaster general in Asquith's government and a minister without portfolio in Lloyd George's government, which succeeded it.

In 1917 he went to Russia as official observer for the British government, and in 1918 broke with Lloyd George over his refusal to send delegates to a big socialist conference in Stockholm. In the same year he initiated a call for a conference at Berne with delegates from the defeated and neutral nations joining those of the victorious nations, with the idea of formulating recommendations to send to Versailles for inclusion in the peace treaty.

In 1924 he was home secretary in MacDonald's cabinet and spent most of his energy on two problems: the implementation of the Dawes Plan and the drafting of the Geneva protocol for the settlement of international disputes by arbitration.

When MacDonald formed his second government, Henderson became foreign secretary. In his two years in that position, he achieved the resumption of Britain's diplomatic relations with Russia, arranged with Briand for the evacuation of French troops from the Rhineland before the date stipulated in the Versailles Treaty, championed the cause of Egyptian independence and attended the tenth and eleventh assemblies of the League of Nations.

Henderson also headed the League's disarmament effort. In January 1931 he persuaded the council to call the Disarmament Conference in 1932; he was president and presided over the opening sessions. The conference, as the world knows, was a failure; Hitler withdrew from it in October 1933, and Henderson was hardly able to hold it together through 1934. The failure of the conference foreshadowed World War II, but as Henderson's biographer, Mary A. Hamilton, wrote, "If any man is clear of responsibility, it is Arthur Henderson."

Henderson remained optimistic to the end, and did not share the views of his friend C. P. Scott, the editor of the *Manchester Guardian*, who wrote: "I hate the very thought of the permanent division and hostility in Europe and if that is all we have to look forward to, I feel as if the future has little interest for me, and I had rather get out of it. It isn't the material loss or even the prospect necessarily involved of future wars and bloodshed; it is the enthronement in Europe . . . of the spirit of hatred and revenge."

Acknowledging the Nobel Prize, Henderson said about the Disarmament Conference, which was just then falling about his ears, "It has been a period of difficulty and delay and disappointments—of hopes deferred. But if success has yet to be achieved, at least that decisive and heartbreaking word 'failure' has not been written. And I cannot conceive that it will be allowed to be written."

In his Nobel lecture, he was less optimistic. "Men and women everywhere are once more asking the old question: is it peace?" he began. "They are asking it with anxiety and fear; for, on the one hand there has never been such a longing for peace and dread of war as there is today. On the other hand, there have never been such awful means of spreading destruction and death as those that are now being prepared in well-nigh every country. To a visitor from another planet the world would present a spectacle as melancholy as it is bewildering. He would see civilization in danger of perishing under the oppression of a gigantic paradox: he would see millions of people starving in the midst of plenty, and nations preparing for war although pledged to peace.

"Perhaps the grimmest aspect of this great paradox is that the very nations that are chiefly responsible for starting and maintaining the Disarmament Conference are also the nations that have begun the new arms race. . . .

"There can be no real disarmament except on the basis of the collective peace system of the League of Nations. The Disarmament Conference has become the focal point of a great struggle between anarchy and world order, between those who are willing to cooperate and those who would be the sole judge of their own case, between those who think in terms of inevitable armed conflict and those who seek to build a universal and durable peace. . . .

"The establishment of a world commonwealth is, in the long run, the only alternative to a relapse into a world war. The psychological obstacles are formidable but not insurmountable. There is already a group of nations in the world between whom war may be considered as ruled out forever. Those nations are the British Commonwealth, the United States, and the surviving European democracies. I would add to that group the Soviet Union which in its international policy has shown that it is devoted to peace, abhors war, and sincerely believes in the ideal of world union and world cooperation, although it is of the opinion that in the long run such a consummation is impossible without a far-reaching change in the present social order. . . ."

In this paean of praise for Soviet Russia, Henderson was overlooking several vital points. Russia at that moment abhorred war because her army had been severely mauled in World War I, and in any event the country was so deeply concerned with the problems of sorting out the deviationists and getting the economy moving again, after the terrible upheavals of revolution and famine, that her statesmen had little time to think about war. Also, at this period, the Communists still believed that the workers of the world would arise and overthrow their masters, as the Russian workers had done, without any assistance or persuasion from outside. But there were plenty of people, even as early as 1934, who did not share Henderson's faith in Russia as a peace-loving, forward-looking nation—nor his optimism about the future.

1935

CARL VON OSSIETZKY (1889–1938), Germany. *A soldier turned pacifist, he was among those who formed a movement with the slogan "No More War." He later became secretary of the German Peace Society and between 1926 and 1933 published numerous articles attacking the Reichswehr for condoning paramilitary organizations and secret German rearmament in violation of the Treaty of Versailles—for which he was convicted of treason and imprisoned in a concentration camp.*

THE CHOICE OF Carl von Ossietzky as the 1935 Peace laureate was probably the most controversial yet, and on two scores. In the democracies a great many people felt that to award the prize intended for "the person who shall have done the most or the best work for fraternity between peoples" to the secretary of a powerless peace society in a dictatorship seemingly determined to wage war indicated that the committee saw him merely as a symbol in the struggle for peace, rather than as a champion. And in Germany the award was regarded as "a shameless insult to the new Germany." The German minister at Oslo described the decision as "a deliberate demonstration against Germany," and the official German news agency declared: "The decision to give the prize to a notorious traitor is a shameless provocation and an insult to the new Germany. . . ."

Frederik Stang, chairman of the Nobel Committee, answered the first objection in the presentation speech. In his opinion, he said, Ossietzky had not been chosen purely as a symbol. "But even if it were so, how great is the significance of the symbol in our life. In religion, in politics, in public affairs, in peace and war, we rally round symbols. . . . Moreover, as a rallying point a symbol may be preferable to a personality. But Ossietzky is not just a symbol. He is something quite different and something much more. He is a deed; he is a man. . . . In awarding this year's Nobel Peace Prize to Carl von Ossietzky we are recognizing his valuable contribution to the cause of peace—nothing more, and certainly nothing less."

Born in Hamburg, the son of a civil servant, Ossietzky left school at seventeen after a rather sporadic education and turned to journalism. His first work appeared in *Das Freie Volk* [The Free People], the weekly organ of the Demokratische Vereingung [Democratic Union]. As early as 1913 an article criticizing a promilitary court decision brought against him charges of "insult to the common good" and a fine.

He was called up for military service in 1916 and served with the Bavarian Pioneer Regiment. After the war, by then a confirmed pacifist, he became president of the local branch of the German Peace Society, and subsequently secretary of the society of which Ludwig Quidde, the 1927 Peace laureate, was president.

Ossietzky soon tired of office work and became foreign editor on the *Berliner Volkszeitung* [Berlin People's Paper], which had a nonpartisan, democratic and antiwar policy.

In 1926 Siegfried Jacobsohn, founder and editor of *Die Weltbühne* [The World Stage], offered Ossietzky a position on his staff. Jacobsohn was already deeply involved in efforts to uncover Germany's secret rearmament policy, and when he died that year Ossietzky assumed his editorship and continued Jacobsohn's highly unpopular crusade. In March 1927 the paper published an article attacking the Reichswehr for condoning paramilitary organizations, and Ossietzky as editor was tried for libel, found guilty and sentenced to one month's imprisonment.

In 1929 he ran a campaign protesting against German rearmament in violation of the Versailles Treaty. He was charged with the betrayal of military secrets, tried in November 1931 and sentenced to eighteen months in Spandau prison, but was released after seven months in the Christmas amnesty of 1932.

On February 28, 1933, the morning after the Reichstag fire, he was arrested at his home by the secret police and sent first to a Berlin prison and then to Sonnenburg and Esterwegen-Papenburg concentration camps.

When the Peace Prize was voted to Ossietzky, who was ill with tuberculosis, the German government refused to release him from the concentration camp and demanded that he refuse the prize. When Ossietzky ignored the German demand, the German Propaganda Ministry stated publicly that he was free to go to Norway to accept the prize but, in fact, he was refused a passport and although he was transferred from the concentration camp, he was kept under close surveillance until his death in May 1938.

After the award had been made, the German government decreed that in future no German could accept any Nobel prize.

Ossietzky's last public appearance was at a court hearing at which his lawyer was sentenced to two years' hard labor for embezzling most of the prize money.

1936

CARLOS SAAVEDRA LAMAS (1878–1959), Argentina: *Statesman, president of the eighth Pan-American Conference and author of an Antiwar Pact signed by eleven nations, which had the effect of bringing countries outside the League of Nations into its work to promote peace and prevent war by imposing less rigid demands on them than those prescribed by the League's covenant. He succeeded in bringing hostilities to an end in the Chaco War between Bolivia and Paraguay (1932–35) and became president of the Assembly of the League of Nations in 1936.*

WHEN THE AWARD of the Nobel Peace Prize was made to Saavedra Lamas, the first South American to receive it, the news took precedence in the Argentinian radio bulletins over reports on the Spanish Civil War and the impending visit of Franklin D. Roosevelt to the Pan-American Conference.

Lamas, a member of the Argentinian aristocracy, became a doctor of law at the University of Buenos Aires, studied in Paris and traveled widely before accepting a professorship of law and constitutional history at the University of La Plata. Later he inaugurated a course in sociology at the University of Buenos Aires, taught political economy and constitutional law in the Law School of the university and eventually became its president.

He began his political career in 1906 as director of public credit and in

1907 he became secretary general for the municipality of Buenos Aires. His main interest, however, lay in foreign affairs and he soon became an unofficial adviser to both the legislature and the foreign office on the implications of various proposed foreign treaties.

He was appointed minister of justice and education in 1915, and foreign minister in 1932. In this capacity he played an important role in every South American diplomatic issue during the middle thirties, persuaded Argentina to rejoin the League after thirteen years (Argentina had withdrawn when the League refused to support a suggestion that its covenant be amended to admit any nation without prior application, and without a vote), and represented Argentina at every important international meeting during this period.

He was responsible for ending the so-called Chaco War (which resulted from a long-standing dispute over the boundaries in the Gran Chaco region) and initiated in Washington, D.C., the Declaration of August 1932 which put the American states on record as refusing to recognize any territorial change in the hemisphere brought about by force. He presented his Antiwar Pact to the League of Nations where it was well received and signed by eleven countries. In 1936 he was elected president of the Assembly of the League.

In a radio address given on his receipt of the Nobel prize, Saavedra Lamas said: "We are living in the aftermath of a great war. The fabric which civilization has been weaving in its efforts of centuries, once broken, is difficult to reconstruct. Under its broken web there appears to be a native barbarism, the impeccable cruelty which in centers of the oldest civilization emerges from the immense depths to which they have fallen, destroying the most beautiful entity in their intoxication of destruction.

"War of aggression, war which does not imply defense of one's country, is a collective crime. In its consequences on the mass of the poor and humble, it does not possess even that blaze of valor, or heroism, that leads to glory. War implies a lack of comprehension of mutual national interests; it means the undermining and even the end of culture. It is the useless sacrifice of courage erroneously applied, opposed to that other silent courage that signifies the effort to aid others to improve existence by raising all in this fleeting moment of ours to higher levels of existence."

1937

EDGAR ALGERNON ROBERT CECIL (1864–1958), Great Britain: *Lawyer, parliamentarian and cabinet minister, one of the architects of the League of Nations and its faithful defender. He played a decisive part both as lawyer and politician in drafting the Covenant of the League, which he felt must form an integral part of the Versailles Peace Treaty, and was responsible for the resolution that the League should meet annually and that all meetings should be held in public. He helped to establish the League of Nations Union in Great Britain in 1915 and became its president. In his seventies, he founded the International Peace Campaign with Pierre Cot, the French politician.*

"THE STATESMEN WHO occupied leading positions during the World War were so deeply struck by the deprivation of human life and economic resources, by the futility of war as a social institution, and by its amorality, that they became convinced pacifists and throughout the rest of their lives spared no effort to prevent such a calamity from ever again overtaking mankind."

So said Christian Lous Lange, chairman of the Nobel Peace Prize Committee, making the 1937 presentation. By then, two of the men he was talking about—Woodrow Wilson and Aristide Briand—were dead, and the prize for that year went to the third: Viscount Cecil of Chelwood, better known as Lord Robert Cecil.

Cecil was a member of one of the oldest and most distinguished families of the English landed gentry. His father, the marquess of Salisbury, was for nearly twenty years the leader of the Conservative party, and for most of this time prime minister.

The education which Cecil received at home until he was thirteen was far more interesting, he wrote in his autobiography, than his four years at Eton. He read law at Oxford and was called to the bar in 1887, at the age of twenty-three.

From the law, he turned, inevitably, to politics, representing East Marylebone in the Commons from 1906 to 1910, then becoming an Independent Conservative member for Hitchin in 1911, a seat he held until 1923.

At the outbreak of the war, aged fifty, he went to work for the Red Cross, but with the formation of the coalition government in 1915 he became undersecretary for foreign affairs and minister of blockade from 1916 to 1918.

During this phase of his life, Cecil became convinced that civilization could survive only if an international system could be devised which would ensure world peace. In September 1916 he circulated a memorandum which was regarded as the basis of the British official advocacy of the League of Nations.

From the inception of the League until 1946, when it finally collapsed, he devoted almost his entire public life to its cause. At the Paris Peace Conference, he was the British representative in charge of negotiations for a League of Nations; between 1920 and 1922 he represented the Dominion of South Africa in the League Assembly; in 1923 he made an extended tour of the United States explaining the importance of the League to American audiences, and thereafter, until 1927, he was the minister responsible for British activities in League affairs.

In 1927 Cecil retired from governmental office and worked independently to secure public support for the League. He was president of the British League of Nations Union from 1923 to 1945, and joint founder and president of the International Peace Campaign.

He was created first viscount of Chelwood in 1923, received the Woodrow Wilson Foundation peace award in 1924, and received honorary degrees from numerous universities including Oxford, Cambridge, Edinburgh, Manchester, Liverpool, Princeton, Columbia and Athens.

In the spring of 1946 he took part in the final meetings of the League in Geneva, ending his speech on this note: "The League is dead: long live the League of Nations." He was eighty-one.

In his Nobel lecture, entitled "The Future of Civilization," Cecil said: "I need hardly remind you of the very distressing events which have followed these two great breaches in the barrier against war which were made by Japan and Italy. [Japan's invasion of Manchuria in 1931, and Italy's invasion of Abyssinia in 1935.] We have seen their consequences in the forcible reoccupation of the Rhineland provinces, the intervention by many nations in the affairs of Spain and the absorption of Austria by Germany. . . . We see the world as it is now, after these defeats of the League, and we can compare it with what it was six or seven years ago. The comparison is certainly depressing: the contrast is terrible. . . .

"There can be little doubt that the armament interests were comparatively quiescent during the early years of the League. It was only when they were directly threatened by the effort to limit armaments that they became active in their efforts to destroy the institution which was responsible for this attack on their fundamental prosperity. I do not mean to exaggerate the power of the armament firms, but I have no doubt that they have contributed to the difficulties of the League.

"Professional opinion is almost inevitably against changes. It has been the operation of these and similar influences which has brought about, as I fear, a return to the old conception of what is called power diplomacy. To these conceptions, it is not too much to say, the idea of the complete opposition of war and peace was really foreign. . . . During the entire period before 1914, Europe and, to a degree, the whole world lived under the perpetual shadow of war, as we are doing, I am afraid, at the present time. . . . We are wasting gigantic sums, sums far greater than we ever wasted before, on preparations for war, because war has become again a very present possibility and, at the same time, its horrors and dangers are enormously greater than they were in 1914. And so the world is spending some three or four thousand million pounds sterling every year on preparations for what we all know will be, if it comes to pass, a tremendous danger to the whole of our civilization, whoever wins and whoever loses. . . .

"May Heaven grant that the statesmen of the world may realize this before it is too late and, by the exertion of the needed courage and prudence, restore again to the position of authority it held only a few years ago that great institution for peace on which the future of civilization so largely depends. I mean, of course, the League of Nations."

1938

THE NANSEN INTERNATIONAL OFFICE FOR REFUGEES: *Authorized by the League of Nations in 1930 and founded in Geneva in 1931, it was the successor of the High Commission for Refugees, the first international agency dealing with refugees and established by the League under the direction of Fridtjof Nansen in 1921.*

NANSEN, WHO TOWERED over all the other Peace laureates in the sheer practicability of his contributions, did not live long enough to see his mission accomplished. In the presentation address to the Nansen International Office for Refugees, Frederik Stang, a member of the Nobel Peace Prize Committee, said: "He was the champion of a cause new to politics, the cause of brotherly love, and he performed wonders, first for the prisoners of war and then for the political refugees. When he died, a great deal had already been accomplished, but much remained to be done. So his work had to be carried on. It has been divided between two organizations, a High Commission in London for German refugees and the Office in Geneva . . . which has this year been awarded the Peace Prize."

In 1923 the original mandate of the High Commission to cover Russian refugees was extended to include Armenian refugees. As the refugee problem grew, the mandate was broadened to include Assyrians, Assyro-Chaldeans and Turkish refugees.

After Nansen's death in 1930 the League Secretariat assumed responsibility for the protection of refugees, and that for material assistance was vested in the Nansen International Office for Refugees, an autonomous body under the authority of the League.

The Nansen office was overwhelmed with difficulties during its entire existence. For a start, it never had any regular system of financing but had to appeal for money on an ad hoc basis whenever a particularly urgent problem arose. The onset of the depression complicated matters further by reducing the opportunities of finding employment for refugees. The decline in the prestige of the League during the thirties made it all the more difficult to raise funds at a time when the tide of refugees from Germany, Italy and Spain was sweeping across Europe. There was also the problem that many member-states of the League were reluctant to permit League activities on behalf of people who were in fact refugees from their own regimes.

The accomplishments of the Nansen Office included the settlement of Saar refugees in Paraguay; the construction of villages to house 40,000 Armenians in Syria and the Lebanon and the resettlement of another 10,000 in Erivan; and the donation of financial, legal and material aid to almost a million refugees.

After the Nazis came to power in Germany, the problem of German refugees became so acute that in 1933 the League established a High Commission for Refugees from Germany. In 1938 this was dissolved and a new agency of the League, the Office of the High Commissioner for Refugees, was opened with headquarters in London.

In his Nobel lecture, Michael Hansson, president of the Nansen International Office for Refugees, made the point that an enormous amount of good can be achieved by the most modest contribution. "Many a refugee has been saved by just a single 100-kroner note, not to mention the countless instances in which a loan or grant of about 200 kroner has enabled the head of a family to take up a trade or start a small business, or save his livelihood at a critical moment.

"The other side of the Nansen operation—that is, the protection of the homeless—has been no less important. . . . The permanent insecurity in which the refugees live, their constant fear of being driven away once again from the humble abodes they have created, is perhaps the worst aspect of their plight. They have lost their homes, their country, their possessions. They have been deprived of their nationality and forced to seek asylum in a foreign country. And even when they are allowed to settle, it is by mere charity, charity that can be withdrawn at any time. . . .

"The first task . . . should be to open negotiations with the German authorities to secure for German refugees the right to take with them a certain part of their assets. . . . In the long run Germany can have no interest in obstructing the emigration it has itself planned.

"Dr. Goebbels said recently that about 180,000 Germans, mainly Jews, have left Germany during the last few years but that the new Germany, with its population of eighty million, still has about 700,000 Jews who must get out.

"In Poland, where about ten percent of the population of some thirty-five million are of Jewish origin . . . a Polish minister has stated in so many words that three million Jews are slowly dying of starvation. . . .

"All in all, we can estimate that the Jewish problem in Europe now includes about five million people. It becomes more and more apparent that they themselves seek an entirely new way of life, but how are they to do it? Palestine is by no means large enough, and in any case there are numerous reasons for questioning whether the emigration of Jews to that country should continue at all to any considerable degree.

"They are therefore seeking a country which they can look upon as their home and which can, after a time, receive a mass immigration of Jews from Europe; whether this be America, Africa or Australia does not really matter as long as they can be together on their own. . . . It will take time, but the world has space enough for everyone. . . .

"Today, the Jews have been outlawed in many countries. This is happening more and more as governments become more unfeeling and the people more fearful and suspicious. . . . The refugee problem has, all in all, become the greatest problem of our time. It can be solved, but only by the energetic cooperation with the League of Nations by governments aware of their responsibility to mankind."

LOOKING BACK ON it from this remove, it seems incredible that so many intelligent and far-sighted men should have ended their lectures with fervent pleas for cooperation with the League and renewed affirmations of their faith in it at a time when the League had been openly scorned by the dictators and was powerless to do any more than issue meek protests,

protests which were lost in the roar of the armament factories, and the U-boats crashing down the launching ramps, and the rumble of the panzer divisions, and the roar of the dive bombers. Perhaps, to be charitable, they believed that up until the moment when the war actually started, it could by some miracle be prevented; and it was with this hope that they still clung to the League as the only instrument with which that miracle might yet be performed. Perhaps, too, they felt that by acknowledging the despair many of them must have felt in their hearts, they would be admitting defeat before the blow actually fell, and thereby, in some small way, contributing to it. As it turned out, however, more than a month before the time came to announce the next champion, World War II had already begun.

1939

No prize awarded.

World War II and the Iron Curtain

THE DECADE THAT ended on December 31, 1949, was probably the most significant of our times: in those ten years were sown the seeds of many of the international problems that have troubled the world since then and most of which, unfortunately, seem no nearer to solution now, a quarter of a century later.

It began with a continuation of the "phony" war which had started the previous September—the British and French crouching defensively behind the Maginot Line, the Germans massing behind the Siegfried Line and nothing decisive happening anywhere.

Once things started happening, however, events moved with numbing rapidity. In April 1940 Germany invaded Norway and Denmark. In May Churchill took over as leader of a national government in Britain, and a few days later Germany invaded Holland, Luxembourg and Belgium, bypassing the impregnable Maginot Line. Before the end of May the British Expeditionary Force was being evacuated from the beaches of Dunkirk and on June 14 the Germans entered Paris.

A week later France signed an armistice with Germany and Britain stood alone. The Battle of Britain, the "blitz" on London and other big English cities, the submarine warfare on British shipping in the Atlantic, the Eighth Army's opening of the offensive in North Africa, Roosevelt's Lend Lease Act and Germany's sudden and inexplicable invasion of Russia in June are all familiar history.

We are, however, inclined to forget details, like Rudolf Hess landing in Scotland as early as May 10, 1941, to try to arrange a separate peace between Germany and Britain. Churchill's meeting with Roosevelt in the Western Atlantic to sign the Atlantic Charter was far more significant than it may have appeared at the time, for it marked a new approach to war on the part of the world's leaders. In World War I the monarchs and government leaders were content to leave the strategy to the generals; in

World War II the leaders met constantly—in Moscow, at Casablanca, in Cairo, at Yalta—to discuss and plan the conduct of the war.

Throughout the spring, summer and autumn, the Germans pushed relentlessly forward into Russia until they were within a few miles of Moscow, and in December the Japanese surprise attack on the American Navy in Pearl Harbor brought the United States into the war. Hong Kong and then Singapore were abandoned to the Japanese but by November 1942 Rommel was in retreat in the desert, Montgomery was in command of the Eighth Army and there had been Allied landings under General Dwight Eisenhower in North Africa.

These momentous events obscured other items which appeared in the newspapers during those crowded months. Terylene was invented; so was ENIAC, the world's first computer. Magnetic tape was developed and the Germans launched their first experimental V2 rocket. Most significant of all, though it didn't seem to matter at the time, was the news that in Chicago in December a scientist called Fermi had succeeded in splitting the atom.

In 1943 the Russians had started to fight back and soon destroyed the German armies surrounding Stalingrad. The RAF had begun its systematic bombing of the Ruhr and of the German railroad system, and the Allies, having driven Rommel out of North Africa, landed in Sicily and began the long push up through Italy. In the same month Mussolini fell from power, and by September 3 Eisenhower, now Supreme Allied Commander, had announced Italy's unconditional surrender.

In the United States the first Henry Kaiser "Liberty" ships were launched; a United Nations Relief and Rehabilitation Administration was set up; the Rodgers and Hammerstein smash hit *Oklahoma!* launched a completely new style of musical; and a crooner called Frank Sinatra became the world's first pop idol.

By June 1944 the Allies had fought their way up as far as Rome and two days after the Fifth Army entered the Italian capital came the D-day landings in Normandy.

In July the German generals tried to assassinate Hitler, there was a rising in Warsaw and the British landed on the French Riviera. By July 25 General de Gaulle, leader of the Free French Forces, was marching down the Champs-Elysées in Paris, in the wake of the Allied troops. By September 5 Brussels had been liberated, and before the end of the year the Russians were advancing into Europe through Yugoslavia and Hungary. In November Roosevelt won the US presidential elections for his fourth term, defeating Thomas Dewey, and on December 16 the final desperate German push started the Battle of the Bulge in the Ardennes.

The "black-out" restrictions in Britain were lifted in September 1944, and at Clinton, Tennessee, a uranium pile was being built to manufacture plutonium for the first atomic bomb.

In February 1945 the Allied troops reached the Rhine, on March 7 they entered Cologne, and on March 28 the last of 1,050 V-bombs fell on Britain.

In April Franklin D. Roosevelt died and was succeeded by Harry S. Truman, his vice-president. The Russians reached Berlin and in San Francisco a meeting was held between Anthony Eden, Molotov and Edward Stettinius to discuss some form of a United Nations Organization. In the same month Mussolini and his mistress were murdered by partisans and their bodies strung up, head downwards, outside a gasoline station.

On May 8, VE Day, Von Keitel surrendered to Zhukov near Berlin, and the following month the Allied Control Commission divided Germany up into occupational zones.

In July Churchill, after all he had done for the British war effort, was rejected by the electorate in a Labor landslide that cleared the way for a new policy of wholesale nationalization in Britain.

On August 6 an American plane dropped the first atomic bomb on Hiroshima and three days later another was dropped on Nagasaki. The war was over, but the world's troubles were only beginning.

In the same month Korea was placed under American and Russian occupation until a democratic government could be established and an independent Vietnam republic was formed with Ho Chi Minh as president.

In September an All-India Congress under Gandhi and Pandit Nehru rejected all British proposals and called on the British to quit India. Egypt demanded the revision of the Anglo-Egyptian 1936 treaty, the end of military occupation and the return of the Sudan.

In October fighting broke out between the Nationalists and the Communists in northern China for the control of Manchuria, and Egypt, Iraq, Syria and the Lebanon warned the United States that the creation of a Jewish state in Palestine would lead to war. The Arab League was founded, and the United Nations officially came into existence when twenty-nine nations ratified its charter.

The trial of the Nazi war criminals began in Nuremberg, Tito took over in Yugoslavia and de Gaulle in France, and the foreign ministers of the United States, Great Britain, and the USSR met in Moscow to call again for a provisional democratic government in Korea.

The deaths in World War II were reckoned up. In Britain there were 244,723 killed and 277,090 wounded; in other Commonwealth countries, 109,929 killed and 197,908 wounded. In the United States there were 230,173 killed and 613,611 wounded; in Germany about three million military and civilians were listed dead or missing and another million wounded; and the Russian casualties amounted to twenty million military and civilians dead. Other casualties of the period, from one cause or another, included Lloyd George, Hitler, Laval and Rommel.

The year 1946 opened with the first session of the United Nations General Assembly in London and the appointment of the Norwegian Socialist, Trygve Lie, as secretary general.

In Britain the Bank of England was nationalized.

In March the first chill draft of the cold war was felt when Churchill, in his Fulton speech, warned the West to stand up to the USSR. In Russia a Soviet Council of Ministers under Josef Stalin replaced the Council of People's Commissars.

In Africa the Gold Coast became the first British colony with a majority of Africans in the legislature.

On April 18 the League of Nations Assembly dissolved itself and an Anglo-American committee advised against the partition of Palestine.

In May a bill was introduced to nationalize the coal mines in Britain, and in July bread rationing was introduced because of a world wheat shortage.

In Nuremberg, Goering escaped execution by killing himself, but eleven other leading Nazis were sentenced to death and Hess to life imprisonment. He is still in jail.

In November the British introduced a National Health program and published a bill to nationalize public transport. New York was chosen to be the permanent headquarters of the United Nations.

During the year the US Supreme Court ruled that the segregation of Negroes on interstate buses was unconstitutional; the Fairey Aviation company perfected the first pilotless, radio-controlled rocket missile and television transmissions were resumed in Britain with an estimated 12,000 viewers. Joe Louis successfully defended his world heavyweight title for the twenty-third time.

In January 1947 the British coal industry was nationalized and Nigeria achieved a modified form of self-government. Egypt broke off diplomatic relations with Britain and referred the question of preparing the Sudan for self-government to the United Nations. The following month a British proposal to divide Palestine into Arab and Jewish zones was rejected by both Arabs and Jews.

In March Truman explained to Congress his plan for economic and military aid to states "threatened" by communism, outlining plans to aid Greece and Turkey.

Britain, in despair, referred the Palestine question to the United Nations and in a speech at Harvard, George Marshall, then US secretary of state, called for a European economic recovery plan, the plan which later became known simply as Marshall Aid.

In August Indian independence was proclaimed, partitioning India and Pakistan; the proclamation was followed by violent riots between Moslems and Hindus.

In November the UN General Assembly recognized Korea's claim to independence; Princess Elizabeth married Philip Mountbatten, the Duke of Edinburgh; a London conference on the future of Germany failed because of Russian reparation demands; and the United Nations announced a plan for the partition of Palestine under UN trusteeship.

This was the year of the first supersonic flight, the first all-automatic transatlantic flight and the inauguration of Britain's first atomic pile at Harwell. The first of the Dead Sea Scrolls were discovered and two pioneers of the automobile—Henry Ford and Ettore Bugatti—died.

In January 1948 Mahatma Gandhi was assassinated, and in March the USSR walked out of a conference of the Allied Control Commission for Germany. The US Congress passed the Marshall Aid Act contributing $5.3 billion for European recovery, and in April the USSR began to interfere with traffic between West Germany and Berlin. The same month saw a meeting in Paris which set up the OEEC (Organization for European Economic Cooperation).

The British mandate in Palestine ended in May and a Jewish provisional government was set up in Israel, with Chaim Weizmann as president and David Ben-Gurion as premier. Immediately the Arab Legion of Transjordania invaded Palestine and entered Jerusalem. Egyptian troops intervened in Palestine on the side of the Arabs.

In South Africa the Smuts coalition was defeated by a nationalist Afrikander bloc with a firm apartheid program. North Korea boycotted a national constitutional convention at Seoul, and Yugoslavia was expelled from the Cominform for "nonconformity."

On July 15 the United Nations ordered a truce in Palestine and on July 24 the USSR stopped all road and rail traffic between Berlin and the West, forcing the Allies to introduce the "airlift."

The British Citizenship Act conferred the status of British subjects on all Commonwealth citizens and led to the first mass emigration of people from Africa, India, Pakistan and the West Indies to Britain.

In August the Republic of Korea was proclaimed in Seoul with Syngman Rhee as president and in September the Communists announced the formation of a North China People's Republic. On September 9 the Korean People's Democratic Republic was formed in North Korea claiming authority over the whole country. Count Bernadotte, the UN mediator in Palestine, was assassinated and the first conference in London of representatives from Britain's African colonies was held. In November Harry Truman defeated Thomas Dewey, Republican, in the presidential elections.

In December, Cardinal Mindszenty of Hungary was imprisoned because of the Catholic church's refusal to make concessions to the Communist government; Archbishop Stepinac of Croatia was already in prison in Yugoslavia for similar reasons.

In the same year the long-playing record was invented by Peter Goldmark, and the Bell Telephone Company scientists came up with a gadget known as a transistor. Kinsey's *Sexual Behavior in the Human Male* was published and inaugurated an era in which the most intimate details of sexual relationships were regarded as matters for open discussion.

The year 1949 began with Chiang Kai-shek's resignation as president of China, following a series of defeats of his Nationalist Armies.

In April an agreement creating the North Atlantic Treaty Organization—a mutual aid and defense body—was signed in Washington by foreign ministers from Britain, France, Belgium, the Netherlands, Italy, Portugal, Denmark, Iceland, Norway, Canada and the United States. Ireland refused to sign on the grounds that she could not participate while still partitioned.

On May 5 a Council of Europe was set up, with Strasbourg as the seat; the consultative assembly included Belgium, France, Denmark, Britain, Ireland, Italy, Luxembourg, the Netherlands, Norway and Sweden (later supplemented by Greece, Iceland and Turkey). On May 11 Israel was admitted to the United Nations and the following day the Berlin blockade was lifted.

The German Federal Republic came into existence on May 23 with Bonn as its capital, and in the same month the Chinese Communists drove the Nationalists off the mainland.

In June the state of Vietnam was established in Saigon under Bao Dai, but conflicts with the Communists in the area continued. The United States completed the withdrawal of occupying forces from South Korea, and in South Africa the apartheid program opened with a ban on mixed marriages between Europeans and non-Europeans.

In July the Chinese Nationalists organized a Supreme Council under Chiang Kai-shek and removed their forces to Formosa, and in September the UN Commission warned of the dangers of a civil war in Korea.

Konrad Adenauer became chancellor of West Germany and Britain devalued the pound sterling from $4.30 to $2.80. The Berlin airlift ended after 277,264 flights, and on October 1 the Communist People's Republic of China was proclaimed under Mao Tse-tung, with Chou En-lai as premier and foreign minister.

In November Britain nationalized the iron and steel industries and India adopted a constitution, becoming a federal republic within the Commonwealth.

It was the year of the first atomic bomb tests in the USSR. It was also the year that Axel Munthe, Maurice Maeterlinck and Richard Strauss died.

Books of the decade included Graham Greene's *The Power and the Glory* and *The Heart of the Matter*, Hemingway's *For Whom the Bell Tolls*, Scott Fitzgerald's *The Last Tycoon*, John Steinbeck's *The Moon Is Down*, Somerset Maugham's *The Razor's Edge*, George Orwell's *Animal Farm* and *Nineteen Eighty-four*, Evelyn Waugh's *Brideshead Revisited*, and Norman Mailer's *The Naked and the Dead*.

Among the films were Chaplin's *The Great Dictator*, Walt Disney's *Fantasia*, the Marx Brothers' *The Big Store*; Orson Welles's *Citizen Kane* and *The Third Man*, *Holiday Inn* with Bing Crosby, *Mrs. Miniver* with Greer Garson, Olivier's *Henry V* and *Hamlet* and de Sica's *Bicycle Thieves*. And plays included Arthur Miller's *Death of a Salesman*, T. S. Eliot's *The Cocktail Party*; Tennessee Williams's *A Streetcar Named Desire* and *The Glass Menagerie*, and Jean Paul Sartre's *Huis Clos* [No Exit].

In the United States bebop was the rhythm everybody was dancing to, but the pop song of the period everywhere was "Lilli Marlene."

1940-1943
Prizes not awarded

1944
International Committee
of the
Red Cross

1945 Cordell Hull

1946 Emily Balch

1946 John Mott

1947
Friends Service Council
and
American Friends
Service Committee

1948
Prize not awarded

1949 John Boyd Orr

1940–1943

No prize awarded.

1944

THE INTERNATIONAL COMMITTEE OF THE RED CROSS: *Previously awarded the prize in 1917.*

FACED WITH THE same dilemma as had faced them during World War I, the Nobel Committee reacted in the same way; they withheld the prize during the first years of the war, keeping the money which would have been awarded in the main fund. And in 1944, as in 1917, they awarded the prize as a contribution to the work of the Red Cross.

In his speech of acceptance, Max Huber, honorary president of the International Committee of the Red Cross, said that when Nobel conceived the Peace Prize, he was thinking particularly of "constructive peace of an international order that makes armed conflict impossible."

"But from the beginning," he went on, "you [the Nobel Committee] have also awarded some prizes to men and institutions that have helped the victims of war and the victims of evils that result from war.

"Although there seems to be a big difference between constructive peace and aid to war victims—indeed, in the eyes of some, an antagonism—there is this implicit and fundamental bond. Helping the victims of war is not the sole objective set by the Red Cross; in giving aid it serves another purpose no less important, that of rescuing in the dark storm of war the idea of human solidarity and respect for the dignity of every human being—precisely at a time when the real or alleged necessities of war push moral values into the background."

The Nobel lecture by Edouard Chapuisat, a member of the International Committee of the Red Cross, took the form of a history of the Red Cross and its achievements during World War II.

At the outbreak of war, the Committee was able to draw on experience gained both in the war in Abyssinia and in the Spanish Civil War; it had learned to take into account that the strategy of combat was keeping step with what has been called "progress" in military techniques.

As the war broke out before provision had been made for legal protection of civilians in enemy territory—this was to be discussed at Geneva in 1940—the Red Cross International Committee proposed on September 4, 1939, that interned civilians should at least be protected by the 1929 convention for prisoners of war. As a result delegates from the Committee were able to visit civilian internment camps as well as prisoner of war camps.

The Central Prisoners of War Agency in Geneva handled a total of over 98 million letters and telegrams, made 3 million photocopies and 250 card indexes in which more than 30 million entries were classified, making possible the methodical and detailed investigations necessary when searching for missing persons. A card index was also maintained on missing medical personnel—up to 1945, 50,000 inquiries in this category were handled.

Circumstances arising from the conflict made the dispatch of food and clothing parcels absolutely necessary for the well-being of prisoners and between 1940 and the end of November 1945 more than 34 million parcels totaling some 407,000 tons of goods were sent to prisoners of war by the collective relief services of the Red Cross. Shipments from overseas were usually routed through Lisbon or other Mediterranean ports where the Committee had special delegates. The Red Cross had in its service thirty-nine ships, including six sailing ships, flying neutral colors and carrying on their hulls the sign of the Red Cross.

An Intellectual Relief Service was set up to distribute over 1.3 million books to the prison camps and to encourage the organization of secondary and university studies.

Throughout the war the Committee endeavored to look after the interests of Jews detained in concentration and labor camps. The delegates tried, sometimes at risk to their own lives, to protect persecuted Jewish populations. Supplies of food, medicine and clothing were taken to certain camps by rail or by convoys of trucks belonging to the Committee. Even when requests to visits camps were met with stubborn refusal, the Committee still tried and in some cases succeeded in bringing relief to certain internees in concentration camps, labor camps and prisons. The Committee was also able to send hundreds of thousands of parcels to deportees.

In 1944 the Parcel Service to Concentration Camps sent collective consignments to camps but towards the end of that year the destruction of the German rail network made such a service increasingly difficult to maintain. In April 1945 the Committee secured trucks and fuel for this work. By that time, chaos in Germany resulted in the trucks carrying most of their aid to columns of prisoners on the march and in this way thousands of lives were saved. At the end of the war they were able to enter the concentration camps not only to unload hundreds of tons of goods, but also to bring back liberated prisoners. Thousands of prisoners were transported in the Committee's trucks, usually to Switzerland, where they could begin their journey back to their homelands. At certain camps Red Cross delegates were able to prevent the shooting of prisoners.

"The International Committee wishes to state publicly," Chapuisat concluded, "that the results the Committee achieved measured up to all its hopes; but it also realizes that what it had been given to do was, in the final analysis, of little significance when compared to the sum total of suffering it encountered in the course of its work. It strove to alleviate what misery it could; it tried to raise its flag above the ruins of the world to show that human hope should never falter."

1945

CORDELL HULL (1871–1955), United States: *Described by Franklin Roosevelt as the "father of the United Nations." As secretary of state for twelve years, he laid the foundations for the "good neighbor" policy among the twenty-one American nations, negotiated reciprocal trade agreements with numerous countries and served as a member and senior adviser to the United Nations Conference in San Francisco in 1945.*

AS THE AWARDS immediately following the end of World War I were given to a succession of men associated with the League of Nations, it might have been expected that men connected with its successor, the United Nations, would dominate the list for the years following World War II. Yet, for a variety of reasons—perhaps paramount among them the fact that the expectations of the United Nations proved largely fruitless—the only UN figure to feature among the immediate postwar laureates was the American secretary of state, Cordell Hull.

Born in a log cabin in Tennessee, Cordell Hull was the son of a farmer who turned lumber merchant. The only one of five sons who showed any interest in learning, Cordell Hull wanted to be a lawyer. He did his elementary school training in a one-room schoolhouse his father had built in Willow Grove, and received his law degree in 1891 at Cumberland University in Lebanon, Tennessee.

He began to practice law at the age of twenty, and when he was twenty-one went into politics. From 1893 to 1897 he was a member of the Tennessee House of Representatives. He then temporarily abandoned politics to serve as captain of the Fourth Tennessee Regiment in the Spanish-American War. In 1903 he became a judge, and in 1907 was elected to Congress from the Fourth Tennessee District. He was a member of the House Ways and Means Committee, a leader of the movement for lower tariffs and the author of the first Federal Income Tax Act in 1913. The United States Supreme Court had decided in 1895 that the introduction of income tax was a breach of the federal constitution; Hull refused to accept this judgment because he was convinced that an income tax as a means of increasing federal revenue was more practical than the tariff system, which in his view created monopolies and enriched the few at the expense of the many. He was also a firm believer in free competition, and drafted a resolution convening a world trade-agreement conference at the end of World War I.

Hull was elected a US senator for the 1931–37 term, but resigned when he was made secretary of state by Franklin Roosevelt in 1933.

In November of that year he headed the American delegation to the seventh Pan-American Conference, held in Montevideo, where he won the trust of the Latin American diplomats and laid the foundations for Roosevelt's "good neighbor" policy. At the same time, through the Trade Agreements Act of 1934, he negotiated reciprocal trade agreements with many countries, lowering tariffs and stimulating trade.

From 1936 onwards, foreseeing the danger to world peace arising from the existence of dictators, he advocated rearmament, made a plea for the implementation of a system of collective security, supported US aid to the Western democracies (though not in the form of military involvement), condemned Japanese encroachment into Indochina and warned all branches of the US military well in advance of the attack on Pearl Harbor to resist simultaneous, surprise attacks at various points. His major effort during World War II was the preparation of a blueprint for an international organization dedicated to the maintenance of peace with sufficient legislative, economic and military power to achieve it.

Hull was forced to resign in November 1944 because of ill health. In a letter to Roosevelt on November 21, 1944, he wrote: "It is a supreme tragedy to me personally that I am unable to continue making my full contribution to such great international undertakings as the creation of the postwar peace organization, the solution of the many other problems involved in the promotion of international cooperation and the final development of a full and complete structure of a world under law."

Roosevelt's reply included the following tribute: "Incidentally, when the organization of the United Nations is set up, I shall continue to pray that you as the Father of the United Nations may preside over its first session.

"That has nothing to do with whether you are secretary of state or not at that time but should go to you as the one person in all the world who has done the most to make this great plan for peace an effective fact. In so many different ways you have contributed to friendly relations among nations that even though you may not remain in a position of executive administration, you will continue to help the world with your moral guidance."

Hull was not well enough to go to Oslo to deliver a Nobel lecture, but in his message of acceptance he said: "The problem of peace is uppermost today in the hearts and minds of all of us as the world emerges from the staggering ordeal of the most widespread and cruel war of all the ages. That war has brought with it a truly incredible development of means of destruction and a terrifying prospect of rapid and almost limitless development in that direction. Triumphant science and technology are only at the threshold of man's command over sources of energy so stupendous that, if used for military purposes, they can wipe out our entire civilization.

". . . I am firmly convinced that, with all its imperfections, the United Nations Organization offers the peace-loving nations of the world, now, a fully workable mechanism which will give them peace, if they want peace. . . . Alfred Nobel, were he alive today, would, I am sure have joined me in the unshakable faith that this crucial test will be met: that the searing lessons of this latest war and the promise of the United Nations Organization will be the cornerstones of a new edifice of enduring peace and the guideposts of a new era of human progress."

1946

EMILY GREENE BALCH (1867–1961), United States: *Social reformer and one of the founders of the Women's Trade Union League of America. She was associated with the Women's International League for Peace and Freedom founded at The Hague during World War I, and was secretary general of the International Women's League in Geneva until 1922 as well as a delegate to the nine congresses of the Women's League which were held between the wars.*

JOHN RALEIGH MOTT (1865–1955), United States: *Traveling secretary for the YMCA among the students of American and Canadian universities cited for creating "worldwide organizations which have united millions of young people in work for the Christian ideals of peace and tolerance between nations."*

IN MAKING THE presentation to Emily Greene Balch, Gunnar Jahn, chairman of the Nobel Committee, made the curious admission that her name might not be familiar to many of those present and that there were probably few people in Europe who still remembered her.

Born in Boston, the daughter of a successful lawyer, she graduated from Bryn Mawr College in 1889, used a European fellowship from Bryn Mawr to study economics in Paris in 1890–91, and completed her formal studies at Harvard and the University of Chicago, spending a further year working on economics in Berlin in 1895–96.

In 1896 she joined the faculty of Wellesley College, becoming a professor of economics and sociology in 1913. She was a member of two municipal boards (on children and on urban planning) and two state commissions (on industrial education and on immigration), and was active in movements for women's suffrage, racial justice, control of child labor, and better labor conditions in general.

Emily Balch became convinced after the outbreak of World War I that she wanted to devote her life to furthering the cause of peace. As a delegate to the International Congress of Women at The Hague in 1915, she played a prominent role in several important projects, among them the founding of the Women's International Committee for Permanent Peace, later named the Women's International League for Peace and Freedom; preparing peace proposals for consideration by the belligerent nations; and serving on a delegation to Russian and Scandinavian countries to urge their governments to initiate mediation offers.

On her return to the United States, she campaigned actively against America's entry into the war, left Wellesley College and worked on the liberal weekly, the *Nation*. She wrote a successful pacifist book, *Approaches to the Great Settlement*, which had a foreword by Norman Angell, the 1933 Peace Prize winner. She also attended the second convention of the International Congress of Women held at Zurich in 1919, and accepted an offer to become secretary of its operating organization, the Women's International League for Peace and Freedom at

Geneva. She donated her Nobel Peace Prize money to this organization and worked for it without salary.

In the period between the wars, she helped in one way or another with many League of Nations projects: among them disarmament, the internationalization of aviation, drug control and the participation of the United States in the affairs of the League.

The growth of the Nazi movement and the fresh war clearly looming on the European horizon brought about an abrupt change in Emily Balch's outlook. She attacked isolationism and American neutrality legislation, placing herself in opposition to the American branch of the Women's League. With the coming of the war, she did not oppose America's entry, as she had done in World War I. She had asked herself the question which faces all those who work for peace: "Shall we submit weakly and be devoured?", and answered it "by rising to defend the fundamental human rights sword in hand," as August Schou put it in *Nobel: The Man and His Prizes.* After the war she was a strong supporter of the United Nations Organization and brought her influence to bear on enlisting the support of American peace organizations, even if the proposed UN did not correspond perfectly with their ideals.

"The future shape of the new organization," she said, "will not depend on what the documents appear to state, but on what the members make of it. Practice in cooperation is what will give the United Nations its character. Plans have not been set up for a utopia, but for Europe, Russia, America and all other countries with their conflicting interests and ideas. And it is precisely because the proposals we have before us are fairly modest that they may perhaps be realized. . . . International unity is not in itself a solution. Unless this international unity has a moral quality, accepts the discipline of moral standards and possesses the quality of humanity, it will not be the unity we are interested in."

In a very lengthy Nobel lecture, she analyzed both the unifying and the divisive trends which then existed in the world and underlined the effect of the two world wars: "These wars also greatly altered the relative standing of the leading countries. The role of Italy and Austria has diminished as has that of France and Britain; Germany and Japan have suffered catastrophically. Meanwhile Russia and America have increased in stature. The world looks with interest to see what may come out of Asia with a new India and (one hopes) a new China; and also out of Australia. While Europe is hard hit and lies at the moment almost prostrate, there is on the horizon promise of a long-needed integration which, if it succeeds, may mean a new European Epoch in which she will remain a 'mother of culture' and no longer be also a 'mother of wars.' . . . It looks as though the systematic assistance proposed in the Marshall Plan to help Europe to recover economically after the shock of the war might be the means of knitting Europe together as it has never been before."

Summing up the problems facing the United Nations Organization, she said: "Most serious of all, unlike the League of Nations, it is called upon to begin its active life before the peace treaties are complete. Germany and Austria and Japan are still occupied. . . . The world is not even technically at peace; an agreement has not yet been reached on the absolutely crucial question of Germany. The United Nations is moreover faced with the necessity for immediate decision and action on several peculiarly poignant and complicated problems in Greece, in Palestine, in Korea and elsewhere. Still more it operates in a world half wrecked by the destruction of war on an unimaginable scale. We are more or less used to famine in India and China (though I suppose it is as painful there as nearer home). Now we see a Europe herself hungry, collectively and separately, covered with masses of broken rubble, charred timber and vast fields that carry white crosses instead of grain. Production and trade are so deeply affected that their reconstruction presents problems which would be almost insuperable even if they were not complicated by political difficulties. At the same time there is an extraordinarily bitter ideological and nationalistic opposition between the Soviet Union, with its friends, and the Western democracies, so that two great powers, or blocs of powers, face one another in mutual suspicion and fear.

"That the new world organization has done as well as it has under such circumstances is surprising. Indeed the fact that it has actually been set up and is actually functioning is, if you think of it, a miracle."

JOHN RALEIGH MOTT, Emily Balch's co-laureate that year, was a bizarre choice by any standards. Making the presentation, Herman Smitt Ingebretsen, a member of the Nobel Committee, admitted that he had never been a politician and had never taken an active part in organized peace work. Mott had been chosen, he said, "because he has been faithful to the call which he answered as a young student, and because he has created worldwide organizations which have united millions of people in work for the Christian ideals of peace and tolerance among the nations. . . . He has always been a living force, a tireless fighter in the service of Christ, opening young minds to the light which he thinks can lead the world to peace and bring men together in understanding and goodwill."

Mott, born of pioneer stock in Livingston Manor, New York, moved with his parents to Postville, Iowa, where his father became a lumber merchant and first mayor of the town. His father hoped that his son would join the family timber trade, but Mott himself vacillated between the law, the church and politics. While he was at Cornell University, a lecture by J. Kyanston Studd in January 1886 made him determined to devote his life to furthering Christianity among the world's students.

In the summer of 1886 he represented Cornell's Young Men's Christian Association at the first international, interdenominational student Christian conference. At that conference, which was attended by 251 men from 89 colleges and universities, a hundred delegates, including Mott, pledged themselves to work in foreign missions. Out of this conference, two years later, sprang the Student Volunteer Movement for Foreign Missions.

During his two remaining years at Cornell, as president of the YMCA he increased the membership threefold and raised money for a university YMCA building. He graduated in 1888, having majored in philosophy and history, and the same year began a twenty-seven-year stint as national secretary of the Intercollegiate YMCA of the US and Canada, and for part of that time was also chairman of the executive committee of the Student Volunteer Movement for Foreign Missions. He was presiding officer at the World Missionary Conference in Edinburgh in 1910; organized the World's Student Christian Federation, and as its general secretary went on a two-year world tour, helping to set up national student movements in India, China, Japan, Australia, New Zealand, and selecting corresponding members of the world federation in Egypt, Hawaii and many European countries.

Mott himself was a Methodist, but the students who flocked to his organizations included Protestants of all kinds, Roman Catholics, and Orthodox Catholics as well as representatives of the Nestorian, Syrian and Coptic churches. His stated aim was to give the Christian world new leaders whose love and tolerance would transcend the old frontiers which had previously separated people.

In 1926 he became president of the World's Alliance of Young Men's Christian Associations. Its membership, drawn from all social classes and occupations, numbered about two million young men and boys from over fifty countries. It represented autonomous national organizations all over the world and of every Christian denomination. It arranged the exchange of delegates and publications, and through planned activities tried to find constructive solutions to the problem of peace among the nations.

During World War I, Mott gathered the resources of his organizations to launch welfare work among the soldiers at the front and bring relief to millions of prisoners of war on both sides. His teams worked to render captivity a bit more bearable mentally and physically for the prisoners, and tried to prepare them for a return to normal life after the war.

During World War II, the YMCA, still under Mott, resumed its operations to improve the conditions of prisoners of war. After the war, though now aged eighty, he set out on yet another world tour to reforge the international links which the war had severed and arrange a world conference of his organization. It was held in Geneva in 1945 under his chairmanship.

In 1913 Woodrow Wilson had tried to persuade Mott to accept the post of US ambassador to China, but Mott declined. He was a member of a delegation sent to Mexico in 1916 to resolve difficulties which had arisen between the United States and Mexico, and was a member of the American diplomatic mission to Russia in 1917.

In 1914 he had presided over the first Christian student conference for blacks in the United States, and during the same year presided over the first US congress for both black and white Christians from northern and southern states. "If we are Christians," Mott said, "we must be able to live side by side as true friends, in equality, justice and mutual respect."

Elihu Root, Nobel Peace laureate of 1912, said of Mott: "His powerful personality and completely self-sacrificing devotion to the cause of peace have, I believe, never been equaled. He does not owe his influence to the official positions he holds; rather, it is the positions which have acquired importance through the work he has accomplished. Over the years he has traveled over the whole world, using his official position to create and strengthen a universal sympathy for the ideas on which peace necessarily depends."

Mott wrote sixteen books on evangelism and the world mission; he crossed the Atlantic over a hundred times and the Pacific fourteen times, averaging thirty-four days on the ocean per year. He received honorary awards from China, Czechoslovakia, Finland, France, Greece, Hungary, Italy, Japan, Jerusalem, Poland, Portugal, Siam, Sweden and the United States; and six honorary degrees from the universities of Brown, Edinburgh, Princeton, Toronto, Yale and Upper Iowa.

In his Nobel lecture, he spoke of the work of Gandhi. "The most trustworthy leader," he said, "is one who adopts and applies guiding principles. He trusts them like the North Star. He follows his principles no matter how many oppose him and no matter how few go with him. This has been the real secret of the wonderful leadership of Mahatma Gandhi. In the midst of most bewildering conditions he has followed, cost what it might, the guiding principles of nonviolence, religious unity, removal of untouchability, and economic independence."

A great many people have wondered, over the years, why Gandhi was never chosen for a Nobel Peace Prize.

1947

THE FRIENDS SERVICE COUNCIL, established in 1927: *The standing committee responsible for the overseas work of the Quakers' Religious Society of Friends in Great Britain and Ireland, dedicated to missionary activity, international service and relief work.*

THE AMERICAN FRIENDS SERVICE COMMITTEE, founded in 1917 in the United States: *Designed to provide young Quakers and other conscientious objectors to war with an opportunity to perform an alternative "service of love" in wartime.*

IT MAY SEEM at first glance curious that the award of the Peace Prize to a man who devoted his life to the Young Men's Christian Association should be followed by its division between the two service committees of the Quakers, a religious group which earned its title from the religious fervor of its forebears which caused them to tremble or "quake" before the Lord. Perhaps the explanation lay in the state of the world at this juncture. With the Russian bloc and the Western democracies glowering balefully at one another over the Iron Curtain, in a world which now had a weapon capable of destroying every living thing, the Nobel Committee may have decided that the wisest present course was to award the Peace Prizes to individuals and organizations with already well-established lines of communication with the Prince of Peace Himself, who alone, they may well have felt, could get humanity out of the mess in which it had landed itself.

This glib explanation would, however, be grossly unfair to the relentless pacifism of the Quakers, whose work for peace and the alleviation of suffering over the years was out of all proportion to the relatively small size of the organization, never more than about 200,000 in all scattered throughout the world, though mainly in England and America.

The Society of Friends was founded in Britain over three hundred years ago by George Fox, the English religious leader and preacher, and was from the beginning a community without a fixed organization. In 1656, the Quakers, escaping persecution in England, found their way to America where at first they met the same fate. By the end of the century, however, they had been accepted. William Penn, probably the best known Quaker in America, had founded the city of Philadelphia and the unarmed colony of Pennsylvania, and there were then about 60,000 Quakers in America and the same number in England.

From the beginning the Quakers were opposed to violence in any form, and although they became involved in some political protests against slavery, in the struggle for social justice, in opposing the Crimean War, it is another side of their activities which earned them the Peace Prize. Making the presentation, Gunnar Jahn, chairman of the Nobel Committee, said: "It is through silent assistance from the nameless to the nameless that they have worked to promote the fraternity between nations cited in the will of Alfred Nobel. Their work began in the prisons. We heard about them from our seamen who spent long years in prison during the Napoleonic Wars. We met them again during the Irish Famine of 1846–47 . . . and we found them again in France after the ravages of the 1870–71 war."

When World War I broke out, many Quakers were thrown into prison as conscientious objectors and were treated like criminals. Others, even as early as 1914, had started relief work on the very battlefields, first on the Marne and later elsewhere along the Western Front. After the war it was the Friends Service Committee which, at the request of Herbert Hoover—then head of the US Food Administration and War Relief commissions—took over the task of obtaining food for the sick and undernourished children of Germany. Their relief corps worked in Poland and Serbia, and during the Spanish Civil War it rendered aid to both sides.

During World War II more relaxed conscription laws allowed all Quakers to undertake relief work as an alternative to military service. Most of the countries occupied by the Germans were closed to them, but they worked wherever they could, first in England during the Blitz, and after that behind the front in many countries of Europe and Asia and even in America, where, after Pearl Harbor, the whole Japanese-American population was evacuated from the West Coast. The Quakers went to their assistance and tried to break down the prevailing prejudice toward the Japanese, most of whom were US citizens.

When the war ended, the Quakers became active in Europe again, bringing relief to prisoners released from concentration camps, helping with the repatriation of people from forced labor or POW camps. They also worked in Asia, in India and Japan, helping people back to normal life and work, and restoring their self-respect and confidence in the future. The Korean War, the Hungarian Revolution, the Algerian War, Vietnam and Biafra all provided fresh openings for the Quaker overseas services.

Concluding his presentation address, Gunnar Jahn said: "The Quakers have shown us that it is possible to translate into action what lies deep in the hearts of many: compassion for others and the desire to help them—that rich expression of the sympathy between all men, regardless of nationality or race, which, transformed into deeds, must form the basis for lasting peace. For this reason alone the Quakers deserve to receive the Nobel Prize today."

Apart from relief work in the field, the Quaker committees, shortly after World War I, inaugurated a series of Quaker International Centers (popularly known as "Quaker Embassies"), which provided neutral and friendly ground for the exchange of information and viewpoints between people of different nationalities, a focus for various activities that aimed at spreading goodwill and understanding, and a base from which the Quaker ambassadors of peace could operate during crises—in short, they constituted an attempt at constructive peacemaking.

In his Nobel lecture, Henry J. Cadbury, chairman of the American Friends Service Committee, said that he had been reading all he could about the views of Alfred Nobel on the subject of peace. "His ideas were not completely consistent and unchanging. . . . Sometimes he thought that war would be stopped by the invention of more terrible weapons, though he did not dream of some of the weapons which are in existence today. Sometimes he thought it would be stopped by collective force, by arbitration, or by international law, and he sometimes mentioned international friendship. These divergent views of his stress the fact that the struggle against war is a struggle which—if I may use a military metaphor—may be carried on on many fronts.

"We believe that war is a habit, a curious habit, a somewhat accidental habit that men have adopted, although in other areas they have found different means for pursuing similar ends. . . . We recognize that there are times when resistance appears at first to be a real virtue, and then only those most deeply rooted in religious pacifism can resist by other than physical means. We have learned that in the end only the spirit can conquer evil and we believe that in many recent situations those who have unwillingly employed force have learned this lesson at the last. . . .

"Today there are millions of men in nearly every great nation who have taken part in war and they still believe that that war, or their part in it, was justified. As long as they hold that view, they seem to me to be a risk against world peace. Those people who have once believed that war is justified can readily be persuaded that it will be justified again. . . . So perhaps in a world like this there is room for a few thousand persons like Quakers who take the opposite view, who begin with the assumption that war is not and has not been and will not be justified on either practical or moral grounds. . . . Of course, Friends have found it necessary to think through their position on this as on many awkward questions. For example, they have had to think whether this view is disloyalty to the state, and they have had to learn to distinguish loyalty to the policy of a government in power from loyalty to the true interests of a nation. . . .

"We have learned that few wars are justified by their results and that victory in war sometimes in itself makes real peace difficult."

1948

No prize awarded.

1949

JOHN BOYD ORR, LORD BOYD ORR OF BRECHIN (1880–1971), Great Britain: *Medical doctor and nutrition expert, whose 1936 report* Food Health and Income *became the basis for the British food policy during World War II. After the war he became director general of the Food and Agricultural Organization of the United Nations, which he was instrumental in founding. In 1945 he was elected president of the National Peace Council, which represents more than fifty British peace organizations, and in 1949 became president of the World Union of Peace Organizations.*

IN 1949 THE Nobel Committee broke with all previous tradition by awarding the prize not to a statesman or an international lawyer, or a politician, or even a pacifist, but to a scientist, Lord Boyd Orr of Brechin, who devoted most of his life to the study of nutrition.

"But however great his scientific contributions may have been, they alone would not have earned him the Peace Prize," said Gunnar Jahn, chairman of the Nobel Committee, in his presentation address. "Scientific discoveries cannot, in themselves, create peace. It is only when they are employed to promote cooperation between nations that they become a valuable factor in the cause of peace. For John Boyd Orr the purpose of his scientific work is to find ways of making men healthier and happier so as to secure peace; he believes that healthy and happy men have no need to resort to arms."

Hunger and want in the midst of plenty constitute one of the fundamental causes of war, Boyd Orr believed. In *Welfare and Peace* he wrote: ". . . it is no use trying to build the new world from the top down, with political ideas of spheres of influence and so on. We have to build it from the bottom upwards, and provide first the primary necessities of life for the people who have never had them. . . . Agreements between nations not to go to war have never lasted, and will never be enough to maintain peace. The nations must construct peace through daily cooperation, with a positive goal in view, a goal which is seen to be mutually advantageous. Only this can remove the principal causes of war."

Born in a rural community in Ayrshire, Scotland, John Boyd Orr went to the village school and became a student teacher there at the age of eighteen. Aided by scholarships, he simultaneously attended a teachers' training college and Glasgow University. After three years of teaching in a secondary school, he returned to Glasgow University, taking degrees in medicine and the biological sciences. After a stint as a ship's surgeon and another as a substitute for a doctor on vacation, he decided to go into research and accepted a two-year Carnegie research fellowship in physiology, arriving in Aberdeen to assume direction of a nutrition institute which did not exist; all that had been approved was a scheme of research. Boyd Orr threw himself enthusiastically into plans for a research facility, but his work was interrupted by World War I during which he served in the Royal Army Medical Corps and subsequently in the Navy.

After the war he returned to the institute, raised money for buildings to house it and its library and to accommodate visiting scientists and research workers; he also established an experimental farm in 1925.

Initially primarily interested in animal nutrition, his interest switched in the 1930s to human nutrition, not only as a researcher but also as a propagandist for healthy diets for people everywhere. His research had shown that even in Great Britain, where the standard of living was higher than in most countries, the diet of a very large part of the population was inferior to that accepted by nutritional physiologists as adequate. He demonstrated that a substantial increase in agricultural production was essential if the population was to receive adequate nourishment.

Although he put forward as early as the 1920s his ideas on the coordination of agricultural and nutritional policies, both to free mankind from want and to create a basis for peaceful cooperation between classes, nations and races, the problems of nutrition were not tackled on a serious scale until the world faced a situation in which famine was decimating entire populations in some countries, while in others agricultural crises were arising from overproduction of food. It was not until 1934 that the League of Nations Assembly took up the question, and appointed an international committee of nutritional physiologists to establish food guidelines for the world. Boyd Orr was a member of this committee, which presented its report in 1936.

During World War II the application of Boyd Orr's ideas on nutrition—set out in his 1936 report, *Food, Health and Income*—by means of rationing and other economic measures, resulted in the British people's receiving a diet that produced a far higher level of health among the population than anyone had expected.

In 1942 Boyd Orr visited the United States in a private capacity to drum up support for his ideas on a plan for world organization of food supplies, and a 1943 conference at Hot Springs—out of which grew the Food and Agricultural Organization of the United Nations—was strongly influenced by his views. The FAO was launched in Quebec in 1945, and Boyd Orr, who took part in the conference, was appointed director general of the organization. He regarded the formation of the FAO as one of the most important steps ever taken to lay the foundation of a lasting peace. "All nations must accept the responsibility of assuring their own people the food which is necessary to maintain life and health. Governments must cooperate to ensure that this goal is attained by people in all countries. This is the first step on the road to fulfilling the Atlantic Charter's promise of freedom from want."

One of the first tasks facing the FAO after the war was to ensure a fair distribution of food supplies which were scarce. The International Emergency Food Council set up for this purpose operated a sort of international rationing system which continued until 1949, and which was responsible for averting the famine which threatened many countries in the immediate postwar period.

Subsequently Boyd Orr suggested a World Food Board to stabilize food prices on the world markets, to create reserves of food to meet local shortages and counteract increases in price in the event of harvest failures, and to raise capital to finance the sale of surplus food supplies to countries in the greatest need. This World Food Board never materialized; neither Great Britain nor the United States would vote for it.

In 1945 Boyd Orr was elected president of the National Peace Council, representing more than fifty British peace organizations, and in 1949 he became president of the World Union of Peace Organizations.

He donated his Peace Prize money to the National Peace Council, the World Movement for Federal Government and several other such organizations.

He made one of the most brilliant and far-ranging Nobel Peace lectures of the postwar period, in which he preached his policy of a world peace based on world plenty. "Permanent peace cannot be attained merely by efforts to prevent war. We will be on the road to world unity and peace when nations begin to cooperate on a world scale to apply science to develop the resources of the earth for the benefit of all. . . . The difficulty is to get a real beginning. Why should we not consider some concrete measure like the elimination of preventable disease through the World Health Organization or doubling the world food supply to meet all human needs through the joint work of the other agencies, with all nations contributing through the World Bank, in proportion to their wealth, to provide the necessary funds? In working together for a concrete world plan for the benefit of all countries, the present misunderstandings which divide nations would gradually become meaningless. . . .

"The new powers which science has let loose cannot be bottled up again. They must be used for constructive ends or they will break loose in another world war which will destroy our European civilization. . . . For Europe at least, peace is inevitable. It can either be the peace of the grave, the peace of the dead empires of the past, which lost their creative spirit and failed to adjust themselves to new conditions, or a new dynamic peace applying science in a great leap forward in the evolution of human society to a new age in which hunger, poverty and preventable diseases will be eliminated from the earth—an age in which the people in every country will rise to a far higher level of intellectual and cultural well-being, an age in which 'iron curtains' will disappear and people, though intensely patriotic for their own country, will be able to travel freely as world citizens. That is the hope science sets before us."

The Frightened Fifties

THE KNOWLEDGE THAT man had finally developed a weapon capable of destroying his entire civilization hung heavily in the atmosphere throughout the fifties. Right at the beginning of the decade most people realized that it was now only a matter of time until nations other than the United States would develop their own atomic bombs, however diligently the secrets might be guarded; and indeed, before the decade ended, both Britain and Russia had tested their first nuclear weapons. And on Bikini Atoll in the Pacific, America had exploded a hydrogen superbomb, so powerful that it made the bombs dropped on Hiroshima and Nagasaki look like mere "conventional" weapons.

It is perhaps significant of the frivolous attitude of "civilized" man that the word *bikini* has entered the English language only by virtue of the fact that today's very brief two-piece swimsuit was named after it because they both, in their way, represented "the ultimate" in the middle fifties.

It was in the middle fifties, too, that mankind first realized that there was a grave danger of polluting the entire environment, not only with atomic waste, but with all the inevitable but deadly by-products of industry and transportation.

In January 1950 Britain recognized Communist China, and capital punishment was reintroduced in the USSR. Alger Hiss was found guilty in the United States of perjury and of concealing his membership of the Communist party. The racist policy in Johannesburg, South Africa, provoked riots. Britain, Norway, Denmark and Sweden signed an agreement for economic cooperation and President Truman instructed the US Atomic Energy Committee to proceed with the development of the hydrogen bomb.

The USSR and Communist China signed a thirty-year treaty in Moscow in February, and in March, in the United States, Carl Fuchs was found guilty of betraying atomic secrets to Russia. A few days later Marshall Voroshilov announced that Russia now possessed its own atomic bomb.

In May came the Schumann Plan for putting the French and German coal, iron and steel industries under a single authority; this was, in effect, the precursor of the Common Market (EEC).

West Germany joined the Council of Europe in June, and in the same month North Korean forces invaded South Korea. Trygve Lie, appointed to a fresh term as secretary general of the United Nations, urged UN members to assist South Korea to repel the invasion.

In July Douglas MacArthur was appointed commander of the United Nations forces in Korea. In September UN forces landed at Inchon, South Korea, and by October 1 South Korean troops had crossed the 38th parallel. Chinese forces occupied Tibet and in November MacArthur reported the massing of Chinese Communists in North Korea. Before the end of the year the United Nations forces were in retreat and the Chinese had crossed the 38th parallel again.

It was the year of Thor Heyerdahl's epic voyage on the balsa-wood raft *Kon-Tiki;* the year that Pope Pius XII pronounced the dogma of the bodily assumption of the Virgin Mary; the year of Billy Wilder's *Sunset Boulevard* and Irving Berlin's *Call Me Madam.* The United Nations building in New York was completed; Jan Smuts, Bernard Shaw and Léon Blum died; and Senator McCarthy was busy sniffing out Communists all over the States.

In January 1951 the North Korean and Chinese troops broke through the United Nations lines and captured Seoul. India and Britain urged a truce in the Korean War. The Six (France, West Germany, Italy, Belgium, the Netherlands and Luxembourg) signed a treaty in Paris, embodying the Schumann Plan and inaugurating the Common Market (EEC).

Guy Burgess and Donald Maclean, two British diplomats were inexplicably found missing from Britain . . . they turned up in Russia.

A peace treaty with Japan was finally signed in September in San Francisco; and in Europe the foreign ministers of Britain, France and the United States discussed plans to combat Soviet aggression and use West German troops in the NATO armies. East and West Germany agreed to send representatives to the United Nations to discuss the question of free elections, but the USSR opposed the project.

A London Congress on Space Travel established the International Astronomical Federation, and electric power was produced from atomic energy in Idaho. Cinerama was invented and the year's best sellers included Nicholas Montsarrat's *The Cruel Sea*, Herman Wouk's *The Caine Mutiny* and J. D. Salinger's *The Catcher in the Rye*. Films of the year included Hitchcock's *Strangers on a Train* and John Huston's *The African Queen*.

In February 1952 King George VI died, and Princess Elizabeth became Queen Elizabeth II; Churchill announced that Britain had her own atomic bomb.

The Chinese Communists accused the United States forces in Korea of using germ warfare. Pandit Nehru formed a government in India after his party won 364 of the 489 seats in the National Assembly. And in October a state of emergency was declared in Kenya following Mau-Mau disturbances. In November, in a Republican landslide, Dwight Eisenhower won the presidential election against Adlai Stevenson.

On December 3 the United Nations accepted India's proposal for an armistice in Korea—it was rejected a few days later by China.

This was the year of the first contraceptive tablet, soon universally known as "the pill"; Britain held her first atomic bomb tests in Western Australia, America exploded the first of a series of hydrogen bombs (which culminated in the Bikini superbomb of March 1954), and Truman laid the keel of the first atomic-powered submarine, *Nautilus*.

A new word—"smog"—entered the language when it was discovered, in places as far apart as London and San Francisco, that what had always been regarded as a purely natural phenomenon was largely of man's own making.

In March 1953 Stalin died aged seventy-three, and was succeeded as chairman of the Council of Ministers by Malenkov. Dag Hammarskjöld, a Swede, was elected secretary general of the UN.

Jomo Kenyatta and five other Kikuyu were convicted in April of masterminding the Mau-Mau disturbances. The UN and the Communists arranged for an exchange of prisoners in Korea and in June South Korea released 26,000 non-Communist North Korean prisoners; the Korean armistice was finally signed at Panmunjom in July 1953.

On June 19 the Rosenbergs, husband and wife, sentenced for atomic espionage in 1951, went to the electric chair.

In August the USSR exploded its first hydrogen bomb.

In September Khrushchev became first secretary of the Central Committee of the Communist party.

In the United States the first experimental color TV transmissions went out. A disease called myxomatosis killed millions of rabbits all over the world. And the news that Hillary and Tensing had reached the summit of Everest reached London on Queen Elizabeth's Coronation Day.

Reg Butler's sculpture *Unknown Political Prisoner* won an art competition in London and Ian Fleming published *Casino Royale,* the first of the James Bond novels.

In January 1954, still striving to bring World War II to a conclusive end and reduce world tension, the foreign ministers of Britain, France, the United States and the USSR met in Berlin, but the USSR rejected proposals from the West for the reunification of Germany through free elections.

In February Colonel Nasser became the vital force in Egypt, and in

April the US Air Force flew a French battalion to Indochina to defend Dien Bien Phu. Dr. Nkrumah formed a government in Ghana, and in July an armistice for Indochina was signed in Geneva. Under the truce's terms France agreed to evacuate North Vietnam; the Communists agreed to evacuate South Vietnam, Cambodia and Laos; and France undertook to respect the independence of Cambodia, Laos and Vietnam.

Before the end of the year, a US Senate committee reported that Senator Joseph McCarthy had acted improperly in making government employees hand over documents; a nine-power conference in London agreed that West Germany should join NATO; the Communists occupied Hanoi; and Britain, France, the United States and the USSR agreed to end the occupation of Germany. The Enosis issue over Cyprus resulted in riots in Athens, and France sent 20,000 troops to Algeria. There was trouble everywhere.

The proliferation of nuclear weapons got far more attention in the press than the formation of the first International Convention for the Prevention of Pollution of the Sea by Oil. The Bell Telephone Company invented a solar battery capable of turning the sun's radiation into electricity, there was widespread concern over the disposal of atomic waste, and doctors began to connect smoking with lung cancer for the first time. The first vertical take-off "flying bedstead" was invented and the first passenger jet airliner, the *Comet*, ran into a series of disturbing disasters.

The religious revivalist Billy Graham was holding mammoth meetings in London, New York and Berlin, and Roger Bannister ran a mile in 3 minutes 59.4 seconds.

Kingsley Amis wrote *Lucky Jim*, J. R. Tolkien published *The Lord of the Rings,* Dylan Thomas's *Under Milk Wood* was broadcast by the BBC, and in France a young girl with the pseudonym of Françoise Sagan wrote *Bonjour, Tristesse.*

It was a year of resignations: Malenkov was replaced by Bulganin in Russia, and Churchill by Anthony Eden in Britain.

Ruth Ellis, the last woman ever to be executed in Britain, was hanged, and a fourteen-year-old boy lynched in Massachusetts. The United States and the USSR announced that they would attempt to launch an earth satellite in the International Geophysical Year of 1957–58. It was the year of *The Diary of Anne Frank,* Nobokov's *Lolita* and Samuel Beckett's *Waiting for Godot.* It was also the year of Bill Haley's *Rock around the Clock.*

In March 1956 Archbishop Makarios was deported from Cyprus to the Seychelles and Greece asked for the Cyprus problem to be put before the UN General Assembly.

In April a cease-fire between Israel and Jordan was arranged by Dag Hammarskjöld.

On June 13 the last British troops left the Suez Canal and a few days later Nasser seized the canal by decree. This produced immediate financial sanctions by Britain, France and the United States, and all British and French nationals were immediately evacuated from Egypt in a massive airlift.

In Ghana, Nkrumah demanded total independence from Britain and got it; Britain was too preoccupied with the Suez Canal and the Egyptian question to argue.

A London conference on the Suez on August 19 was boycotted by Nasser, who also rejected an eighteen-nation UN plan for Suez suggested by Pandit Nehru.

On September 23 Britain and France referred the Suez question to the UN Security Council.

In October the people of Budapest rebelled against the Russians, demanding democratic government, the withdrawal of Soviet troops and the release of Cardinal Mindszenty; the Russian reply, etched forever in the minds of everybody who remembers those newspaper photographs, was to send the tanks into the streets of Budapest and shell the unarmed students.

On October 30 an Anglo-French ultimatum to Egypt and Israel called for an immediate cease-fire and a withdrawal ten miles from the Suez. Only Israel accepted and the following day Anglo-French forces bombed Egyptian airfields. There was an immediate outcry in Britain and France, a UN emergency peace-keeping force was sent in, and within a few days Britain and France bowed to public opinion, accepted the United Nations peace-keeping force and quietly withdrew.

On November 4 Soviet troops attacked Budapest in earnest, and the USSR threatened the use of rockets if Britain and France failed to accept the cease-fire in Suez. The situation between the East and West had reached a new low.

Dwight Eisenhower was reelected president, defeating Adlai Stevenson yet again. A couple of days later the UN General Assembly demanded the withdrawal of Soviet troops from Hungary. In Hungary a call for a national strike led to the proclamation of martial law and mass arrests, and in Suez a UN naval force started to clear the canal.

Calder Hall, Britain's largest nuclear station, began operations and by the end of the year was supplying 65,000 kilowatts; it was also the year of the first Aldermaston March to protest against nuclear armament and the general dangers of atomic radiation.

In January 1957 Anthony Eden, badly battered by his part in the Suez fiasco, resigned and Macmillan became premier of Great Britain.

There was a state of emergency in Indonesia and Thailand; Israeli troops handed over the Gaza strip to the UN; Ghana became an independent state and was admitted to the UN. EOKA [the National Organization of Cypriot Combatants] offered to suspend terrorist activities on the release of President Makarios; and Albert Schweitzer sent a letter to the Nobel Committee urging mobilization of world opinion against nuclear tests.

In May, in spite of Schweitzer's appeal and in spite of a Soviet appeal to the United States and Britain to stop nuclear tests, Britain exploded her first thermonuclear bomb in the megaton range in the Central Pacific.

Russia launched the first earth satellite, Sputnik I, on October 4 and a month later put Sputnik II in orbit, with an Eskimo dog called Laika on board to enable Russian scientists to study living conditions in space. The first Sputnik circled the globe in ninety-five minutes.

Down below, on earth, the show that everybody was talking about was *My Fair Lady*, a musical based on Bernard Shaw's *Pygmalion*; the popular plays were John Osborne's *Look Back in Anger* and *The Entertainer;* and the films of the year included David Lean's *The Bridge over the River Kwai.*

In January 1958 the European Common Market and Euratom came into force; and the West German forces came under NATO command.

The USSR threatened Greece with economic sanctions if she agreed to the installation of NATO bases on her territory, and Egypt and Sudan were united as the United Arab Republic with Nasser as head of state.

North Korea proposed the withdrawal of all foreign troops from North and South Korea; this was completed by the end of October.

In March Khrushchev succeeded Bulganin as chairman of the USSR Council of Ministers, and in April Fidel Castro and his guerrillas began a policy of total war against President Batista in Cuba.

In Southern Rhodesia, Garfield Todd, former premier, was ousted for making a stand to extend the franchise to Africans. A state of emergency was declared in Aden and another in Ceylon, and in May General de Gaulle formed a government of national safety in France. Iceland decreased her fishing limits to twelve miles and began to harass British trawlers fishing within these limits.

Imre Nagy was executed in Hungary on June 9 after a secret trial. There was an Eight-Power Conference in Geneva to discuss the detection of nuclear explosions, Alaska became the forty-ninth state of the United States, and trouble broke out in the Middle East again, with British paratroops landing in Jordan at the request of King Hussein. The United Arab Republic and Iraq signed a treaty of mutual defense and the former severed all relations with Jordan. Macmillan rejected Khrushchev's proposal for a summit meeting on the Middle East and suggested a special meeting of the Security Council.

Prince Charles became Prince of Wales, and on June 26 the last of the debs were presented at the British Court. There were race disturbances in Nottingham and Notting Hill, London, and the US Supreme Court ordered Little Rock School in Little Rock, Arkansas, to admit Negroes. On the death of Pope Pius XII, Cardinal Roncalli became Pope John XXIII.

In December the first All Africa Peoples' Conference was held in Accra, in Ghana; General Salan was appointed inspector general of national defense in Algeria; and General de Gaulle was elected president of France.

The American nuclear submarine *Nautilus* passed under the ice cap of the North Pole, the "beatnik" wave spread from California to Britain; the first stereo records were produced, and the popular plays of the year were Graham Greene's *The Potting Shed*, Harold Pinter's *The Birthday Party* and Bernstein's musical *West Side Story*. By the end of the year there were 1,000 electronic computers in use in the United States, 160 in Europe.

The year 1959 began with disturbances at Leopoldville in the Congo; Laos announced that she would recognize the United Nations as sole arbiter of disputes, provoking a denunciation from North Vietnam; Fidel Castro became premier of Cuba; and there were more disturbances in Nyasaland [Malawi] where Dr. Hastings Banda and other leaders of the Nyasaland African Congress were arrested.

Hawaii became the fiftieth state of the USA, jet fighters "buzzed" a US aircraft in the Berlin corridor and Cuba invaded Panama. Communist China invaded India's northeast frontier, and on September 22 the UN voted against the admission of Communist China. In November the UN General Assembly condemned apartheid in Africa and racial discrimination in any part of the world.

On November 20 a European Free Trade Association (Britain, Norway, Portugal, Switzerland, Austria, Denmark and Sweden, otherwise known as "The Seven") was formed. Britain and the United Arab Republic resumed diplomatic relations which had been severed since November 1956, and the UN decided not to interfere in Algeria.

The war had been over for more than ten years, but as yet no peace treaty with Germany had been signed; there was turmoil all over the Far East and the Middle East, impending signs of serious trouble in Africa and Cuba and between the Western Powers and the Russian bloc—victorious allies such a short time earlier—a state of grudging, uncooperative hostility that came to be known as "the cold war."

It was a difficult period for the Nobel Peace Prize Committee, and many of the speeches and the lectures given during the decade reflected the underlying disillusionment. The League of Nations had been a bitter disappointment; and now, it seemed, the United Nations, for all the high hopes once held for it, was going the same way.

1950 Ralph Bunche

1951 Léon Jouhaux

1952 Albert Schweitzer

1953 George Marshall

1954
Office of the
United Nations
High Commissioner
for Refugees

1955-1956
Prizes not awarded

1957 Lester Pearson

1958 Georges Pire

1959 Philip Noel-Baker

1950

RALPH JOHNSON BUNCHE (1904–1971), United States: *The first black Nobel laureate. An expert in colonial affairs in the State Department, he was a member of the US delegation to the UN conferences in London in 1945 and 1946 and one of the representatives to the 1946 ILO conference in Paris. In 1946 he was also appointed director of the Trusteeship Department of the UN Secretariat. He was Count Bernadotte's collaborator in the UN Truce Commission to the Palestine conflict of 1948, and on Bernadotte's assassination became his successor and succeeded in achieving an armistice.*

BUNCHE WAS THE first black man to win a Nobel Prize, and, at forty-six, with Carl von Ossietzky (the 1935 winner), the youngest Peace laureate to date. He was born in Detroit, became a messenger boy at the age of seven, and at twelve worked long hours in a bakery, often until midnight. He sold newspapers, worked in a carpet-laying firm and did various other odd jobs, both in Detroit and in Los Angeles, where he moved with his grandmother "Nana" and the other children when his parents died. In later years he could not remember a time when his family had not lived in abject poverty.

His grandmother, a former slave, was a natural philosopher and always encouraged Bunche to fight for his rights, but without rancor. Years after, he explained her philosophy: "The right to be treated as an equal by all other men . . . who indeed is a better protector of the American heritage than he who demands the fullest measure of respect for those cardinal principles on which our society is reared?

"Never compromise what you know to be the right. Never pick a fight, but never run from one if your principles are at stake. Go out into the world with your head high, and keep it high at all times."

In the fact that he had to work in order to study and live, Ralph Bunche's story is no different from that of thousands of American kids; as he recalls, seventy percent of the students at the University of California were obliged to do the same. He supported himself from the proceeds of an athletic scholarship and a janitor's job.

With a scholarship from Harvard University and a fund of a thousand dollars raised by the black community of Los Angeles, he began his graduate studies in political science. He completed his master's degree in 1928 and for the next six years alternated between teaching at Howard

University in Washington, D.C., first as an instructor and then as a professor, and working towards his doctorate at Harvard. The Rosenwald Fellowship, which he held in 1932–33, enabled him to go to Africa to research colonial and racial problems in Togoland and Dahomey.

In 1936 he received a grant from the Social Science Research Council to examine colonial policy and for two years did postdoctoral research in anthropology at Northwestern University, the London School of Economics and Capetown University in South Africa, where he also did a great deal of field research among the African tribes.

From his experience as co-director of the Institute of Race Relations at Swarthmore College in 1936 and his field research, he wrote *A World View of Race* (1936). He also collaborated with the Swedish sociologist Gunnar Myrdal in the Carnegie Corporation's well-known survey of the black in America, which resulted in the publication of Myrdal's *An American Dilemma* (1944).

He soon caught the attention of the American administration, and in 1941 was offered a post in the Office of Strategic Services as a colonial-affairs expert. In 1944 he was appointed territorial specialist in colonial affairs under the State Department, and in 1945 became head of the division, the first black to reach such a position in the American administration.

He achieved this position largely as a result of his work as adviser to the State Department and to the military on African and other colonial areas of strategic military importance during World War II. He also served on the US delegations to the UN Conferences in London in 1945 and 1946, and was a representative to the 1946 ILO conference in Paris. The same year he was appointed director of the Trusteeship Department of the UN Secretariat, with the task of handling problems of the world's peoples who had not yet attained self-government.

From June 1947 to August 1949, Bunche worked on the most important assignment of his career and the one which resulted in his award of the Nobel Peace Prize.

When the British mandate over Palestine ended in May 1948, open warfare broke out between the Arabs and the Jews. A Truce Commission sent out in April failed to make any headway, and the United Nations appointed Count Folke Bernadotte, grandson of King Oscar II of Sweden, as mediator with Bunche as his chief aide. Four months later, on September 17, 1948, Count Bernadotte was assassinated, and Bunche became the UN's acting mediator on Palestine. After eleven months of negotiation between seven Arab states on the one hand and the Jews on the other, none of whom would sit down together in conference, Bunche succeeded in obtaining an armistice.

He returned home to a hero's welcome, with a "ticker tape" parade along Broadway in New York City. Los Angeles declared a "Ralph Bunche Day," and he received over thirty honorary degrees, plus the Nobel Peace Prize. After that he performed many special UN assignments, in the Congo with Dag Hammarskjöld in 1960, and in Cyprus, Kashmir and the Yemen.

An outspoken man, when asked by an interviewer about the UN's intervention in international crises, he said "The United Nations has had the courage that the League of Nations lacked—to step in and tackle the buzz saw."

Bunche was a member of the "Black Cabinet," consulted on minority problems during Franklin Roosevelt's administration, but he later declined President Truman's offer of assistant secretary of state because of the segregated housing conditions in Washington, D.C. In 1956 he helped to lead the civil rights march organized by Martin Luther King, Jr., the 1964 laureate, in Montgomery, Alabama, and supported the action programs of the National Association for the Advancement of Colored People.

"Never in human history have so many peoples experienced freedom," he said in his Nobel lecture. "Yet human freedom itself is a crucial issue and is widely endangered. Indeed, by some peoples, it has already been gained and lost.

". . . Very many would hold that the loss of human dignity and self-respect, the chains of enslavement, are too high a price to pay even for peace. But the horrible realities of modern warfare scarcely afford even this fatal choice. There is only suicidal escape, not freedom, in the death and destruction of modern war. This is mankind's great dilemma. . . .

"Alfred Nobel, half a century ago, foresaw with prophetic vision that if the complacent mankind of his day could, with equanimity, contemplate war, the day would inevitably come when man would be confronted with the fateful alternative of peace or reversion to the Dark Ages. Man may well ponder whether he has now reached that stage. Man's inventive genius has so far outreached his reason—not his capacity to reason but his willingness to apply reason—that the peoples of the world find themselves precariously on the brink of disaster."

Unlike many of the other Peace Prize laureates, Bunche clearly recognized that in order to achieve peace, the United Nations would have to be prepared to use force, and plenty of it.

Taking Korea as an example, he pointed out that there the United Nations' processes of peaceful intervention had failed because the North Korean regime refused to give them a chance to work and resorted to aggressive force to resist them. In these circumstances the United Nations had no alternative but to check an aggressive national force with an international one. Unfortunately, because vast numbers of Chinese troops intervened on the North Korean side, the UN effort came to nothing. In future, he warned, to make world peace secure, the UN must have at its disposal, as a result of firm commitments undertaken by all its members, "military strength of sufficient dimensions to make it certain that it can meet aggressively military force with international military force speedily and conclusively. . . ."

He then turned to a problem which was increasingly to occupy the attention both of the UN and of the Nobel Committee: the importance to future world peace of conditions in the emerging Third World.

". . . Europe, and the Western world generally, must become fully aware that the massive and restive millions of Asia and Africa are henceforth a new and highly significant factor in all peace calculations. The hitherto suppressed masses are rapidly awakening and are demanding, and are entitled to enjoy, a full share in the future fruits of peace, freedom and security. . . . Peace is no mere matter of men fighting or not fighting. Peace, to have meaning for many who have known only suffering in both peace and war, must be translated into bread or rice, shelter, health and education, as well as freedom and human dignity—a steadily better life."

1951

LÉON JOUHAUX (1879–1954), France: *International labor leader who believed that peace could be achieved through unity in the international labor movement. He spent his life working for that ideal through the International Federation of Trade Unions, the International Labor Organization (ILO), which he was instrumental in founding, the League of Nations, the United Nations and the European Movement, of which he was made president in 1949.*

LÉON JOUHAUX, DEAN of the French labor movement for forty-five years, was born in Paris; his grandfather had fought in the Revolution of 1848 and his father had been part of the Commune that ruled Paris briefly in the immediate aftermath of the Franco-Prussian War.

His father worked in a match factory in Aubervilliers, where Léon joined him at the age of sixteen after a schooling interrupted by periods of poverty when his father was on strike.

After a stint of military service in Algeria, from which he was recalled when his father went blind after years of working with the white phosphorous which was then used in the manufacture of matches, Jouhaux rejoined the match factory. In 1900 he took part in his first strike there, a protest against the use of this material. He was blacklisted and dismissed, and drifted through a succession of jobs until he was reinstated in the match factory through the intervention of the union. He then immediately embarked on his career as a labor leader. In 1906 his local union elected him to be their representative on the Confédération Générale du Travail (CGT) [General Confederation of Labor] and from 1909 to 1947 he served as its secretary general.

In 1936 he was a signatory to the Martignon Agreement, giving French workers an eight-hour day, paid vacations and the right to organize and bargain collectively.

From 1911 to 1921 he edited *La Bataille Syndicaliste* [The Syndicalist Battle], the principal organ of the CGT, and in the years immediately before the war he traveled extensively in Germany, Switzerland, England and Belgium, urging labor unions to unite in the cause of international peace.

Jouhaux encouraged the CGT to develop a peace program calling for arms limitation, international arbitration and an end to secret treaties, and in 1916 at the Leeds Conference he presented a report which laid the foundation for the International Labor Organization. When war broke out, he declared his support for the war effort, and served on several government committees. He also served in the French army.

At the Peace Conference in Paris in 1919 he was partly responsible for getting the constitutional basis of the ILO incorporated in the Versailles Treaty, and in the same year was chosen as a worker-representative member of the ILO's governing body.

He was first vice-president of the International Federation of Trade Unions in 1919 and later was vice-president of the Confederation of Free Trade Unions. Between 1925 and 1928 he was a French delegate to the League of Nations.

After the fall of France in 1940, the CGT was dissolved. Jouhaux joined the Resistance, was eventually captured and sent to Buchenwald prison camp in Germany in 1943. When he was liberated in May 1945 he was sixty-six, but still active enough to become involved in peace work again, first as a French delegate to the United Nations and, in 1949, as president of the European Movement, which established the Council of Europe as a first step on the road to a Federated Europe. One of the most important offices Jouhaux held after the war was the presidency of the French National Economic Council, an advisory body which he had suggested as early as 1907; its objective was to integrate the economic forces within France.

Jouhaux believed that cooperation reaching across national frontiers and the removal of social and economic inequalities both within nations and between nations represented the most important means of combating war. But he had an even broader objective: to mold a social environment capable of breeding a new sort of man who would create a society in which war would no longer be possible.

"The final and essential goal, the only valid goal," he said in his Nobel lecture, "is to extend the well-being of the worker, to give him a more equitable share of the products of collective work, to make Europe a social democracy, and to ensure the peace desired by men of every race and tongue by proving that the democracies can bring about social justice through the rational organization of production without sacrificing the liberty and the dignity of the individual. . . .

"The free trade union movement is called upon to play an essential part in the fight against international crisis and for the advent of true peace. The scope of the task is enormous, matched only by its urgency. Our movement intends to devote its efforts to this task regardless of cost. I must add that it was enormously encouraged [to see] that certain official circles had adopted the idea which we have been propagating for years and which we have already succeeded in putting into the Treaty of Versailles: the idea that economic disorder and misery are among the determinative causes of wars. . . ."

Jouhaux was the author of a pacifist book *Le Désarmement* [Disarmament] published in 1927, as well as a number of books on the trade union movement.

1952

ALBERT SCHWEITZER (1875–1965), Germany (Alsace): *Philosopher, theologist, musician and musicologist, medical missionary, pastor and founder of a hospital at Lambaréné in French Equatorial Africa.*

ALBERT SCHWEITZER WAS the first German to receive the Nobel Peace Prize since Carl von Ossietzky accepted it in 1935 while in a German concentration camp, an action which caused the Hitler government to decree that in the future no German could accept the prize.

Schweitzer was born in Alsace in 1875, a few years after the province had become part of the German empire. He saw it reincorporated with France, overrun again by the Germans during World War II and yet again united with France. Since he was brought up in this border country, he spoke both German and French fluently, as well as the Alsatian dialect, and his upbringing gave him a deep insight into both French and German cultures.

In making the presentation, Gunnar Jahn, chairman of the Nobel Committee, emphasized that Albert Schweitzer "will never belong to any one nation. His whole life and all his work are a message addressed to all men regardless of nationality or race." Summing up Schweitzer's work and giving, in effect, the reason behind his being chosen for the award, he remarked, "Even in these troubled and uncertain times, men are searching for something which will allow them to believe that mankind will one day enjoy the reign of peace and goodwill. If altruism, reverence for life, and the idea of brotherhood can become living realities in the hearts of men, we will have laid the very foundations of lasting peace between individuals, nations and races."

If this seems a very far cry from the specific conditions for a champion of peace that Nobel laid down in his will, one can only argue that Schweitzer, judged from any point of view, was a special case. If the philosophy he developed and the example he set with his own life caused even a handful of people to think more profoundly about the nature of the world and man's responsibilities to his fellow man, then who can say that his contribution to the overall cause of peace on earth was not at least as positive as that of all those who spent their lives organizing conferences, passing resolutions and writing pamphlets?

The son of a pastor, Schweitzer grew up in the little village of Günsbach, went to the village school with the sons of the local peasants, then studied in Münster and Mulhausen where he admitted he was not a very promising pupil—"too much of a dreamer" was his own diagnosis. He goes on: "Between the ages of fourteen and sixteen I had a compelling desire to discuss everything. The joy of seeking the truth and the purpose of things became almost an obsession with me." But even as early as that, his observations disturbed him, and he conceived a deep feeling of obligation to help those who lived less happy lives. "As far back as I can remember, the thought of all the misery in the world has been a source of pain to me."

He studied theology from 1893 in the University of Strasbourg, where he obtained his doctorate in philosophy in 1899 with a thesis on the philosophy of Kant. He received his licentiate in theology in 1900, after which he preached in St. Nicholas Church in Strasbourg, held several administrative posts in the Theological College of St. Thomas at Strasbourg and in 1906 published *The Quest of the Historical Jesus*, the book on which much of his fame as a theological scholar rests.

At the same time, he was developing into a talented musician of international stature. From the age of nine he had played the organ in his father's church, and from early manhood was in considerable demand as a concert organist. Indeed, out of his concert hall earnings, he was able to pay not only for his education and particularly for his later medical schooling, but also to lay the foundations for the fund which was to start his hospital in Africa. A musicologist as well as a musician, he wrote a biography of Bach in French in 1905, rewrote it in German in 1908, and in the interim wrote a book on organ building and playing.

One day in 1904, when he was twenty-nine, Albert Schweitzer came across an appeal from the French Protestant Missionary Society in Paris asking for help for the Negroes in French Equatorial Africa. Immediately he decided that this was the way he could contribute his share to paying the debt he felt the white man owed the black, and he decided to disburse the debt, not primarily as a priest but as a medical doctor; to do this, he had first to study medicine. "I wanted to become a doctor in order to be able to work without words. For years I had used the word. My new occupation would be not to talk about the gospel of love, but to put it into practice."

For seven years, from 1905 to 1913, Schweitzer studied medicine. "The pursuit of natural sciences gave me more than just the knowledge I sought. It was for me a spiritual experience. I had always felt that the so-called humanities with which I had been concerned present a psychic danger because they rarely reveal self-evident truths, but often present value judgments which masquerade as truth because of the way in which they are clothed. . . . Now, suddenly, I stood in another world. I was now working with truths based on realities, and I was among men who took it for granted that every statement had to be supported by fact."

In 1913 Schweitzer qualified as a doctor of medicine. The Protestant Missionary Society whose appeal had initially stirred him into this activity was now extremely dubious about his unorthodox views and, before the society would accept him, he had to give it a formal promise that he would confine himself to medical work in Africa and not try to influence the religious faith of the Christian blacks. He also had to raise funds from his friends and acquaintances to augment his savings to pay for the journey and for the rudimentary hospital he planned to build.

At last, on Good Friday in 1913, he set out for Lambaréné in West

Africa, a small village on the banks of the River Ogowé close to the Equator, about one hundred miles from the coast. There he began a completely new life, deep in the primeval forest, far removed from the lecture rooms and the concert halls that until then had been his whole life. To his own surprise he proved surprisingly adept at organizing the natives and even at such physical tasks as the building of huts in which to house and treat them.

His initial sojourn in Africa was, however, short lived. On the outbreak of war in 1914, he was placed under surveillance as a German citizen and in 1917 he and his wife were brought back to be interned in France. When he was released in 1918, he was ill and stayed in Europe, studying and playing the organ until 1924. From that date until his death he lived in Africa, leaving to take only an occasional trip to Europe to give a series of concerts or lectures to help finance his activities at Lambaréné. With the royalties he earned from the several books he wrote during his period in Europe and from his personal appearance fees and donations from all over the world, he was able to expand the hospital to seventy buildings, which by the early 1960s could accommodate some five hundred patients. With the Nobel Peace Prize money he started the leprosarium at Lambaréné. He died in Africa in 1965, at the age of ninety.

Schweitzer's unique philosophy is probably best synthesized in August Schou's essay on the Peace Prize in *Nobel: The Man and His Prizes*. According to Schou, Schweitzer believed, in essence, that "civilization consists in the strivings of individual and community to achieve perfection. Intellectual and material progress are undoubtedly important to the development of civilization. However, unless progress of this kind is based on some universal ethical principle, it will not advance civilization but, on the contrary, contribute to its dissolution. Schweitzer believed that this latter state of affairs had been reached in western civilization at the end of the nineteenth century.

"As Schweitzer saw it, the question was as follows: Is dissolution an inevitable process, or is it possible to arrive at a universal ethical principle, which can once again animate our civilization, and create harmony between the actions and thoughts of civilized man? Schweitzer has described how, in 1915, after years of pondering, he hit on the redeeming formula: 'respect for life.' What, he asked himself, does this respect for life mean and how does it arise in the individual? Schweitzer's answer was: If the individual is to understand himself and his relationship to the world, he must constantly and continuously look beyond everything that knowledge and science has created in him, and penetrate to that which is elemental. A truly organic explanation of the problem of life is to be found in the elementary craving for life. This deepens, intensifies and heightens the will to live. On the basis of an absolute ethical principle, the individual will conceive 'good' as the act of maintaining, promoting and ennobling all life that is capable of development, and 'evil' as the destruction and suppression of life. Schweitzer considered that all ethical systems, which until his own time had been built up, suffered from one decisive flaw—they confined themselves to the mutual relations between human beings, and failed to take into account all living things, i.e., plants and animals. Only an ethical system with a pantheistic basis of this nature would have a universal and binding character."

One can readily see why the Protestant Missionary Society was a bit doubtful about allowing him to preach his views to natives whom they had painstakingly converted to orthodox Christianity.

Schweitzer took "The Problem of Peace" as the subject for his Nobel lecture. He pointed out that whereas in the past war was an evil which men tolerated because it served progress (he gave several cases in point: among them the fact that Alexander the Great's victory had opened the way, from the Nile to the Indus, for Greek civilization), war was now so dangerous that it involved the future of all mankind. He did not, however, believe that international laws, even with organizations like the League of Nations and UN to "enforce" them, could ever be effective in preventing war.

Kant, he said, was unremitting in his insistence that the idea of a league of nations could not be hoped for as the outcome of ethical argument, but only as a result of perfecting the law.

"Today we can judge the efficacy of international institutions by the experience we have had with the League of Nations in Geneva and with the United Nations. . . . These two institutions have been unable to bring about peace. Their efforts were doomed because they were obliged to undertake them in a world in which there was no prevailing spirit directed toward peace. And being only legal institutions, they were unable to create such a spirit. The ethical spirit alone has the power to generate it. Kant deceived himself in thinking that he could dispense with it in his search for peace. We must follow the road on which he turned his back. . . .

"Is the spirit capable of achieving what we in our distress must expect of it?" he asked, and replied: ". . . The height to which the spirit can ascend was revealed in the seventeenth and eighteenth centuries. It led those peoples of Europe who possessed it out of the Middle Ages, putting an end to superstition, witch hunts, torture and a multitude of other forms of cruelty or traditional folly. It replaced the old with the new in an evolutionary way that never ceases to astonish those who observe it. All that we have ever possessed of true civilization, and indeed all that we still possess, can be traced to a manifestation of this spirit.

"The idea that the reign of peace must come one day has been given expression by a number of peoples who have attained a certain level of civilization. . . . People have labeled it a utopia. But the situation today is that it must become reality in one way or another; otherwise mankind will perish. . . . The only originality I claim is . . . the intellectual certainty that the human spirit is capable of creating in our time a new mentality, an ethical mentality. Inspired by this certainty, I too proclaim this truth in the hope that my testimony may help to prevent its rejection as an admirable sentiment but a practical impossibility. Many a truth has lain unnoticed for a long time, ignored simply because no one perceived its potential for becoming reality.

"Only when an ideal of peace is born in the minds of the peoples will the institutions set up to maintain this peace effectively fulfill the function expected of them."

1953

GEORGE CATLETT MARSHALL (1880—1959), United States: *Chief of staff of the US Army from 1939 to 1945, General Marshall built up and directed the largest army in the history of the world. He was secretary of state from 1947 to 1949, during which time he formulated the Marshall Plan, a program of economic and military aid to Europe.*

GENERAL GEORGE MARSHALL was probably the most controversial of all the Nobel Peace laureates. There was sharp press criticism all over the world and student riots in the streets of Oslo, where public buildings were draped with banners linking Marshall's name with Hiroshima and Nagasaki. As chief of staff of the US Army, and a member of the policy committee that supervised the atomic researches engaged in by American and British scientists from 1941, Marshall certainly must qualify, by any standards, as primarily a man of war. Yet long before the first atomic bomb had been dropped (and with less justification, the second one), he had reached a clear and passionate understanding that the final objective to be obtained by war, the only justifiable goal, is to make another war impossible. More important, he had also reached the firm understanding that there could be no political stability or secure basis for peace in a world deprived of a normal economic life. It was with this guiding belief that he conceived his "Marshall Plan" to provide a vast program of economic and military aid to the war-devastated countries of Europe—the contribution for which he was awarded the Peace Prize.

George Marshall was keenly aware of the anomaly of such a man as himself receiving the prize. "There has been considerable comment over the awarding of the Nobel Peace Prize to a soldier. I am afraid this does not seem quite so remarkable to me as it quite evidently appears to others. . . . The cost of war in human lives is constantly spread before me, written neatly in many ledgers whose columns are gravestones. I am deeply moved to find some means or method of avoiding another calamity of war."

Marshall's father ran a flourishing coal business in Pennsylvania, but his son was determined to be a soldier and enrolled at the Virginia Military Institute. After serving in posts in the Philippines and the United States, he graduated with honors from the Infantry-Cavalry School at Fort Leavenworth in 1907 and from the Army Staff College in 1908.

When he completed one tour as training officer of a camp in Utah, his commanding officer was required to make the usual efficiency report on young Marshall. In answer to one of the standard questions in the report—"Would you desire to have him under your immediate command in peace and in war?"—the camp commander, Lt. Colonel Johnson Hagood, replied: "Yes, but I would prefer to serve under *his* command."

Marshall sailed for France in June 1917 with the first ship in the convoy carrying the first division of American troops to France. He became chief of operations of the division and aide to General Pershing, commander in chief of the American armies in Europe. To the end of his life Marshall was haunted by the fact that of that first division of 27,000 men, 25,000 became casualties. In rapid succession, he was made temporary major, lieutenant colonel and colonel and was recommended for promotion to brigadier general by Pershing. But Pershing's recommendation was not accepted and after the war ended Marshall reverted to the rank of captain. He had to wait fifteen years before reaching the rank of colonel again, due to the strict rules of seniority under American military practice. As soon as he became chief of staff in 1939 he immediately altered the regulations: one result was that within a year Major Dwight Eisenhower was promoted to colonel and then brigadier general, jumping 366 senior officers.

Between the wars, Marshall had been stationed at Tientsin, where he became so fluent in Chinese that he was able to examine Chinese witnesses without the aid of interpreters.

In his position as chief of staff, he constantly preached a policy of preparedness, foreseeing the possibility of a surprise strike like the Pearl Harbor attack of 1941. When the United States entered the war, he became the architect and overall commander of an army of eight million soldiers, the largest the world had ever seen. He resigned at the end of the war, in 1945. During his military career he had been involved in many diplomatic situations; he had taken part, as chief of staff, in the conference on the Atlantic Charter, and those at Casablanca, Quebec, Yalta and Potsdam. In late 1945 and in 1946 he represented President Truman on a special mission to China, then torn by civil war, and the following year he became secretary of state. It was in this capacity, in the spring of 1947, that he outlined his Marshall Aid plan in a speech at Harvard University.

"Our policy," he said on that occasion, "is directed not against any country or doctrine, but against hunger, poverty, desperation and chaos. Its purpose should be the revival of a working economy in the world so as to permit the emergence of political and social conditions in which free institutions can exist. Such assistance, I am convinced, must not be on any piecemeal basis as various crises develop. Any assistance that this government may render in the future should provide a cure rather than a mere palliative."

Marshall carried his plan into effect, fighting for it for two years both in public and in Congress, and in the spring of 1948, Congress voted $5.3 billion towards European recovery based on the "Marshall Plan."

For one year, during the Korean War, he was made secretary of defense, a civilian post in the cabinet; during this time he put into effect his idea of basing the future defense of the United States on conscription rather than on a standing professional army. He retired in September 1951 to his small estate in Virginia.

In his Nobel speech, Marshall referred to the "rapid disintegration between 1945 and 1950 of our once vast power for maintaining the peace." He went on: "As a direct consequence, in my opinion, there resulted the brutal invasion of South Korea, which for a time threatened the complete defeat of our hastily arranged forces in that field. . . . For the moment the maintenance of peace in the present hazardous world situation does depend in a very large measure on military power, together with Allied cohesion. But the maintenance of large armies for an indefinite period is not a practical or a promising basis for policy."

His lecture included an appeal for better education, particularly in the field of history. "There are innumerable instructive lessons out of the past, but all too frequently their presentation is highly colored or distorted in the effort to present a favorable national point of view. . . . Maybe in this age we can find a way of facing the facts and discounting the distorted records of the past."

But his final and main point reflected his whole thinking, the thinking that lay behind the Marshall Plan. "We must present democracy as a force holding within itself the seeds of unlimited progress by the human race," he said. "By our actions we should make it clear that such a democracy is a means to a better way of life, together with a better understanding among nations. Tyranny inevitably must retire before the tremendous moral strength of the gospel of freedom and self-respect for the individual, but we have to recognize that these democratic principles do not flourish on empty stomachs, and that people turn to false promises of dictators because they are hopeless and anything promises something better than the miserable existence that they endure. However, material assistance alone is not sufficient. The most important thing for the world today in my opinion is a spiritual regeneration which would reestablish a feeling of good faith among men generally."

1954

THE OFFICE OF THE UNITED NATIONS HIGH COMMISSIONER FOR REFUGEES: *Established by the UN General Assembly in 1951, its aim is to promote international legal regulations for the benefit of refugees and to ensure that they are treated in accordance with such regulations, in particular as regards the right to work, social security and the freedom to travel.*

THE EXTENT TO which the care and resettlement of refugees can be regarded as work for the promotion of world peace is, to say the least of it, a debatable one, and although in a sense a precedent had been set when the Peace Prize was awarded to Nansen in 1922, Gunnar Jahn, chairman of the Nobel Committee, appeared to be conscious of this when making the presentation. "There may perhaps be some," he said, "who do not believe that work for the refugees is work in the cause of peace. . . . But it *is* work for peace, if to heal the wounds of war is to work for peace, if to promote brotherhood among men is to work for peace. For this work shows us that the unfortunate foreigner is one of us; it teaches us to understand that sympathy with other human beings, even if they are separated from us by national frontiers, is the foundation upon which a lasting peace must be built."

Dr. Gerrit Jan van Heuven Goedhart, UN High Commissioner for Refugees, made a more valid point perhaps, in his acceptance speech. "There can be no real peace in this world," he said, "as long as hundreds of thousands of men, women and children, through no fault of their own, but only because they sacrificed all they possessed for the sake of what they believed, still remain in camps and live in misery, and in the greatest uncertainty of their future. Eventually, if we wait too long, the uprooted are bound to become easy prey for political adventurers, from whom the world has suffered too much already."

Gunnar Jahn painted a very depressing picture in his presentation address, and the sad truth is that although the locations may have changed somewhat in the years between, the refugee problem has grown more rather than less acute.

"It has been estimated," he said, "that there were between thirty and forty million homeless at the end of the war." And he went on to explain that a forerunner of the present organization, the United Nations Relief and Rehabilitation Administration (UNRRA) set up by the Allies in 1943, spent $3.9 billion—contributed by various governments, ninety percent of it from the United States and the United Kingdom—repatriating six million people by the autumn of 1945. But they came up against the problem of many people who did not want to return to their own countries, either because they no longer had ties there or because they feared reprisals. These became the new refugees, people for whom a chance of a new life would have to be found outside their own countries.

Refugee work was taken over in 1947 by the International Refugee Organization (IRO), which assumed responsibility both for the refugees which UNRRA had been looking after and for those rendered homeless for other reasons, taking under its care 1.7 million people. A million refugees were helped to emigrate and thousands in camps were rescued from hardship or even death. But in the two short years before it was wound up in 1949, it had spent $470 million.

The IRO was replaced by the Office of the United Nations High Commissioner for Refugees (UNHCR), which unlike IRO is a promotional rather than an operational body, and merely coordinates international action for refugees, establishing liaisons with governments, with UN specialized agencies, and with intergovernmental and private organizations. The UN provides the administrative expenses involved in running the head office in Geneva and some thirty branch offices throughout the world, with a combined staff of no more than 123 people. Their work is otherwise financed by contributions from private sources, and the funding target for any given year is determined by the executive committee on the recommendation of the high commissioner and according to the special needs of the period. For example, early in the 1950s, the Ford Foundation gave a grant of about $3 million (increased to $8 million with funds from other sources) to carry out pilot projects in the economic integration of refugees in Austria, Germany, France and Trieste and on the resettlement of refugees in Canada, Latin America and Australia. Annual programs vary between $3 million and $7 million, though in 1960, World Refugee Year, the program amounted to $12 million.

The term "refugee" is strictly defined in UNHCR's mandate as "a person who, because of fear of persecution arising from his race, creed, or political philosophy, is living outside his former home country and is unable or unwilling to avail himself of that country's protection." UNHCR provides such refugees with international protection in accordance with a convention operative since 1954 and ratified by sixty countries. If the refugees cannot be persuaded to become integrated in their country of origin, and for one reason or another cannot emigrate (a solution that is becoming more difficult each year as the problems of potential "host" countries become more acute), UNHCR aims to promote action which will help the refugees to become self-supporting and eventually, through naturalization, cease being refugees. Assistance given in achieving this aim may include emergency aid and rural settlement projects in Africa and Asia; housing and establishment assistance in European countries; and advice, education and retraining in most other areas.

Put like that, it sounds cold and statistical, but in accepting the award, the High Commissioner van Heuven Goedhart, spelled out the problem in human terms. "The refugee problem has nothing to do with charity," he said. "It is not the problem of people to be pitied, but far more the problem of people to be admired. It is the problem of people who somewhere, somehow, sometime, had the courage to give up the feeling of belonging, which they possessed, rather than abandon the human freedom which they valued more highly. It is the problem of rebuilding their existences. . . . Under the mandate of the Office of the UNHCR come about 2.2 million refugees, more than 50 percent of whom are in Europe. Of these, some 300,000 had at the beginning of this year not been able to solve the problem of their independent existence; 70,000 of them are still living in some two hundred camps in Germany, Austria, Italy and Greece; and some 15,000 of them are unfit for economic integration anywhere, as they are too old or for some other reason disabled."

He also referred to the unsolved problems in other areas, in the Middle East, the Far East, particularly the Chinese mainland where some 13,000 refugees of European origin were trying to leave China and settle elsewhere. He talked about refugees from East Germany now living in the

Federal Republic, the Moslem refugees who had fled from India to Pakistan, the Hindu refugees who had fled from Pakistan to India. "Theoretically," he said, "it could be regretted that these latter groups are excluded from the United Nations' mandate, but practically it must be admitted that a wider definition would include so many millions of uprooted people as to paralyze the office and make it quite impossible to work out any program."

He went into detail on one aspect of the program: the dissolution of the existing refugee camps, in which 70,000 refugees had been living for up to ten years.

". . . The dissolution of camps is a process which is much more complicated than appears at first sight. The building of houses is by no means enough. The refugee, in order to solve his problem, must be able to maintain his family and himself. He must, if he has lost his skill, be retrained in a trade for which there is a demand, and his house must be within reasonable distance of his work. If he intends to set himself up in a small business, he may need a loan at a moderate interest. If he is not sure how he can solve his problem, he will need counseling. If he hopes to emigrate, his papers must be put in order before he can leave."

All this, he emphasized, costs money. The governments appealed to had so far not made available more than 55 percent of the target requirement. "An office which has just been awarded the Nobel Peace Prize has perhaps no right to be discouraged, but should it be necessary for the United Nations High Commissioner for Refugees to spend such a considerable part of his time fund raising? In a world where there are so many insoluble problems we can ill afford to neglect one which is soluble."

1955–1956

Prizes not awarded.

1957

LESTER BOWLES PEARSON (1897–1972), Canadian: *Politician, diplomat and Canada's foreign minister from 1948 to 1957. He was present at most of the major international conferences in the thirties and at many sessions of the League of Nations, participated in the establishment of both UNRRA and the FAO in 1943 and attended the San Francisco Conference on the establishment of the United Nations in 1945. He headed the Canadian delegation to the UN from 1946 and was largely responsible for creating the UN emergency peace-keeping force, first used during the Suez crisis of 1956.*

LESTER PEARSON, THE first Canadian to be awarded the Peace Prize, won the distinction, not as a politician but, in the words of Gunnar Jahn, chairman of the committee, as a man, "because of his personal qualities—the powerful initiative, strength and perseverance he has displayed in attempting to prevent or limit war operations and to restore peace in situations where quick, tactful and wise action has been necessary to prevent unrest from spreading and developing into a worldwide conflagration."

Born in Toronto of Irish stock, Lester Pearson acquired the nickname "Mike" from his flying instructor in World War I. He entered the University of Toronto in 1913, and when war broke out in 1914, though too young to enlist, he served with an ambulance unit sponsored by the university. He spent two years in England, Egypt and Greece before transferring to the Royal Flying Corps. Injured in a plane crash, he was invalided home, and served as a training instructor for the remainder of the war. He took a degree in history in Toronto in 1919, worked for two years in his father's meat-processing firm, and during that time won a two-year scholarship to Oxford, where he continued to study history, taking his master's degree.

In 1924 he joined the staff of the history department of the University of Toronto, leaving it four years later to become first secretary in the Canadian Department of External Affairs. It was during the next several years that he attended The Hague Conference on International Law and various other international conferences, including the Geneva World Disarmament Conference (1933–34) and meetings of the League of Nations.

From 1935 to 1941 he served in the Office of the High Commissioner for

Canada in London, became assistant undersecretary of state for external affairs at Ottawa in 1941 and rapidly rose to the rank of ambassador. While minister-counselor at the Canadian Legation in Washington between 1942 and 1944, he was involved in the formation both of UNRRA and the FAO, and he attended the San Francisco Conference on the establishment of the United Nations in 1945.

In 1948 he became minister for external affairs, a portfolio which he held for nine years until the fall of the Liberal government.

It was Pearson who drafted the speech in which his prime minister, Louis St. Laurent, proposed the establishment of NATO; he headed the Canadian delegation to NATO until 1957 and was chairman of the NATO Council in 1951–52. He also headed the Canadian delegation to the United Nations from 1946 to 1956 and was president of the Seventh Session of the General Assembly in 1952–53. During the fighting in Korea he took the line that all hostilities should be limited as soon as the North Koreans had been forced back. "The action of free nations against aggression in Korea," he said, ". . . has had as its purpose not the destruction of the North Korean and Chinese peoples, but the localizing of hostilities, repelling the attack, and then negotiating cease-fire arrangements as a prelude to peace."

When the UN had to decide on the Palestine question in 1947, Pearson was active and outspoken on the committee which recommended that the British mandate over Palestine should be discontinued and the country divided into an Arab and a Jewish state.

One of his biggest victories came in 1956 when Nasser suddenly nationalized the Suez Canal. Israel invaded the area, and Britain and France bombed Egyptian airfields. The Security Council could do nothing because of a veto by Great Britain and France. Pearson submitted a resolution putting forward a plan for a neutral international UN peace-keeping force to contain the fighting and supervise the cessation of hostilities. Israel's immediate withdrawal and the end of hostilities on the part of Britain and France added up to the United Nations' first really successful peace move.

Although always a firm supporter of NATO, Lester Pearson never believed that military force could secure peace in the long run. In 1955 he said: "In all the long story of mankind, arms alone, however powerful, have never been sufficient to guarantee security for any length of time. Your strength for defense becomes the weakness of those against whom you feel you must be ready to defend yourself. Your security becomes their insecurity; so they in turn seek safety in increased arms. A vicious circle commences which in the past has cost untold misery and destruction and might now, if we cannot cut through it, cause mankind's extinction. Even adequate collective defense, then, is no final solution. It is merely a means to an end—peace based on something more enduring than force."

In his Nobel lecture which he called "The Four Faces of Peace," he dealt in turn with the four factors which in his view are vital in any discussion of peace: prosperity, power, policy and people. Poverty and distress—especially with the awakening of the submerged millions of Africa and Asia—make the risks of war today far greater, he argued. "It is already difficult to realize that a mere twenty years ago poverty was taken almost for granted over most of the earth's surface. There were always a few visionaries, but before 1939 there was little consideration given to the possibility of raising the living standards of Asia and Africa in a way that we now regard as indispensable. Perhaps only in North America every man feels entitled to a motor car, but in Asia hundreds of millions of people do now expect to eat and be free. They no longer will accept colonialism, destitution, and distress as preordained. That may be the most significant of all the revolutionary changes in the international fabric of our times. . . . If we ignore this, there will be no peace."

On the question of force, he argued that the force which a nation and its allies collect for its own security can, in a bad international climate, increase, or seem to increase, somebody else's insecurity. "A vicious chain reaction results. In the past the end result has always been, not peace, but the explosion of war. . . . I am not arguing against the short-run necessity [of military forces]. I am arguing against their long-run effectiveness. At best they give us a breathing space during which we can search for a better foundation for the kind of security which would itself bring about arms reduction.

"Today, less than ever, can we defend ourselves by force, for there is no effective defense against the all-destroying effect of nuclear missile weapons. Indeed, their very power has made their use intolerable, even unthinkable, because of the annihilative retaliation in kind that such use would invoke. So peace remains . . . balanced uneasily on terror, and the use of maximum force is frustrated by the certainty that it will be used in reply with a totally devastating effect. Peace . . . must surely be more than this trembling rejection of universal suicide."

On policy: "The grim fact is that we prepare for war like precocious giants and for peace like retarded pygmies. Our policy and diplomacy—as the two sides in the cold war face each other—are becoming as rigid and defensive as the trench warfare of forty years ago, when the two sides dug in, dug deeper, and lived in their ditches. . . .

"What I plead for is no spectacular meeting of a Big Two or a Big Three or a Big Four at the summit, where the footing is precarious and the winds blow hard, but for frank, serious and complete exchanges of views — especially between Moscow and Washington—through diplomatic and political channels.

"Essential to the success of any such exchanges is the recognition by the West that there are certain issues such as the unification of Germany and the stabilization of the Middle East which are not likely to be settled in any satisfactory way without the participation of the USSR. Where that country has a legitimate security interest in an area or a problem, that must be taken into account.

"It is also essential that the Soviet Union, in its turn, recognize the right of people to choose their own form of government without interference from outside forces or subversive domestic forces encouraged and assisted from outside. . . .

"Perhaps a diplomatic effort of this kind would not succeed. I have no illusions about its complexity or even its risks. Speaking as a North American, I merely state that we should be sure that the responsibility for any such failure is not ours. The first failure would be to refuse to make the attempt."

On the question of people and their attitude to wars, alone of all the Nobel laureates, Lester Pearson acknowledged the fact that men *like* war. He quoted the Canadian psychiatrist, Dr. G. H. Stevenson, who once wrote: "We like the excitement of it, its thrill and glamor, its freedom from restraint. We like its opportunities for socially approved violence. . . . We like its economic security and its relief from the monotony of civilian toil. We like its reward for bravery, its opportunities for travel, its companionship of men in a man's world, its intoxicating novelty. And we like taking chances with death. This psychological weakness is a constant menace to peaceful behavior. We need to be protected against this weakness, and against the leaders who capitalize on this weakness."

Pearson commented: "Perhaps this has all changed now. Surely the glamor has gone out of war. The thin but heroic red line of the nineteenth century is now the production line. The warrior is the man with the test tube or the one who pushes the nuclear button. This should have a salutary effect on men's emotions. A realization of the consequences that must follow if and when he does press the button should have a salutary effect also on his reason. . . .

"I believe myself that the Russian people—to cite one example—wish for peace. I believe also that many of them think that the Americans are threatening them with war, that they are in danger of attack. So might I, if I had as little chance to get objective and balanced information about what is going on in the United States. Similarly, our Western fears of the Soviet Union have been partly based on a lack of understanding or of information about the people of that country. Misunderstanding of this kind, arising from ignorance, breeds fear, and fear remains the greatest enemy of peace."

1958

GEORGES CHARLES CLEMENT GHISLAIN PIRE (1910 — 1969), Belgium: *Dominican priest, chaplain to the resistance movement in World War II, cited for his efforts to help refugees to leave their camps and return to a life of freedom and dignity. He founded four homes for old people and seven European villages for the resettlement of refugees.*

WITH THE COLD war at its height (if that's the word for the extremity in a cold war), with trouble brewing in Algeria, in the Middle East, in India, in Africa, it is perhaps not surprising that the Nobel Peace Committee turned once again to the still unsolved problem of the refugees and awarded the prize to a man who, like Albert Schweitzer, made a statistically small but spiritually vast contribution to the plight of his fellow man.

It is possible that his interest in refugee work came from a subconscious memory of his own childhood: when he was four and a half, he and his family had to flee before the advancing Germans in 1914. They spent four years in France and returned to find their home in ruins.

Georges Pire was born in Dinant, where his father was a civic official. He studied classics and philosophy at the Collège de Bellevue before entering the Dominican monastery of La Sarte in Huy, Belgium, where he took the name Henri Dominique and made his final vows in 1932. He continued his studies in Rome, was ordained in 1934 and became a doctor of theology two years later.

In 1938 Father Pire began his long service of organizational work by founding the Service d'Entr'aide Familiale [Mutual Family Aid Service] and the Stations de Plein Air de Huy [Open Air Camps of Huy] for children. During and after the war these camps became missions that fed thousands of Belgian and French children.

In World War II he was chaplain to the resistance movement and an agent for the intelligence service; he was one of the organizers of the escape system by which Allied airmen were returned to their own forces.

For his work in this area, he was awarded the Military Cross with Palms, the Resistance Medal with Crossed Swords, the War Medal and the National Recognition Medal.

In 1949, when he was thirty-nine years old, he suddenly became deeply aware of the refugee problem, more particularly the problem of the old and infirm who had little hope of building up a new life for themselves and their families by their own efforts. He described their plight in a magnificent phrase: "They have been sitting on their luggage and waiting twelve or fourteen years for a train that never comes."

It is obvious that effective help for this category of refugee is extremely difficult to arrange because it is impossible to think in terms of loans, often arranged in the case of young refugees, fit, well-trained and able to work to repay their debts. Help for the old and infirm, on the other hand, must be a matter of pure charity.

Father Pire began with a sponsorship scheme: he put refugee families living in camps in touch with private families who were willing to correspond with them and send them gifts and perhaps money. By 1958, 15,000 "godparents," as he called them, in twenty countries, were corresponding with 15,000 refugees in camps. It was a start, but the refugees were still in camp.

In 1950 he began his work to try to enable as many refugees as possible to leave the camps. He dealt first with the problem of the old people and within four years had succeeded in founding four homes for them, all in Belgium, where they could be provided with shelter, clothing, food and medicine, as well as all the care they needed, until they died.

During the next three years, he founded seven European villages, each for 150 people, at Aachen, Germany; Bregenz, Austria; Augsburg, Germany; Berchem-Sainte-Agathe, Belgium (called the Fridtjof Nansen village); Spiesen in the Saar (called the Albert Schweitzer village); Wuppertal, Germany (the Anne Frank village); and Euskirchen, Germany.

In 1950, he had formed a society named L'Aide aux Personnes Deplacées [Aid to Displaced Persons]. This became an international organization in 1957, which aimed to provide stateless refugees, regardless of nationality or religion, "with material and moral support in every form, . . . especially through assistance by sponsorship, nursing homes and European villages," thus forging "a chain of forces for good around the refugees who are without country, in the form of a 'Europe of the Heart.'"

Father Pire's Nobel lecture consisted for the most part of messages which he had received from all over the world, encouraging him in his work. But he did make one valid point. "The Aid to Displaced Persons is a splendid medium and an original one," he said. "For us who have so little influence on the great decisions taken at the UN and elsewhere, this is as effective a means as any of working for peace, albeit within Europe alone. Whereas the man in the street despairs of having a say in major political questions, he has every say and every opportunity to put his words into practice on the displaced persons problem.

"I am unmoved by the pessimists who say that the Nobel Peace Prize has failed to avert violence. I believe that the world is making progress spiritually, slowly no doubt but still making progress. We proceed, as it were, at the rate of three steps forward and two steps back. The important thing is to take that third extra step. In this lies man's only chance. . . ."

Nevertheless, a lot of people felt then, and still feel, that the provision of homes for refugees, as worthy an endeavor as it may well be, is not precisely what Nobel had in mind when he wrote about "the person who shall have done the most or the best work for fraternity between peoples."

1959

PHILIP JOHN NOEL-BAKER (1889–   ), Great Britain: *Politician and statesman, who participated in the formation, administration and legislative deliberations of both the League of Nations and the United Nations and was adviser to Nansen in his prisoner-of-war and refugee work.*

IN A SENSE, Noel-Baker harks back to an earlier generation of Nobel laureates; he was awarded the prize not for a specific piece of work but for a lifetime of service, first for the League of Nations and then for the United Nations. He had been Nansen's adviser and assistant in his prisoner-of-war and refugee work, and was a close and valued friend.

One of seven children of a Canadian-born Quaker who moved to England to establish a machine-manufacturing firm, Noel-Baker took honors in history (1910) and economics (1912) at King's College, Cambridge. He accepted the post of vice-principal of Ruskin College at Oxford in 1914, but when war broke out, he organized and commanded the Friends' Ambulance Unit on the Western Front (1914–15) and subsequently became adjutant of the first British Ambulance Unit for Italy (1915–18).

In 1918–19 during the Peace Conference in Paris, he was principal assistant to Lord Robert Cecil on the committee which drafted the League of Nations Covenant; from 1920 to 1922 a member of the Secretariat of the League and principal assistant to Sir Eric Drummond, first secretary general of the League; and from 1922 to 1924 he was private secretary to the British representative on the League's Council and Assembly. In the meantime he was acting as adviser and assistant to Nansen. From 1929 to 1931 he was a member of the British delegation to the Assembly of the League and for a year was assistant to Arthur Henderson, chairman of the Disarmament Conference and Nobel Peace Prize laureate for 1934.

He was also a prolific writer and a politician. Among the books he wrote during this period are *The League of Nations at Work* (1926) and *Disarmament* (1926). From 1929 to 1931 he sat in the House of Commons as Labor member for Coventry. Subsequently he represented Derby and Derby South, was elected to the National Executive Committee of the Labor party in 1937 and in 1946 succeeded Harold Laski as chairman of the party. In the Attlee postwar government he was minister of state in the Foreign Office (1945–46), secretary of state for air (1946–47), secretary of state for commonwealth relations (1947–50) and minister of fuel and power (1950–51).

He was in charge of British preparatory work for the United Nations, helped to draft the UN Charter in San Francisco in 1945 and was a member of the British delegation. He supported the regulation of traffic in arms, atomic control, economic aid for refugees and the reintroduction of the Nansen "passport."

In the fifties, he returned to his studies on armament and published *The Arms Race: A Program for World Disarmament*, which summarized a lifetime of research and experience. The book won the Albert Schweitzer Book Prize in 1961. In it, he traces all the attempts which have been made to reach agreement on disarmament since World War I and describes the repeated efforts to find an acceptable system of control. He believes that up to 1955, the Soviet attitude was responsible for the failure but holds the view that in more recent years the West has been too adamant in its demands. Disarmament, he wrote, must be complete and must include all kinds of weapons if it is to be effective. He also deals with the possibilities which exist for effective control and makes a number of concrete proposals, both for disarmament and for mutual control. Instead of dismissing the objections that are made, he counters them; above all, he argues that even if a control system is not completely watertight, the risk involved is a small one compared to the present situation of aimlessly drifting along.

Noel-Baker took the arms race as the subject for his Nobel lecture, and the figures he presented were frightening. In 1914 the nations had something over five million men in their standing peacetime forces; in 1960 they had more than sixteen million. In 1914 they were spending about £500 million a year on preparing for war; in 1960 the figure was £40,000 million. In 1945 the Hiroshima weapon multiplied by 2,000 the explosive power of the ten-ton "block-buster" which the Allied pilots had dropped on Berlin. "It killed 100,000 people in an instant of time; it crippled, burned, blinded, riddled with radiation sickness 100,000 more; in 1959 scores of people have died a lingering, hideous death as the result of a bomb dropped fourteen years ago. A city as big as Oslo was utterly destroyed: houses, factories, offices, barracks, docks—nothing remained.

"In 1954 the so-called H-bomb—the first primitive, unliftable thermo-nuclear device—multiplied by almost a thousand the power of the Hiroshima bomb. A British Home Office Manual on Civil Defense tells us that a ten-megaton bomb—ten million tons of Nobel's high explosive, much smaller than the weapon of 1954—would wipe out London: total annihilation of the center, and around it an unbroken circle of roaring flame from which it would be a miracle if anything escaped."

He referred to poison gas and "biological" warfare. "Goering tried a nerve gas which he called 'Tabun,' on a herd of goats; they went mad and massacred each other, before the few survivors died, after hours of agonizing pain. An American general has told us that our nerve gas is ten times as potent now; others say even more. 'Biologicals' may be just as potent, and, if they start a large-scale epidemic, more horrifying still."

He believed that unless there was an iron resolution to make disarmament the supreme object of international policy and to realize it now, all talks about disarmament would fail. This ruled out attempts to "limit" war by new laws or understandings about how weapons would be used.

"Some people honestly believe that small steps will be easier to take than large ones," he continued. "They quote proverbs to support their point—the crude English, 'Don't bite off more than you can chew'; the elegant French, 'The better is the enemy of the good'; the Russian, 'The slower you ride, the further you go.' . . . I prefer the words of our great economist and political thinker John Stuart Mill: 'Against a great evil, a small remedy does not produce a small result; it produces no result at all.' Or the saying of Lloyd George: 'The most dangerous thing in the world is to try to leap a chasm in two jumps.' There is a great chasm, a great gulf, between the armed world of today and the disarmed world which we must have on some near tomorrow."

The Stormy Sixties

THE STORMS OF the sixties were not confined to the havoc caused by the "wind of change," referred to by British premier Harold Macmillan on a visit to Africa in January 1960, which howled across that continent and swept away all but a few isolated outposts of colonialism.

The decade began ominously with a United States protest to Cuba about the expropriation of American property there which before long had escalated, to use a phrase of the period, into the most dangerous exercise in brinksmanship (another phrase of the period) since the invention of the atomic bomb: Castro's Cuba was bristling with Russian nuclear missiles all pointing at America, and the US Navy, on a war footing, was blockading the island.

It was a decade during which American involvement in Vietnam escalated from 685 military advisers to 542,000 combat troops by the end of 1969, by which time American casualties had far exceeded those in the Korean War.

It was a time of continuing riots—student riots, race riots, riots in protest against nuclear weapons and the Vietnam War, riots between opposing factions in emerging African states and among starving Asians, riots between the people and police in Belfast and Londonderry. Terrorism—in Cyprus, in Israel, in Palestine and in Northern Ireland—became so familiar on our television screens that it lost all its power to shock. On those small screens, too, we saw an American president assassinated and his assassin murdered; and we learned to accept hijacking as one of the hazards of traveling by air.

It was the decade in which man first left this planet (and his spacecraft) and walked weightless up there somewhere among the stars, and set foot for the first time on the bleak, alien ashes of the moon. In the beginning we would crouch breathlessly around the TV set, gasping at each new countdown and goggling incredulously at blurred black and white glimpses of heavily helmeted men strapped in strange positions. Long before the decade ended we had become blasé and could hardly spare the time to glance at perfect color pictures of the astronauts larking about with the earth spinning away, and us on it, miles below their dangling feet, or emerging from the bobbing capsules after yet another perfect splashdown in the Pacific. Spacecraft after spacecraft was tossed into orbit with casual, unerring accuracy and the litter began to accumulate, all whirling around up there—copper needles and communications satellites, discarded rocket stages and lunar modules and all the débris that discovery of this new world entailed.

To most ordinary people, unable or perhaps unwilling to accept the implications of what was really happening, these were the swinging sixties—an era of blue jeans and mini-skirts, of nude shows like *Hair* and *Oh, Calcutta!,* the high noon of the permissive society. The sound of the sixties was made in Liverpool, England—by four boys calling themselves the Beatles; they soon became, as one of them immodestly but accurately put it, better known than Jesus Christ. It was a time when, in the words of the British Conservative slogan, we "never had it so good"; "it was the best of times, it was the worst of times," as Dickens had said of an earlier period.

It was, although we didn't realize it at the time, the end of yet another era. . . .

In January 1960 Brussels agreed to give the Belgian Congo full independence *within six months,* making no preparations at all for what would happen after the withdrawal of Belgian troops. In February there was rioting in Algiers where the French *colons* were still desperately trying to cling on to an empire they believed they had built and in which they felt they had a stake. Britain and the United States agreed to build an "early warning system" to detect hostile missiles headed in their direction. At Sharpeville in South Africa in March police fired into a crowd of Pan-African demonstrators; they killed 69 and wounded 180. In America blacks began a passive "sit-in" campaign in all-white sections of luncheonettes as a protest against segregation. On April 1 the South African government banned both the African National Congress and the Pan-African Congress, the two African anti-apartheid movements.

Togo became an independent republic and Sierra Leone announced that it would follow suit by 1961.

On May 1 an American U2 "spy" aircraft flown by Francis Powers was shot down over the Urals by the USSR; in May the Kariba Dam was opened, Israel announced the arrest of Eichmann, the former Gestapo chief, and Princess Margaret married Tony Armstrong Jones, a photographer.

In June Madagascar, Somaliland and the Belgian Congo all became independent republics; in the Congo, Kasavubu became president and Patrice Lumumba premier. Within a few days there was a mutiny in the Congolese army, Europeans were fleeing from Léopoldville to Brazzaville and Belgium had sent troops back to the Congo. Lumumba appealed to the UN and by June 8 Moise Tshombe, premier of the mineral-rich province of Katanga, proclaimed it a separate and independent republic.

France agreed to the independence of Dahomey, Niger, Upper Volta, Ivory Coast, Chad, French Central Africa and the French Congo; Mauretania soon followed, becoming an independent Islamic republic, and Cyprus declared her independence with Archbishop Makarios as president. A UN emergency force landed in the Belgian Congo.

In September the news that the USSR had agreed to provide aircraft for Lumumba was followed almost immediately by an announcement that President Kasavubu had dismissed Lumumba.

In November John F. Kennedy continued to fight Richard Nixon on the television screens of America and won the presidential elections by ninety-four electoral votes.

Surgeons at Birmingham, England, developed the pacemaker for keeping a human heart beating; the first microwave laser was constructed and there was a "kneel-in" campaign by blacks in segregated churches in the southern United States.

America had 85 million TV sets, Britain 10.4 million and West Germany came next with 2 million. It was the year of Fellini's *La Dolce Vita* and Antonioni's *L'Avventura*.

In February 1961 the US broke off relations with Cuba, and the UN Security Council urged the use of force to prevent civil war in the Congo and ordered an inquiry into Lumumba's mysterious death.

In March South African premier Verwoerd announced that his nation would leave the Commonwealth by the end of May. In May, Tanganyika achieved full independence with Julius Nyerere as premier, and Kwame Nkrumah took over in Ghana. A month earlier, there had been an army revolt in Algeria, and an attempted invasion of Cuba by rebel forces which was defeated by Castro.

On May 28 the Simplon-Orient Express, which had been carrying VIPs between Paris and Bucharest for seventy-eight years, made its final full-length journey. Khrushchev proposed a peace conference in June, to conclude a treaty and establish Berlin as a free city. The West rejected the proposal and in August, East Germany sealed off the border between East and West Germany, closed the Brandenburg Gate and began to build the Berlin wall.

In September heavy fighting broke out between UN peace-keeping troops and Katanga rebels; Hammarskjöld was killed in a plane crash near the Katanga border on September 17/18 on his way to see Tshombe. On December 18 there was a cease-fire in the Congo and Tshombe agreed to end the secession of Katanga. But the fighting did not stop—it went on sporadically throughout the decade.

In England, throughout the year, the CND (Campaign for Nuclear Disarmament) had been active; 1,314 people were arrested after a sit-down protest in London in September. There were "freedom rides" by young blacks on segregated buses in the southern states of the US and the first conference, in Tanganyika, on the preservation of Africa's vanishing wildlife.

In April Yuri Gagarin of Russia became the first man to orbit the earth and in May Alan Shepherd of the US became the first American astronaut to make a re-entry through the atmosphere in a space capsule.

An English review called *Beyond the Fringe* brought a new kind of comedy both to the West End of London and to Broadway; films of the year included Truman Capote's *Breakfast at Tiffany's* with Audrey Hepburn and Truffaut's *Jules et Jim* with Jeanne Moreau. Carl Gustav Jung and Sir Thomas Beecham died, and Ernest Hemingway shot himself.

On February 8, 1962, a US military council was established in Vietnam. In August, Jamaica became an independent republic; and Algeria, now independent of France, was admitted to the Arab League. Trinidad and Tobago became independent and even the little island of Malta demanded independence.

On October 22 President Kennedy announced that Russia had been installing missile bases on Cuba and ordered a naval blockade (which, for diplomatic reasons, was called a "quarantine"). The United States went on to full war alert for over a week until November 2, when Kennedy announced that the Russians had been observed dismantling their bases in Cuba. On November 22, when Khrushchev agreed to withdraw all Illyushin bombers from Cuba, the incident was over and the whole civilized world breathed a sigh of relief.

By the end of the year Northern Rhodesia (later to be renamed Zambia) had its first African-dominated government under Kenneth Kaunda and the UN troops were again fighting in Katanga.

During the year two American astronauts, John Glenn (February) and Malcolm Scott (May), were sent into orbit and in July, Telstar was launched and circled the earth every 157.8 minutes, enabling live TV pictures to be exchanged between the United States and Europe. Other satellites were dispatched to explore Venus and study cosmic radiation and other properties of outer space.

An epidemic of congenital defects in infants was found to be due to the use of the drug thalidomide, which was promptly, if belatedly, banned.

Alexander Solzhenitsyn published *One Day in the Life of Ivan Denisovitch*; the play of the year was Edward Albee's *Who's Afraid of Virginia Woolfe?*; and the most spectacular film was David Lean's *Lawrence of Arabia*.

On August 5, 1963, Britain, the United States and the USSR signed a nuclear test ban treaty, subsequently signed by ninety-six nations, but not by France or China. On August 28, 200,000 blacks took part in a peaceful demonstration for civil rights in Washington, and in September there were riots over school desegregation in Birmingham, Alabama.

John F. Kennedy was assassinated in Dallas, Texas, on November 22 and Lyndon B. Johnson was sworn in as president.

It was the year of the Great Train Robbery in Cheddington, in Buckinghamshire, England (a gang got away with £2,500,000), the year that the Russians put a woman, Valentina Tereshkova, into orbit for three days (in June), and the year of *The Silent Spring*, a book in which Rachel Carson warned of the dangers of excessive pest control. Films of the year included the £12,000,000 epic *Cleopatra* with Elizabeth Taylor, Visconti's *The Leopard* and Tony Richardson's *Tom Jones*.

January 1964 opened with anti-American riots in Panama and a rebellion in Zanzibar, which became a republic. There were riots, too, in Salisbury, Southern Rhodesia, and fighting between the Greeks and Turks in Cyprus where, in February, a UN peace-keeping force took over.

In April, Ian Smith became premier of Southern Rhodesia and immediately placed Nkomo, the African leader, under restriction. Tanganyika and Zanzibar were united as Tanzania and in July the Nyasaland Protectorate became independent Malawi. The following month a US destroyer was attacked off North Vietnam and US aircraft attacked North Vietnamese bases in reprisal.

Harold Wilson became prime minister of Britain for the first time in October, and on October 16 the Chinese exploded an atomic bomb.

In the November presidential elections in the US, Lyndon B. Johnson scored a sweeping victory over Barry Goldwater.

Great Britain issued the first licenses to drill in the North Sea for natural gas, US divers began to explore the ocean environment, living for nine days in a "sealab" to study the effects of depth on man's mind and body, and the Roman Catholic hierarchy, fully aware that the world was no longer capable of producing enough food for the population explosion that was taking place, ruled firmly against the contraceptive pill.

The films of the year included the Beatles' *A Hard Day's Night* and Stanley Kubrick's *Dr. Strangelove*. Cole Porter, Brendan Behan, Sean O'Casey, Douglas MacArthur, Herbert Hoover and Ian Fleming, author of the James Bond novels, all died.

Winston Churchill died in January 1965, and his state funeral, on January 30, was watched by millions all over the world. US aircraft continued to bomb North Vietnam, and in Manhattan, Malcolm X, the black Muslim leader, was shot dead.

On March 8, 3,500 US Marines landed in South Vietnam.

Racial violence broke out in Selma, Alabama, where whites killed a white civil rights worker. On March 21 Martin Luther King, Jr., led a procession of civil rights workers from Selma to Birmingham to deliver a petition of black grievances. Four days later the Ku Klux Klan shot Viola Liuzzo, a white civil rights worker in Selma.

In April there were student demonstrations in Washington against the bombing of Vietnam; there was fighting in India, an outbreak of terrorist activity in Aden and rioting in Los Angeles.

In September the USSR admitted supplying arms to Hanoi. In November, Ian Smith of Rhodesia made a unilateral declaration of independence. Britain declared the regime illegal and introduced exchange and trade restrictions and an oil embargo. General Mobutu of the Congolese army deposed President Kasavubu, and President Ho Chi Minh of North Vietnam rejected a US offer to begin unconditional peace talks.

During the year Soviet cosmonaut Leoney became the first man to walk in space (in March), followed by Edward White of the US (in June).

In a blaze of ecumenical fervor, the Eastern Orthodox Church annulled the excommunication of the Church of Rome, which had been in operation from 1054A.D. On May 25 a heavyweight boxer called Cassius Clay (later known as Muhammed Ali) knocked out Sonny Liston in the first round of a fight at Lewiston, Maine.

Nine African states broke off relations with Britain in 1966 for not taking a firmer line over Rhodesia, where Smith had introduced penalties for listening to "subversive" broadcasts. In the US an extended call-up for military service was introduced, and Kosygin, who had replaced Khrushchev as prime minister, negotiated an agreement between India and Pakistan at Tashkent.

There were more unsuccessful peace moves in Vietnam by North Vietnam, the USSR, Canada and Italy. A US hydrogen bomb was recovered off the coast of Spain in April, after thirteen weeks in the sea. China exploded her third atomic bomb and the first "soft" landings on the moon were made by Russia and the US.

In the United States, in July, the Polaris fleet of forty-one submarines was completed when the last vessel, the *Will Rogers*, was launched at Groton, Connecticut. In the same month the British Colonial Office ceased to exist.

There were riots in Belfast and the Reverend Ian Paisley chose to go to jail rather than keep the peace for two years. In China there was a Great Proletarian Cultural Revolution.

The worst floods in the history of Italy covered Florence with several feet of water and caused millions of dollars' worth of damage to art treasures. The US attacked targets around Hanoi for the first time, an action condemned by U Thant, the UN secretary general.

In January 1967 Israeli forces used tanks for the first time in the steadily worsening conflict with Syria. On January 27 three US astronauts died in a flash fire in the first Apollo spacecraft before it left the launching pad; the same day, representatives of sixty nations, including the US and the USSR signed a UN treaty guaranteeing the peaceful use of outer space and a ban on nuclear weapons in space.

In February, Peking was placed under military rule, Kosygin expressed sympathy with the anti-Maoists in China in a TV interview and the Soviet embassy was attacked in Peking. In Japan, Eisaku Sato, a future Nobel Peace Prize winner (1974), was elected premier.

In Aden, Arab nationalists were fighting the British and one another; there were riots in Athens followed by a military coup d'état; racial disorders in Jackson on the State College campus and riots in Hong Kong; and 70,000 people marched down Fifth Avenue in New York in support of the soldiers fighting in Vietnam. Heavyweight Muhammed Ali (Cassius Clay) was indicted by a federal grand jury in Texas for refusing to be inducted into the US armed forces.

The US Marines and South Vietnam forces made their first attack within the demilitarized zone and Hanoi itself was bombed for the first time.

In Africa the eastern region of Nigeria announced its secession as the independent state of Biafra.

On June 5 a full-scale war broke out between Israel and the Arab nations, and Nasser closed the Suez Canal. The war was over in six days, during which the Israelis had made deep inroads into Arab territory.

In the States the National Guard was called out to cope with riots in Tampa, Florida, and Cincinnati, Ohio. China announced the successful explosion of a hydrogen bomb, and Israel passed a law making Jerusalem a united city where Arabs and Israelis could mingle freely for the first time in nineteen years.

Day and night rioting rocked Newark, New Jersey, for three days and nights of racial violence in which 26 people were killed, 1,500 injured and 1,397 arrested. This was followed by two days of rioting in Minneapolis and Detroit, where the army was called in. The disturbances in Detroit lasted for five days, during which 40 people were killed, 2,000 injured,

5,000 arrested and another 5,000 rendered homeless. Later in August there were five days of fierce rioting in New Haven, Connecticut.

In September the US forces were bombing targets within seven miles of the Chinese border and US Defense Secretary McNamara announced the establishment of a "light" missile network capable of providing defense against the sort of limited attack that Communist China would be able to mount within five years.

In October, Che Guevara, the Cuban revolutionary leader, was killed in a clash between guerrillas and the Bolivian army. In Washington, D.C., a crowd of 50,000 held demonstrations at the Pentagon and the Lincoln Memorial to protest against the Vietnam War.

In December, South African surgeons headed by Christiaan Barnard successfully achieved the world's first heart transplant operation.

In January 1968 Cambodia received a shipment of planes and anti-aircraft guns from China. A North Vietnamese mission in Paris repeated that the US would have to stop bombing North Vietnam before Hanoi would start conversations in Paris on relevant problems. On January 23, the *Pueblo*, a US naval intelligence ship, was seized off the North Korean coast; President Johnson ordered 14,787 air force and naval reservists to stand by for active duty and sent the nuclear aircraft carrier *Enterprise* to Korean waters.

There were riots in Poland, Mauritius became an independent state, and the US Command in Saigon announced that US casualties in Vietnam now exceeded those in the whole of the Korean War.

More than two hundred people were injured in student riots in Rome, and a protest march in Memphis, Tennessee, led by Martin Luther King, Jr., in support of striking garbage workers ended in violence, with one black youth killed. On April 4 Martin Luther King himself was assassinated in Memphis. His death was followed by further race riots in Chicago and Washington.

On April 8, 100,000 troops began the biggest drive of the war to clear the Communist forces out of the eleven provinces around Saigon.

There were student demonstrations in West Berlin, and Columbia University in New York was closed for two days after student riots. The US secretary of defense established a riot control center at the Pentagon.

In May the Paris students went on strike, occupying a lecture hall in the university's Nanterre Center, and fighting the police with paving stones in the Latin Quarter; they were joined by French workers in a 24-hour general strike. The civil war had been going on in Biafra now for ten months and there was famine in Nigeria.

On June 5 Senator Robert Kennedy was shot dead in Los Angeles by a Jordanian Arab. Students occupied university buildings in Milan, and the police cleared out some two hundred students who had taken over the Sorbonne in Paris.

At the end of June, sixty-two nations, including the US, the UK and the USSR, signed a nuclear nonproliferation treaty, and President Johnson announced that the US and the USSR had agreed to begin talks on the means of limiting and reducing their arsenals of nuclear weapons. A few days later France resumed its nuclear tests in the South Pacific.

In July the British House of Commons passed a government bill to outlaw racial discrimination. An Israeli airliner was hijacked over Italy by members of an Arab commando group and forced to land in Algeria.

After a series of "Warsaw Pact" exercises on the Czech border, Czechoslovakia was invaded late on the night of August 20 by troops of the USSR, East Germany, Poland, Hungary and Bulgaria. In the UN Security Council three days later, the USSR cast its 105th veto to defeat a resolution condemning the invasion of Czechoslovakia.

On September 11 Soviet tanks and military units began to withdraw from Prague. President Johnson ordered a complete halt to all US air, naval and artillery bombardment in North Vietnam on October 31, as a preliminary to the Paris peace talks.

Richard Nixon was elected thirty-seventh president of the United States on November 5. In December the eighty-two crewmen of the *Pueblo* were released after signing a document, denounced as false, admitting that the ship had violated North Korean waters.

During the year Jacqueline Kennedy married Aristotle Onassis, the Cunard line refused to take the completed QE2, probably the world's last transatlantic ocean liner, because of defects, and the Beatles' guru, Maharishi Malesh, yogi director of an academy of transcendental meditation in Swargshram, India, was much in demand everywhere for television interviews and private and group consultations.

The films of the year included *Star!*, *Camelot*, *Funny Girl* (all musicals), *Reflections in a Golden Eye* and *The Graduate*. Books in the news included Gore Vidal's *Myra Breckenridge* and John Updike's *Couples*.

Ramon Novarro, Talullah Bankhead, Edna Ferber, John Steinbeck and Yuri Gagarin—the first man in space—all died in 1968.

The year 1969 opened with violent civil disorder in Northern Ireland when Protestants attacked a peaceful civil rights march from Belfast to Londonderry. San Francisco State College was closed for three weeks in the face of continuing student strikes.

In February members of the Palestine Liberation Organization elected Yasir Arafat as leader. There was fighting in the streets of Istanbul as 20,000 people clashed over a visit of the US 6th Fleet. The London School of Economics was closed for three weeks because of student disorders.

Concorde, the British-French supersonic airliner, made its first test flight in France on March 2. On March 14 President Nixon said that there was no prospect of reducing the forces in Vietnam. Marines moved into the demilitarized zone for the first time since the cease-fire of 1968 and there were clashes between the USSR and Chinese troops along the Ussuri River.

Golda Meir became prime minister of Israel, there was a student revolt at Harvard and on April 20 black students seized the student union at Cornell University. British troops were sent to Northern Ireland to help the police to restore order.

There was rioting at Howard University, Washington, D.C., and in Berkeley, California.

In June President Nixon met South Vietnam President Van Thieu on Midway Island and announced that 25,000 troops would be withdrawn by August 31.

In July the first troops to be withdrawn from Vietnam were flown back to the States, where the spacecraft Apollo II set off for the moon with three astronauts on board; on July 20 Neil Armstrong and Buzz Aldrin became the first men to set foot on the surface of the moon.

In September the North Vietnamese premier Ho Chi Minh died, to be succeeded by "collective leadership." Nixon announced the withdrawal of another 35,000 troops.

On November 11 the UN General Assembly rejected, for the twentieth time, a proposal to admit Communist China as a member. On November 13 came the "march against death" in which 46,000 people carried the names of US soldiers killed in Vietnam past the White House and antiwar protesters, estimated at 250,000, staged a peaceful rally in Washington, D.C.

On November 24 President Nixon and Podgorny of the USSR ratified the nuclear nonproliferation treaty at ceremonies in Moscow and Washington. The following day President Nixon ordered the destruction of all US germ-warfare stocks.

In December Nixon announced a third reduction in the US combat troops despite reports of increased enemy infiltration in South Vietnam.

The films of the year included *Isadora* (with Vanessa Redgrave); *Bonnie and Clyde*; *Midnight Cowboy*; *Oh, What a Lovely War!* and Fellini's *Satyricon*. Books: *Portnoy's Complaint* by Philip Roth and Mario Puzo's *The Godfather*.

The deaths of the year included Dwight Eisenhower, Judy Garland, Boris Karloff and Mary Jo Kopechne (who drowned when a car driven by Senator Edward Kennedy plunged off a bridge at Chappaquiddick).

A. S. NORSK TELEGRAMBYRA

1960 Albert Luthuli

1961 Dag Hammarskjöld

1962 Linus Pauling

1963
International Committee
of the Red Cross
and League of
Red Cross Societies

1964 Martin Luther King, Jr.

1965
United Nations
Children's Fund (UNICEF)

1966-1967
Prizes not awarded

1968 René-Samuel Cassin

1969
International Labor
Organization

1960

ALBERT JOHN LUTHULI (1898–1967), South Africa: *As chief of his tribe and president-general of the African National Congress, he led ten million black Africans in a nonviolent campaign for civil rights in South Africa.*

IN AWARDING THE 1960 Peace Prize to Albert Luthuli, the Zulu tribal chieftain and civil rights leader of ten million black Africans, the Nobel Committee broke with tradition in two respects: Luthuli was the first black from the African continent to be chosen as a laureate and he was the first Nobel Peace Prize winner concerned purely with the question of civil rights within his own country. He had never served on any international conferences or committees and, until he received the Peace Prize, had taken no interest in the problem of world peace; his concern was solely for the ideals expressed in the declaration of human rights embodied in the Charter of the United Nations.

Luthuli came from a long line of Zulu chiefs, but he was deeply influenced by Christianity in the local Congregationalist mission school he attended in Groutville. He then studied at a boarding school called Ohlange Institute before transferring to a Methodist teachers' training college. After passing his examinations at Adams College in Natal, he joined the faculty of the college where he taught several subjects, including the history of the Zulu people. He was a teacher for seventeen years; during all this time he took no part in politics, though as secretary and then as president of the African Teachers' Association he frequently argued that education should be made available to all Africans, and that its quality should be equal to that of the education available to white children in South Africa.

In 1935 he was invited by the tribal elders to become chief of his tribe. In 1936 he accepted, and for almost seventeen years, until removed by the government of the Union in 1952 (the chief, although chosen by the tribe, was paid by the government and could therefore be "sacked"), he devoted himself to the 5,000 people in the tribe, acting as magistrate and as sole representative of his people in their dealings with the white overlords as well as appearing as presiding dignitary at traditional functions.

The increasing pressures which the ruling whites imposed on all the other races in South Africa caused Luthuli to abandon his passive stance and enter politics. In 1944 he became a member of the African National

Congress, an organization which had been founded in 1912 to secure universal enfranchisement and legal observance of human rights. In 1952 he was elected president, and he held that office until the Congress was banned in 1960.

The Union of South Africa, set up as an independent British Dominion in 1910, had developed rapidly from an agricultural community into one in which mining, industry and trade predominated and in which the urban population rapidly increased.

The population of South Africa is roughly 14 or 15 million, of whom only about 3 million are white. Of the remainder, 9 to 10 million are black, about 0.5 million are Asian (mainly Indians imported by the British to work the sugar plantations), and about 1.5 million are mixed races, the so-called colored people. Of the 10 million Africans, about a third live in African reservations, a third in the agricultural districts owned by the whites, and a third in the cities.

At the time when Luthuli became a tribal chieftain, nonwhites were denied all right to participate in the government. They were discriminated against legally in every possible way. The nonwhite had no vote and no part in determining his own status. Under the "pass" system, he was deprived not only of the right to live where he chose but also of the right to choose his employer. He had no protection against police tyranny and was not entitled to the same education as the white children; sexual relationship between white and nonwhite entailed punishment for both parties.

It was this discrimination that led to the formation of the African National Congress, founded by nonwhite Africans who had been able to secure a higher education, either abroad or in the days when the regulations were not so strict. Initially, the Congress tried to make its influence felt by petitions and deputations to the government of the Union, but when that made no headway—on the contrary, the discrimination between whites and nonwhites grew steadily in the years between 1912 and 1960—the Congress decided to adopt a more active line. When Luthuli joined the Congress, it had moved in the direction of passive resistance through boycotts, defiance campaigns and strikes. The Congress never passed any resolution to confine its demonstrations to nonviolent ones, but Luthuli was always completely opposed to the use of violence and frequently had to hold back the younger, more hot-headed members who wanted to use force to make South Africa an entirely nonwhite state.

Because of Luthuli's involvement in the Congress at this period, the government told him that he must either give up his position as tribal chief or resign from the Congress. He refused to do either, and was deposed.

In a declaration of his views, entitled "The Chief Speaks," he said: "What have been the fruits of my many years of moderation? Has there been any reciprocal tolerance or moderation from the government, be it Nationalist or United Party? No. On the contrary, the past thirty years have seen the greatest number of laws restricting our rights and progress until today we have reached a stage where we have almost no rights at all: no adequate land for our occupation; our only asset, cattle, dwindling; no security of homes; no decent and remunerative employment; more restrictions to freedom of movement through passes, curfew regulations, influx control measures. In short, we have witnessed in these years an intensification of our subjection to insure and protect white supremacy. It is with this background and with a full sense of responsibility that . . . I have joined my people in the new spirit that moves them today, the spirit that revolts openly and boldly against injustice and expresses itself in a determined and nonviolent manner. . . ."

In 1952, after he had been deposed and had been elected president of the Congress, he was banned for two years from all the larger centers of population of the Union and forbidden to attend public gatherings. In 1954 he went to Johannesburg to address a meeting which had been called to protest against the forced evacuation of colored people from Sophiatown to Meadowland; he was turned back at the airport and confined to an area within a twenty-five-mile radius of his home for another two years. When this second ban expired, he attended a Congress meeting in 1956 and was arrested, along with 155 others, and charged with treason. He was held in custody for about a year during the preliminary hearings and was released in December 1957, with all charges against him and 64 of the others dropped; the remainder were acquitted in 1961. Luthuli was among those arrested after the Sharpeville disturbances when 69 people were shot dead and 180 wounded in one afternoon, after the police had fired on a Pan-African crowd demonstrating against the pass laws. In 1960 both the Pan-African Congress and the African National Congress were dissolved by order of the government.

Before Luthuli went to Oslo in 1961 to receive the prize, South Africa had become a republic and was no longer a member of the British Commonwealth, but the relations between whites and nonwhites had not appreciably improved. In making the presentation, Gunnar Jahn, chairman of the committee, said: "If the nonwhite people of South Africa ever lift themselves from their humiliation without resorting to violence and terror, then it will be above all because of the work of Luthuli, their fearless and incorruptible leader who, thanks to his own high ethical standards, has rallied his people in support of this policy, and who throughout his adult life has staked everything and suffered everything without bitterness and without allowing hatred and aggression to replace his abiding love of his fellowmen."

"Africa presently is most deeply torn with strife and most bitterly stricken with racial conflict," Luthuli said in his Nobel lecture. "How strange then it is that a man of Africa should be here to receive an award given for service to the cause of peace and brotherhood between men. There has been little peace in Africa in our time. . . . Our continent has been carved up by the great powers; alien governments have been forced upon the African people by military conquest and by economic domination; strivings for nationhood and national dignity have been beaten down by force; traditional economies and ancient customs have been disrupted, and human skills and energy have been harnessed for the advantage of our conquerors. In these times there has been no peace; there could be no brotherhood between men.

"But now, the revolutionary stirrings of our continent are setting the past aside. Our people everywhere from north to south of the continent are reclaiming their land, their right to participate in government, their dignity as men, their nationhood . . . by comparison with Europe, our African revolution—to our credit—is proving to be orderly, quick and comparatively bloodless.

"In a strife-torn world, tottering on the brink of destruction by man-made nuclear weapons, a free and independent Africa . . . acting in concert with other nations . . . is man's last hope for a mediator between the East and West. Africa's qualification for this noble task is incontestable, for her own fight has never been and is not now a fight for conquest of land, for accumulation of wealth, or domination of peoples, but for the recognition and preservation of the rights of man and the establishment of a truly free world for a free people."

Luthuli, on his return to South Africa, was intermittently harassed by the authorities and limited to a radius of twenty-five miles from his home. In July 1967, at the age of sixty-nine, he was struck by a freight train as he walked on a trestle bridge near his home and was fatally injured.

1961

DAG HJALMAR AGNE CARL HAMMARSKJÖLD (1905–1961), Sweden: *Secretary general of the United Nations from 1953 until his death.*

THE 1961 PEACE PRIZE was awarded to Dag Hammarskjöld posthumously, after his death in an air crash in Katanga in what was then the Congo on the night of September 17–18, 1961.

The youngest of four sons of Hjalmar Hammarskjöld, prime minister of Sweden, a member of the Hague Tribunal and chairman of the board of the Nobel Foundation, Dag Hammarskjöld was the outstanding student of his day at Uppsala University, where he took his degree in 1925 in the humanities, concentrating on languages, literature and history. In 1928 he took a second degree at Uppsala in economics and a law degree in 1930; he became a doctor of economics in 1934.

He taught economics for a year at the University of Stockholm but there was never very much doubt that he would go into public affairs. In 1953 on a radio program, he said, "From generations of soldiers and government officials on my father's side I inherited a belief that no life was more satisfactory than one of selfless service to your country—or humanity. This service required a sacrifice of all personal interests, but likewise the courage to stand up unflinchingly for your convictions."

His first public position—as secretary from 1930 to 1934 to a government commission on unemployment—drew the attention of the Bank of Sweden, and he became secretary to the Bank in 1935. From 1936 to 1945 he was undersecretary at the Ministry of Finance, and from 1941 to 1948, head of the Bank of Sweden. These positions overlapped as did his appointment in 1946 as financial adviser to the Swedish Ministry of Foreign Affairs. In 1951 he became deputy foreign minister, with cabinet rank, and one of his successes during this period was in steering Sweden clear of military commitment to NATO while collaborating on the Council of Europe and the Organization for European Economic Community (OEEC). He represented Sweden as delegate to the United Nations in 1949 and again between 1951 and 1953. In the latter year he was elected secretary general for a five-year term, and re-elected in 1957. He succeeded the Norwegian lawyer and statesman Trygve Lie, who had made the office of secretary general a more independent and important position than had originally been envisaged. Dag Hammarskjöld had no illusions about the magnitude of the task or of its difficulties. In a letter written shortly after his almost unanimous election, he said: "To know that the goal is so significant that everything else must be set aside gives a great sense of liberation and makes one indifferent to anything that may happen to oneself."

He regarded himself as an international civil servant with only one master: the United Nations. From the first, he believed in solving any problems that arose by means of private discussions between representatives of the countries concerned, a process he called "quiet diplomacy."

He first came into the international spotlight when in 1955 he negotiated an agreement between Israel and the Arab states, setting up demarcation lines and UN observation posts. He was not over-sanguine about the effectiveness of these measures, and subsequent events proved him right.

In 1956, when Nasser nationalized the Suez Canal and a dispute over the canal territory arose which involved Britain and France, Dag Hammarskjöld did his best to find a solution through "quiet diplomacy." However, when Israel attacked Egypt at the end of October, and Britain and France vetoed a resolution calling on Israel to withdraw her troops and then attacked Egyptian air bases, Hammarskjöld threatened to resign unless all the member states stood firm by the UN Charter. By November 3 Hammarskjöld was able to announce that he had secured agreement from France and Britain to suspend hostilities and accept the formation of the UN peace-keeping force suggested by Lester Pearson, winner of the Peace Prize in 1957.

In 1958 Hammarskjöld suggested a solution to the continuing crises in Lebanon and Jordan—the establishment of observation groups in both countries. This reduced tension considerably for a time.

His most difficult problem arose in July 1960, in the recently liberated Belgian Congo. The new government with Kasavubu as president and Lumumba as prime minister wanted a unified Congo; but the administration, which had been in Belgian hands, broke down as soon as the Belgians abruptly left. The army mutinied; a large proportion of the white population fled; the Belgian army intervened, ostensibly to protect the white inhabitants still remaining; and on July 11 the province of Katanga broke away. Kasavubu and Lumumba appealed to the UN for aid, including military assistance to protect the Congo against the Belgian troops. The UN responded by sending a peace-keeping force consisting of contingents from African nations and from neutral Sweden and Ireland. No troops from the Soviet or the old colonial blocs were included, and the UN troops had instructions to use their arms only in self-defense.

Everything went tragically wrong in the Congo. Suddenly and inexplicably, Lumumba sent a cable to Khrushchev, the Russian premier, suggesting that he might ask for Russian aid if the Western powers continued their aggression. Khrushchev sent him an encouraging reply and, at the UN meetings, became bitterly opposed to Hammarskjöld, more than once demanding his resignation.

Still Hammarskjöld battled on, now in the face of disagreement among the Congolese themselves on the terms on which they would agree to federation. He also had to contend with the support that mineral-rich Katanga was receiving from Belgium; the possibility of Soviet aid to

Lumumba; the military regime of Mobutu, commander in chief of the Congolese army; and the murder of Lumumba. And all the time he was under heavy personal attack at the UN.

He spent a good deal of time in the Congo and finally, when fighting broke out between the peace-keeping UN force and the Katanga troops, decided to seek a personal conference with President Tshombe of Katanga. He left Léopoldville on the night of September 17–18, 1961, and he and fifteen others were killed when their plane crashed somewhere near the border between Katanga and North Rhodesia.

It is perhaps significant that Dag Hammarskjöld should have been killed in Africa. He had once said that the next decade must belong to Africa or to the atom bomb. Africa was to be the great test for the philosophy he wanted to bring to life through the United Nations.

In accepting the award, Rolf Edberg, Swedish ambassador to Norway, remembered: "He would remind us of how man once organized himself into families, how families joined together in tribes and villages, and how tribes and villages developed into people and nations. But the nation could not be the end of such a development. In the Charter of the United Nations he saw a guide to what he called an organized international community."

1962

LINUS PAULING (1901–   ), United States: *Winner of the Nobel Prize for Chemistry in 1954 and since 1946 a ceaseless campaigner against the development and spread of nuclear weapons. He drew up an appeal, signed by 10,000 scientists from forty-nine countries, against tests in the atmosphere and was largely responsible for the Nuclear Test Ban Treaty signed in July 1963.*

LINUS PAULING, THE only man to have won two undivided Nobel prizes, was born in Portland, Oregon, the son of a pharmacist. His career as a chemist need not much concern us here; his prime interest was in physical chemistry and he won the Nobel prize "for his research into the nature of the chemical bond and its application to the elucidation of the structure of complex substances." He has published papers on the effects of certain blood cell abnormalities, the relationship between molecular abnormality and heredity, the possible chemical basis of mental retardation and the functioning of anaesthetics. He is also well-known for his book *Vitamin C and the Common Cold,* in which he maintains that the common cold could be controlled in certain countries within a few years through an adequate intake of ascorbic acid (Vitamin C).

In 1946, at the request of Albert Einstein, Pauling and seven other leading scientists formed the Emergency Committee of Atomic Scientists with the object of bringing to the attention of the public everywhere the dangers in any further development of atomic weapons. But before they had achieved anything, Russia was building her own atom bomb, and the sinister phrase "balance of fear" had replaced the more conventional "balance of power."

Linus Pauling then switched to the dangers of producing a hydrogen bomb, warning, as early as 1947, that this bomb "may have a destructive effect, a hundred, a thousand, nay ten thousand times greater than the bombs dropped on Hiroshima and Nagasaki. Its effect will depend on how great the bomb is and at what height above the earth it is exploded."

In 1950 he addressed a large audience in Carnegie Hall in New York City, still pleading against the development of the hydrogen bomb.

"It is not necessary," he said, "that the social and economic system in Russia be identical with that in the United States in order that these two great nations can be at peace with one another. It is only necessary that the people of the United States and the people of Russia should have respect for one another, a deep desire to work for progress and a mutual recognition that war has finally ruled itself out as the arbiter of the destiny of humanity."

The United States tested its first hydrogen bomb in November 1952 and the Soviet Union exploded another the following year.

Pauling continued to fight. His next move was the Mainau Declaration of July 15, 1955, signed by fifty-two Nobel laureates, most of them scientists. "We do not deny that perhaps peace is being preserved precisely by the fear of these weapons," the declaration admitted. "Nevertheless, we think it is a delusion if governments believe that they can avoid war for a long time through the fear of these weapons. Fear and tension have often engendered wars. Similarly it seems to us a delusion to believe that small conflicts could in the future always be decided by traditional weapons. In extreme danger no nation will deny itself the use of any weapon that scientific technology can produce. All nations must come to the decision to renounce force as a final resort of policy. If they are not prepared to do this, they will cease to exist."

This was the period when America lived in what was almost a paranoic fear of Communist infiltration. Pauling had his passport withheld on several occasions when he wanted to go abroad, and in 1955 had to appear before a committee of the United States Senate that was investigating the Passport Office. He was questioned about his Communist tendencies and had to swear, as he had done earlier, under oath, that he was not a Communist and had never been one.

Meanwhile, as the nuclear tests continued, Pauling turned his energies to yet another danger: the effects of radioactive fall-out on human health and its hereditary aspects. He now began to campaign for an end to nuclear tests.

In a speech at Washington University in May 1957, he said: "I believe that no human being should be sacrificed . . . to the project of perfecting nuclear weapons that could kill hundreds of millions of human beings, could devastate this beautiful world in which we live."

It was after this speech that he drew up what became known as the Pauling Appeal; it was signed by 2,000 American scientists and 8,000 foreign scientists, from a total of forty-nine countries, and it urged an international agreement to stop the testing of nuclear bombs.

In 1958, without entering into an agreement, the Soviet Union, followed by the United States and Great Britain, suddenly stopped conducting nuclear tests.

Now again, an Internal Security Subcommittee of the United States Senate summoned him for interrogation; they wanted to know how the 10,000 signatures had been obtained. It was clear that they regarded the whole appeal as Communist-inspired. Pauling reiterated that he was not and had never been a Communist, but refused to name the many young people who had worked for peace by helping him to collect the signatures. He was risking a prison sentence for contempt of Congress, but was adamant because he felt that they could be victimized if he gave their names. The Senate subcommittee finally dropped the matter.

In 1961 the Soviet Union resumed nuclear testing in the atmosphere, and in March 1962—despite letters which Pauling sent both to Khrushchev and President Kennedy—the United States also resumed its test program. By October 1962 Pauling was pointing out that the tests carried out by the Soviet Union and the United States during the previous year had released twice as much radioactive fallout as all the tests undertaken in the previous sixteen years.

In 1963 discussions on a nuclear test ban had finally made some progress when the United States, the Soviet Union and Great Britain signed an agreement in Moscow not to carry out any further nuclear tests in the atmosphere. Most countries subsequently signed the agreement, though not France or China.

In his Nobel lecture, Pauling referred to Nobel's desire to invent a substance or machine with such terrible power of mass destruction as to render war impossible. "Two-thirds of a century later scientists discovered the explosive substances that Nobel wanted to invent—the fissionable substances uranium and plutonium with explosive energy ten million times that of Nobel's favorite explosive, nitroglycerin; and the fissionable substance lithium deuteride, with explosive energy fifty million times that of nitroglycerin. . . . The 1954 superbomb [the 20-megaton Bikini bomb] contained less than one ton of nuclear explosive. The energy released in the explosion of this bomb was greater than that of all the explosives used in all of the wars that have taken place during the entire history of the world, including the First World War and the Second World War. . . . Thus the machines envisaged by Nobel have come into existence, and war has been made impossible forever."

He quoted a statement made in 1946 by Einstein: "Today the atomic bomb has altered profoundly the nature of the world as we know it, and the human race consequently finds itself in a new habitat to which it must adapt its teaching. . . . Never before was it possible for one nation to make war on another without sending armies across borders. Now with rockets and atomic bombs no center of population on the earth's surface is secure from surprise destruction in a single attack. . . . Few men have ever seen the bomb. But all men if told a few facts can understand that this bomb and the danger of war is a very real thing and not something far away. It directly concerns every person in the civilized world. We cannot leave it to generals, senators and diplomats to work out a solution over a period of generations . . . there is no defense in science against the weapon which can destroy civilization. Our defense is not in armaments, nor in science, nor in going underground. Our defense is law and order. . . . Future thinking must prevent wars."

Pauling referred to the dangers of radiation in increasing the number of mutations and the number of defective children born in future years, which would be approximately proportional to the amount of exposure. On the question of stockpiling, he said that a single 25-megaton bomb could largely destroy any city on earth and kill most of its inhabitants. Yet thousands of these bombs had been manufactured, along with vehicles to deliver them. Precise information about existing stockpiles were not available, but his estimate for 1963 was 320,000 megatons. The significance of that estimated total, he added, might be brought out by the following statement: "If there were to take place tomorrow a 6-megaton war, equivalent to the Second World War in the total power of all explosives used, and another such war the following day and so on, day after day, for 146 years, the present stockpile would be exhausted—but in

270

fact, this stockpile might be used in one single day, the day of the Third World War."

1963

THE INTERNATIONAL COMMITTEE OF THE RED CROSS: *Previously awarded the Peace Prize in 1917 and 1944.*

THE LEAGUE OF RED CROSS SOCIETIES: *Founded in 1919.*

WE HAVE ALREADY dealt with the foundation and early work of the International Committee of the Red Cross; it celebrated its centenary in 1963, and in that year the Nobel Peace Prize was divided between the Committee and the League of Red Cross Societies, founded in May 1919 as an international federation of National Red Cross Societies. By 1963 there were 102 active National Red Cross Societies, comprising about 170,000,000 individual members.

The Red Cross remained through the years wholly independent of any government. Its highest authority is the Red Cross Conference which meets every four years and consists of delegates from the National Red Cross Societies, the International Red Cross Committee, the League of Red Cross Societies and representatives of the governments which have signed the Geneva Convention. A permanent International Red Cross Commission of nine members discusses every problem which arises between conferences and decides where the next conference shall meet.

In making the presentation, Carl Joachim Hambro, a member of the Nobel Committee, drew the distinction between the International Committee and the League. "In many quarters there has been an idea that the Committee as a Swiss body is more completely neutral and impartial than the League. It was the Committee that was asked to take care of all the transportation of aid in Hungary for the uprising of the people, but it was the League that took care of the refugees, at a cost of more than a hundred million Swiss francs; and correspondingly large sums of money were given to the Algerian refugees and to the Congo—and it was a delegate of the Committee who was killed at Katanga.

"It was the Committee that was permitted by the government of Nepal to give aid to the refugees from Tibet—for Switzerland, not being a member of the United Nations, had taken no part in any decision against Communist China. In the same way, it was on the invitation of the Japanese Red Cross, that the Committee repatriated North Korean prisoners of war in Japan. . . . The work of the Committee is so closely coordinated with that of the League that for all practical purposes they form a unity, and in many fields they work hand in hand with the United Nations. The great worldwide humanitarian work of the League falls outside the sphere of the Peace Prize," he admitted, adding that "the cooperation between the Red Cross societies of over ninety different countries of different races, creeds and color is of very real importance to international understanding and peace."

Léopold Boissier, a member of the International Committee of the Red Cross, emphasized the importance of the neutrality of the Committee: they were admitted on the territory of belligerents "for the sole reason that its members are citizens of a small country, with no political ambitions . . . governments can, therefore, have full confidence in its impartiality. The International Committee has no material power. It has no arms and would not even know how to resort to diplomatic maneuver. But its apparent weakness is offset by its moral authority. For just one hundred years now, governments have considered the existence of the International Committee useful. They expect it to carry out tasks which cannot be accomplished by anyone else."

He went on to talk about the changing function of the Red Cross in a changing world. After making the point that there was no complete, up-to-date Convention in force to protect civilians when World War II broke out, he said that since 1949 civilians are entitled to treatment of at least the same standard as that which is meted out to prisoners of war, and that certain guarantees are now given, under Article Three, to combatants in civil wars. Article Three prohibits the taking of hostages and summary executions without fair trial. It lays down humane conditions of internment and the right to protection by the International Committee. This article, he said, had enabled the Committee to intervene in India at the time of its division into India and Pakistan; in Latin America, Algeria, Vietnam, Laos and the Congo.

This article, however, is applicable only in the event of armed conflicts, and the International Committee, he said, was seeking to extend the scope of the convention to bring assistance to persons interned in their own countries as a result of international tensions. "Today, individuals are often treated in their own countries less favorably than enemy soldiers captured with weapons in their hands."

In the autumn of 1962 the International Committee undertook an unusual peace mission: to set up a system to control all ships bound for

Cuba to ensure, through a force of some thirty inspectors, that no long-range atomic weapons were being delivered to Cuba. This was during the Cuban missile crisis when the world seemed on the brink of a "push-button" nuclear war. The International Committee succeeded in getting consent to the search not only from the three main parties concerned—the United States, the Soviet Union and Cuba—but from all maritime powers whose ships called at Cuba. The tension finally subsided before the International Committee was required to intervene, but the exercise represented a peace-maintenance task which perhaps it alone could have successfully performed.

"When war creates its tragic gap between nations," Boissier said, "the Red Cross remains the last link. . . . The Red Cross, therefore, makes a powerful appeal to all men in favor of peace."

1964

MARTIN LUTHER KING, JR. (1929–1968), United States: *Leader of the first great nonviolent demonstration of contemporary times in the southern states of America, a member of the executive committee of the National Association for the Advancement of Colored People and the man primarily responsible for the Civil Rights Bill of 1964.*

IN DECEMBER 1955 a Mrs. Rosa Parks, a black American housewife, was sitting in a bus in Montgomery, Alabama, in the section reserved for blacks; she was occupying one of the seats just behind the white section, which was filled. She was ordered to give up her seat to a white man and when she refused, she was arrested.

This tiny incident sparked off a great wave of nonviolent demonstration that swept through the South and culminated in a Civil Rights Act making segregation illegal. The leader of this movement was a Baptist pastor, Martin Luther King, Jr. He was only twenty-six when he organized a ban on the buses in protest against Mrs. Parks's treatment—for 382 days not a single black traveled on a bus in Montgomery—and only thirty-five when he was awarded the Nobel Peace Prize, making him the youngest laureate in the history of the prize.

Both his father and his grandfather had been Baptist pastors in Atlanta, Georgia. King attended segregated public schools in Georgia and received his B.A. degree in 1948 at Morehouse College, a black institution in Atlanta from which both his father and grandfather had graduated. He then spent three years at Crozer Theological Seminary in Pennsylvania, where he was awarded a B.D. and a fellowship. He enrolled in graduate studies at Boston University taking his doctorate in philosophy in 1955.

From 1954 he was pastor of the Dexter Avenue Baptist Church in Montgomery, Alabama. He was by this time deeply involved in the struggle for civil rights for his people and a member of the executive committee of the National Association for the Advancement of Colored People (NAACP), the leading organization of its kind in America.

During the bus boycott of 1955, he emerged as a natural leader and was subjected to a great deal of abuse; he was arrested, his home was bombed, and there were threats against his family. But on December 21, 1956, after the Supreme Court had decided that the laws enforcing segregation on buses were unconstitutional, blacks and whites were free to ride on buses everywhere as equals, though that did not necessarily stop their harassment.

His speeches during the campaign started a nonviolent war on the discrimination between blacks and whites in restaurants, shops, schools, public parks and playgrounds.

In his presentation speech, the chairman of the Nobel Committee said: "Despite laws passed by Congress and judgments given by the American Supreme Court, this struggle has not proved successful everywhere, since these laws and judgments have been sabotaged, as anyone who has followed the course of events subsequent to 1955 knows. Despite sabotage and imprisonment, the Negroes have continued their unarmed struggle. Only rarely have they acted against the principle given to them by requiting violence with violence, even though for many of us this would have been the natural reaction. What can we say of the young students who sat down in an eating place reserved for whites? They were not served, but they remained seated. White teenagers mocked and insulted them, and stubbed their lighted cigarettes out on their necks. The black students sat unmoving. They possessed the strength that only belief can give, the belief that they fight in a just cause and that their struggle will lead to victory because they wage it with peaceful means."

Though a devout Christian, King was deeply influenced by the life and work of Mahatma Gandhi. "Gandhi," he once said, "was probably the first person in history to lift the love ethic of Jesus above mere interaction between individuals to a powerful and effective social force. . . . I found in the nonviolent resistance philosophy of Gandhi . . . the only morally and practically sound method open to oppressed people in their struggle for freedom."

In the eleven-year period between 1957 and 1968, King traveled over six million miles, gave over 2,500 lectures and speeches, wrote five books and innumerable articles. He planned the campaign in Alabama for the registration of blacks as voters, led the peaceful march on Washington, D.C., in August 1963 of 250,000 people, and was largely responsible for the Civil Rights Bill introduced by President Kennedy and signed into law by President Johnson in 1964. He was arrested more than twenty times and assaulted at least four times.

In the presentation address he was described as "the first person in the Western world to have shown us that a struggle can be waged without violence." He continued to further that struggle by donating his prize money to the civil rights movement.

In his Nobel lecture King explained his philosophy of nonviolence: "[It] . . . has meant that my people in the agonizing struggles of recent years have taken suffering upon themselves instead of inflicting it on others. It has meant . . . that we are no longer afraid and cowed. But in some substantial degree it has meant that we do not want to instill fear in others or into the society of which we are a part. The movement does not seek to liberate Negroes at the expense of the humiliation and enslavement of the whites. It seeks no victory over anyone. It seeks to liberate American society and to share in the self-liberation of all the people. . . . It seeks to secure moral ends through moral means. Nonviolence is a powerful and just weapon. Indeed, it is a weapon unique in history, which cuts without wounding and ennobles the man who wields it."

On the evening of April 4, 1968, as he was standing on the balcony of a motel in Memphis, Tennessee—where he was going to lead a peaceful protest march the next day in sympathy with striking garbage workers—King was shot dead by a sniper.

1965

THE UNITED NATIONS CHILDREN'S FUND* (UNICEF): *Founded in December 1946.*

AWARE PERHAPS THAT some people would argue that an organization set up initially to distribute food, clothing and medical aid to children suffering in the aftermath of World War II cannot really be regarded as

* Formerly the United Nations International Children's Emergency Fund.

contributing in any positive way to world peace, Mrs. Aase Lionaes, a member of the Nobel Committee, stated that UNICEF fulfilled one condition of Nobel's will: the promotion of brotherhood among the nations. Indeed, she recalled that when UNICEF was founded, there was a great deal of argument in the United Nations itself as to whether what was basically a political forum should concern itself with such peripheral problems as aid to children. During the war, UNRRA had carried out humanitarian work on behalf of children, prisoners and refugees; in 1946, when the organization was being wound up, many people in the United Nations thought that the care of children in peace time could well be left to the various national children's organizations.

The problem in Europe, however, proved too acute to be solved by local organizations. After five years of war and occupation, there were twenty million children in urgent need of care in refugee camps and in bombed towns and villages in Hungary, Yugoslavia, Albania, Poland, Italy, Greece, Rumania and Austria. During the winter of 1947–48, UNICEF gave six million children and mothers in fourteen countries at least one meal a day as well as providing clothing and medical supplies for them.

In Europe economic recovery was rapid; and within four or five years, most countries were able to look after their own children. However, by that time, another, much graver problem faced UNICEF: the plight of the children in the countries in Africa and Asia that were suddenly and abruptly breaking away from colonial rule. In one single year, 1960, seventeen new states appeared on the map of Africa; and the ever-present problem of hunger in India was exacerbated by the bitter fighting that broke out between the Hindus and the Moslems in the years immediately after the British cleared out in 1947.

Originally UNICEF had been envisaged purely as a temporary measure to solve the problem of Europe's children; in 1953 it became a permanent child-aid organization, with its main focus on the developing countries. UNICEF can, of course, only work in countries whose governments are agreeable to its operations, and an initial stipulation was that all countries receiving aid must match the UNICEF contribution in each aid program. The idea was that UNICEF would provide technical assistance and advice as well as commodities and equipment which had to be purchased with foreign currency, while the recipient country would make an equal contribution in the form of its own products, local personnel, transport facilities and so on. In fact, the scheme has worked so well that most countries receiving UNICEF aid now contribute the equivalent of two and a half dollars for every dollar contributed by UNICEF.

UNICEF is financed by gifts from governments, private individuals and organizations all over the world. In 1964, the year before the award was made, it had received 33 million dollars from 118 countries, to finance programs embracing 115 developing countries with a total population of 750 million children.

Initially, there was no general agreement in UNICEF on the question of priorities. Some members believed that a start should be made by combating such national scourges as malaria, trachoma, tuberculosis, and yaws. Others felt that the prime requirement was adequate nourishment, and were convinced that once malnutrition had been eliminated, disease would be that much easier to control. Both of these courses of action seemed feasible in view of the rapid advance in medical science and the tremendous surplus stores of grain and meat in the Western countries. On the other hand, a third group felt that the prime urgency was to overcome illiteracy since an uneducated population would never be able to achieve the economic growth ultimately necessary to take care of its own problems.

In effect, the problems were approached simultaneously, in the World Health Organization (WHO) and the Food and Agricultural Association (FAO).

The statistics representing the first twenty-five years of UNICEF activity are impressive: 71 million children examined for trachoma and 43 million treated; 425 million examined for yaws and 23 million treated; 400 million vaccinated against tuberculosis; countless millions protected from malaria, and 415,000 discharged as cured of leprosy; 12,000 health centers and several thousand maternity wards established in eighty-five countries; help given to provide equipment for 2,500 teacher training schools, 56,000 primary and secondary schools, 965 vocational schools, 31 schools for training vocational instructors, 600 for training dietary personnel; equipment supplied for 4,000 nutrition centers and community gardens, and for 9,000 school gardens and canteens; supplementary meals and articles of clothing dispensed in billions—quite apart from emergency aid to hundreds of thousands victimized by floods, earthquakes and other national disasters.

Mrs. Lionaes ended her talk by referring to the cost of the operation and the difficulty of finding funds to finance new programs. "Possibilities for viable projects far exceed UNICEF's financial capabilities, and it has been necessary to impose a ceiling on allocations. It is an agonizing predicament to know that millions of children will die each year, who might have lived if it were not for lack of funds." She added bitterly that there was little hope, at the present rate of contributions, of an annual budget from all sources exceeding a total of thirty-five million dollars, and yet there is no world shortage of nuclear submarines, which cost $200 million each.

1966-1967

Prizes not awarded.

1968

RENÉ-SAMUEL CASSIN (1887–   ), France: *International jurist, humanitarian, French delegate to the League of Nations, de Gaulle's minister of justice in exile during the war, and architect, with Eleanor Roosevelt, of the United Nations Charter of Human Rights.*

CASSIN, AT EIGHTY-ONE, was among the oldest of the Nobel laureates; he was awarded the prize, according to the citation, for his "respect for human worth, irrespective of nationality, sex or social position . . . and for his contribution to the protection of human worth and the rights of man, as set out in the Universal Declaration of Human Rights."

Borne in Bayonne, France, the son of a merchant, he studied at the Lycée in Nice and took a degree in humanities and another in law at the University of Aix-en-Provence. In 1914 he became a doctor in juridical, economic and political sciences. He had begun his career as a counsel in Paris when war broke out and he was called up for service with the infantry. Severely wounded in 1916 by German shrapnel, he was only saved by the coincidence that his mother happened to be serving as a nurse in the field hospital to which he was taken, and was able to persuade the surgeons to operate.

"That war put its indelible and unmistakable stamp on me, as it did on many of my contemporaries," Cassin said. "It wasn't so much the spectacular horror of the battlefields or the suffering in the hospitals that marked us, it was the agonized perception of the lasting and wasteful consequences of the war: the disabled soldiers, the families deprived of their last supporting member—dead for the welfare of all. I was not able to accept the idea that national solidarity with those victims should limit itself to a kind of charitable alms. That is why I soon joined those who fought—and victoriously—for recognition of the right to compensation for personal damages incurred in the service of the national community. Human dignity and the general welfare of our country, then depleted in manpower, demanded that in addition to being given the traditional pensions our numerous disabled veterans be reintegrated into society by such measures as artificial limb banks, professional retraining programs, and loans for establishing small businesses, and that our 800,000 orphaned minors be brought up and educated under the special protection of the nation.''

To carry out this work he formed and directed the Union Fédérale des Associations des Mutilés et d'Anciens Combattants [Federal Union of Associations of Disabled War Veterans] and was vice-president of the Conseil Supérieur des Pupilles de la Nation [High Council for Wards of the Nation].

His work on behalf of war victims was not limited to France. From 1921 he arranged conferences of war veterans from Italy, Poland, Germany, Czechoslovakia and Austria, and tried, through the International Labor Organization, to organize war veterans who had formerly been enemies to demonstrate together in support of the Disarmament Conference of 1932; he also worked for disarmament as a French delegate within the League of Nations.

When the German invasion of France in 1940 was followed by a brief armistice, René Cassin was among the first to leave Bordeaux in response to General de Gaulle's plea. He became de Gaulle's minister of justice in exile and was responsible for drawing up the agreement between Churchill and de Gaulle which became the charter of the Free French forces.

In private life he had been a professor of law, first at Lille and then in Paris, and when France was liberated in 1945 he became president of the Council of the National School of Administration. In 1960 he became president of the French National Overseas Center of Advanced Studies. He also served as president of several organizations, among them the French branch of the World Federation of Democratic Jurists, the Society of Comparative Legislation and the International Institute of Diplomatic Studies and Research. From 1944 to 1960 he was vice-president of the Council of State, and a member of the Constitutional Council, which like the American Supreme Court adjudicates on whether laws passed by the legislature are constitutional. He was a member of the Court of Arbitration at The Hague from 1950 to 1960 and president of the European Court of Human Rights at Strasbourg from 1965 to 1968.

But the award was made specifically for his work in connection with the Declaration of Human Rights. After World War II when the full horrors of the Nazi concentration camps and the planned extermination of the Jews became widely known, the general reaction found its expression in demands made on all governments to prevent a repetition by adopting an International Bill of Rights.

In 1945 the United Nations included the establishment of a Commission on Human Rights in its charter. The Commission's job was to compose a Universal Declaration of Human Rights and an international convention which would bind the states to preserve these rights.

Eleanor Roosevelt—widow of Franklin Roosevelt—became chairman of the Commission, and René Cassin its vice-chairman; and it was Cassin who actually drafted the declaration. It was, perhaps, a curious coincidence that these two people represented two nations which, about a hundred and fifty years earlier, had adopted the first declarations setting out the basic rights of man: the American Declaration of Independence of 1776 and the French Declaration of the Rights of Man of 1789.

In her presentation speech, Mrs. Aase Lionaes, chairman of the Nobel Committee, pointed out what a difficult task confronted them.

"To be sure," she said, "the United Nations Charter does mention several times that it will promote human rights. But we do not find these rights defined anywhere in the Charter. So the question was: what did human rights mean to the people from these fifty or sixty nations, coming as they did from all parts of the world, and from different levels of cultural development, with diverse traditions, religions and ideologies. The western European peoples have a somewhat similar understanding of this concept. But what do the Chinese, the Indonesians, and the people on Haiti see in the words *freedom, equality* and *cultural and economic rights*? Were there in general any points of contact between the welfare states' conception of those terms and that of the developing countries? For example, in the European countries, we can agree readily on what we mean by 'the woman's legal position in society.' But how is it interpreted by the people in those parts of the world where a woman's value is equated with that of four camels?"

In view of these difficulties it is perhaps not surprising that the Commission took two years to formulate a declaration which everyone could accept at the UN General Assembly in Paris in 1948. Even with a completely prepared draft before it, the UN spent two months—ninety-seven meetings and 1,200 ballots on proposed amendments—finally approving Cassin's draft.

The countries which voted for the Declaration did not commit themselves but declared themselves "in agreement" that all people should have the right to life, liberty and security of person; that all are equal before the law; that everyone is entitled to freedom of conscience, of religion, of expression, and of assembly; that everyone is entitled to work, to equal compensation for equal work, to reasonable working hours and to free education.

In an effort to make the declaration binding on the states which had agreed to it in principle, René Cassin prepared twin Covenants* which were unanimously adopted by the United Nations' General Assembly in December 1966, eighteen years after acceptance of the Declaration.

Twenty years later, Cassin, in the year he won the Peace Prize, wrote in an article in the *Jerusalem Post*: "The Declaration holds up an ideal for us, and it draws the guide lines for our actions. But a glance at reality today is enough to show us that we are far from the ideal. No country, not even the most advanced, can pride itself on fulfilling all the articles of the Declaration. Once the war and the ideals for which we fought have faded into the distance and new states have gained their independence, they are inclined to conduct their domestic affairs as they wish, without regard to human rights.

"We are witnessing the violation of the right to live. Murders and massacres are perpetrated with impunity. The exploitation of women, mass hunger, widespread racial discrimination—all these evils are too prevalent to be overlooked."

The sentiment was echoed by Mrs. Lionaes, in the conclusion of her presentation speech: "Today, where there is no respect for human rights and freedom, there is no peace either. Every day youth falls on the battlefield. Every day prisoners are led to prisons and torture chambers. They fight and they suffer for the ideals which the Declaration of Human Rights proclaims."

In his Nobel speech, René Cassin seemed more sanguine. He described the Declaration as "the first document of an ethical sort that organized humanity has ever adopted, and precisely at a time when man's power over nature became vastly increased because of scientific discoveries and when it was essential to decide to what constructive ends these powers should be put.

"The debates before the General Assembly of the United Nations went on for eighteen years. . . . The most powerful cause of delay was the desire of certain powers to put off as long as possible discussion of the—paradoxically quite modest—enforcement measures voted by the Commission on Human Rights, which were considered encroachments on the sovereignty of the states. The final vote attained unanimity in 1966 only because it became inconceivable on the very eve of the International Human Rights Year to prolong the filibuster any further.

*One concerning civil and political rights; the other concerning economic, social and cultural rights.

". . . Henceforth, there should be no doubt about the fundamental question, that of knowing whether the various sovereign states have retained or lost their traditionally exclusive sphere of authority over the manner of dealing with those under their jurisdiction. That jurisdiction of the states will always be a fundamental principle. But it will no longer be exclusive. It will in some situations, as in the case of a complaint formulated under certain conditions and presented before certain international agencies, be possible to transfer it to these agencies, that is to say, to the whole of juridically organized mankind. This will mean two things: first, the permanent accession of every human being to the rank of a member of human society—in legal parlance one would say to the rank of subject of international law; second, it will mean that the states consent to exercise their sovereignty under the authority of international law. . . ."

Fine words, yet today they are still torturing prisoners and interning suspects and executing political opponents in Africa, in South America and in parts of both the Near and the Far East. And behind the Iron Curtain, who knows how many concentration camps still exist?

1969

THE INTERNATIONAL LABOR ORGANIZATION (ILO): *Created in 1919, by the Versailles Treaty.*

FULLY AWARE THAT an organization set up to meet the demands of the world's working people for social justice and a higher standard of living is not, on the face of it, a major contribution to world peace, Mrs. Aase Lionaes, chairman of the Nobel Committee, dropped all reference to peace in her presentation address and flatly remarked that Nobel "states in his will that the Peace Prize is to be awarded to the person who has done the most to promote fraternity among the nations," adding that it was with this consideration in mind that they had decided to award the Peace Prize to the International Labor Organization. Beneath the foundation stone in the ILO's office in Geneva, she added, as a further justification, lies a document on which is written: *"Si vis pacem, cole justitiam"* [If you desire peace, cultivate justice].

During World War I, tens of thousands of working class people had flocked to the colors, laying aside their own pressing claims for a better deal in order to serve their countries. In the course of the fighting they bore the brunt of the suffering and even the most docile, nonmilitant of them couldn't fail to see that their "masters" were not the intelligent, far-sighted supermen they had previously assumed them to be.

Consequently, when the war ended, at the trade union congresses of 1916, 1917 and 1918, urgent demands were made that the trade union movement should participate in the discussions on the peace treaty.

And with the examples of the Russian Revolution of 1917 and the German Revolution of 1918 ever before their eyes, the architects of the Versailles Treaty realized that if they wanted to avoid the same thing in their own countries, the treaty should include provisions which aimed to secure peace not only among the nations but between the classes.

As a result, the Peace Conference set up an international committee for labor legislation. This included not only delegates from the various governments concerned, but also representatives both of employers and employees, including Samuel Gompers, president of the American Federation of Labor, and Léon Jouhaux, the French trade unionist who was Nobel Peace Prize Winner for 1951.

The Versailles Treaty contained nine points which are regarded as the Magna Carta of the working class. They include the rights of employees as well as employers, to organize themselves; the right of workers to receive a reasonable wage; an eight-hour day or forty-eight-hour week; a ban on child labor; equal pay for men and women doing the same work; and a system of labor inspection in which women, too, should be allowed to play their part in insuring adherence to labor legislation.

During World War II, the ILO moved its organization to Montreal, Canada, and after the war it was linked to the United Nations Organization as an independent specialized body.

In the postwar period the disintegration of the European colonies had a profound effect on the ILO. The flood of new member states, principally from Africa, meant that it was no longer an essentially European organization concerned with conditions in industrialized Europe but had to cope with the problems of people representing all races and religions in the world, with traditions, cultures, and economic and social patterns very different from those with which the ILO had previously been dealing.

On the surface, this called primarily for a program of technical aid for the developing countries, and indeed, working in cooperation with the UN and its other specialized branches, FAO, UNESCO, WHO and with financial support from the UN, the International Labor Organization has carried out research projects and made basic investments in a number of underdeveloped countries, with the object of assisting them to increase their agricultural and industrial output.

There have, however, been major problems arising out of ILO's structure, with independent delegates representing governments, free trade unions and employers' associations. Many of the new states in Africa and Asia have not yet developed any free labor organizations, and the governments nominate both workers' and employers' representatives, a system which runs directly counter to everything that the ILO stands for. Another problem is the fact that although a certain growth can be achieved in the economic life of these countries, improved medical care has resulted in a population explosion which looks like vitiating the whole effort.

By 1969, when the ILO received the Peace Prize, it had more than nine hundred experts of fifty-five different nationalities working on more than three hundred technical cooperation projects in over a hundred countries around the world, trying to find an answer to these problems.

The third activity of the ILO, standard-setting and technical cooperation, is backed up by an extensive research, training, education and publications program. The ILO headquarters in Geneva, Switzerland, is a major source of publications and documentation on labor and social matters, and has established two educational institutions: the International Institute for Labor Studies in Geneva, and the International Center for Advanced Technical and Vocational Training in Turin, Italy.

The ILO is staffed by three thousand people of different nationalities: its deliberative body is the annual International Labor Conference, composed of four representatives from each member country, two government delegates, one trade union delegate and one delegate representing the employers. Between conferences, the work of the ILO is guided by a governing body composed of twenty-four government, twelve worker and twelve employer members.

David A. Morse, an American lawyer, former secretary of labor, and director general of the ILO from 1948 to 1970, stressed in his Nobel lecture the importance of social justice as a basic foundation for secure world peace. "The workers' demands for effective international action have often been in contrast with the views of governments, which have seen in the ILO an instrument for strengthening the stability of the sovereign national state. And while the ILO has of course lived and operated in a world of sovereign states, it has nevertheless extended the scope and possibilities of transnational action. In this way, and in spite of the political calamities, failures and disappointments of the past half-century, it has patiently, undramatically, but not unsuccessfully, worked to build an *infrastructure of peace.*

"The ILO is still the only worldwide organization where international cooperation is the business not only of diplomats and government representatives, but also of representatives of employers and workers. It thus provides opportunities for contacts and for greater understanding within as well as among the three groups. It is only within the ILO that the different trends in the international trade union movement . . . can come together and seek common solutions to common problems. And it is only in the ILO that free-enterprise employers meet regularly with managers of state enterprises in socialist countries. . . . Today, despite the very great differences among ILO's member states, governments, workers and employers have at least learned to live together in the ILO and, after years of mutual suspicion, are beginning to find a larger measure of common ground."

Towards the end of his lecture, David Morse referred to a problem which had become increasingly disturbing in the highly developed, urban industrial societies throughout the sixties: the student revolts which in many cases have spread and involved workers of all kinds.

"This is a novel situation, because the men and women are not in revolt because they are victims of poverty, injustice or oppression. . . . I venture to suggest that it may be a sign of widespread boredom and frustration at the colorless technological civilization in which we live and in which we are prepared to make too many sacrifices to material progress; that it may be frustration over the seeming inability of the existing institutions of industrial societies to seize the almost unlimited opportunities offered by today's technology, opportunities for greater freedom and for all people to lead fuller and richer lives in a spiritual as well as a material sense. . . . The challenge before us now is to make industrialized societies more human, to make man the master rather than the slave of modern technology, to offer more possibilities for the constructive use of leisure, for greater freedom, for greater participation, for more effective dialogue. For there is a serious danger that the fabric of these societies will be torn asunder by the complete disruption of the economic, social and political life of the nation, unless new ways can be found of developing new institutions, new forms of authority, even new social values, which are acceptable to the population as a whole."

The Sobering Seventies

I DO NOT propose to trace the course of events during the first five years of this decade in the same detail as I have done in earlier chapters. For one thing, the events are still so close that it is hard to be objective. For another, they are still close enough to remember clearly. Can anyone have forgotten Watergate and that desperate, haggard look on Richard Nixon's face as he lied again and again and again into the TV cameras? Or the fall of Saigon and the sight of all those helicopters carrying South Vietnamese American sympathizers, American embassy officials, and American and foreign newsmen out to the waiting aircraft carriers? Or the sudden flare-up in the Sinai Desert and along the Golan Heights in October 1973, now known as the Yom Kippur War, which resulted indirectly in the oil crisis that brought about a world recession, the effects of which are with us yet and may, some people believe, herald the beginning of the end of the Western way of life?

It has been, above all, a time of disillusion. Most of us suspected that our politicians were a little corrupt—it's in the nature of the game—but few were prepared for the depths of degradation that were revealed during the endless days of the Watergate trials. Such revelations will make it difficult for people in the Western world to put very much trust in their leaders for a long time.

The fall of Saigon and the sudden collapse of the whole American commitment in the Far East was another shattering blow to American prestige and self-respect. That so many American lives should have been lost in Vietnam was tragedy enough; that they should have been lost for nothing was intolerable. Henry Kissinger received the Nobel Peace Prize for his part in achieving the peace, but the reward was not a popular one: many people felt that, as Nixon's principal adviser, he must also have been instrumental in the heavy bombing that continued almost until the end; and they sensed also that peace, when it came, would amount to leaving the South Vietnamese to their fate, whatever that turned out to be. That there wasn't the blood bath which many people expected is to the credit of the North Vietnamese; so, too, is the fact that the North Vietnamese negotiator Le Duc Tho turned down his share of the Nobel Peace Prize because he felt that no real peace had been achieved.

Nor can anyone have forgotten what happened in Portugal in the period following Salazar's death in July 1970, or the Turkish invasion of Cyprus in 1974; or that on May 31 of that year India exploded an atomic device, making her the sixth nuclear power after the US, Russia, the United Kingdom, France and China; or the arrival on the African scene of Idi Amin, who shored up his arrogant authority with unspeakable atrocities and sent the Indian traders in Uganda packing; or the continuing terrorism everywhere—at Lod International Airport in Israel on May 30, 1972, when three Japanese gunmen employed by Palestinian guerrillas killed 25 people and wounded 76; in Northern Ireland, where in one day on July 21, 1972, twenty-two bombs exploded in eighty minutes, killing 13 persons and wounding 130; at the Munich Olympic Games on September 5, 1972, when Black September Palestinian guerrillas forced their way into the Israeli village, shot two athletes and held nine others hostage for several hours before they were transported to Munich where the hostages, five terrorists and one West German policeman all died.

The space program went on, largely unheeded. In April 1972 Apollo 16 splashed down in the Pacific after John Young and Charles Duke had spent seventy-one hours and two minutes on the moon. Things did sometimes go wrong in space: two Soyuz 11 cosmonauts were found dead in their re-entry capsule after a flight that had set a new space endurance record. But by now people were far less concerned with space exploration than with the very survival of their way of life on the earth. Britain adopted a decimal currency based on the one-pound note rather than the ten-shilling note, and the result was an inflationary epidemic that resulted eventually in a floating pound, which by the spring of 1976 had dropped well below the two-dollar mark. In April 1971 the United States Council of Economic Advisers issued its third inflation-alert warning and in July of that year the US Secretary of Commerce warned Congress that the United States might expect a deficit in the balance of trade for the first time this century.

As early as that, long before the Yom Kippur War even, the oil-exporting countries and representatives of the Western oil companies had begun talks to discuss "more realistic" payments for the now rapidly diminishing supplies of oil. Britain found oil of her own in the North Sea, but the cost of developing the rigs and techniques to get it out from under the seabed meant mortgaging most of the profit long before the first pint was piped ashore in 1975.

And when, after the Yom Kippur War, the oil sheiks started to get really tough, there was overreaction for a few weeks—gasoline ration cards were printed, speed restrictions imposed in some countries, Sunday motoring banned in others—but superficially, the only lasting effect was that all over the world oil prices almost doubled. I say superficially, because the oil crisis has had deeper implications which have had a very sobering effect on the whole Western world. For the first time perhaps, we have begun to wonder about the wisdom of an economy based not only on precarious supplies of a dwindling fuel, but also based on the assumption that the gross national product of every developed and developing country could and should go on increasing indefinitely.

It was also a period of détente. Relations between Russia and the United States had never seemed more cordial; in February 1972 Nixon traveled to China to meet Mao Tse-tung; and in October 1974, incredibly, Yasir Arafat, the Palestinian terrorist leader, was invited to address the United Nations for the first time.

Harry Truman and Lester Pearson and Lyndon B. Johnson and Louis Armstrong died; and Solzhenitsyn, the 1970 Nobel Literary laureate, settled down in the West and turned prophet of doom, using the hospitality of the Western world's radio and television networks to castigate his listeners and viewers for their flippant complacency as they stood on the very brink of catastrophe.

With the US commitment in the Far East at last ended, the focus of attention naturally shifted to Africa, a continent in which, until now, America had shown no interest whatever.

The Portuguese left Angola late in 1975 and a few months later a very confused situation between competing native factions was resolved by the unexpected arrival of well-disciplined Cuban forces, armed with the latest Russian weapons. Britain immediately put new pressure on Smith of Rhodesia to prepare the way for majority (black) rule—"not in a thousand years" was Smith's typically tactless and inflammatory reply—and Henry Kissinger suddenly developed a keen concern for the rights of black African majorities. It looks like there is going to be an anxious time in Africa for anybody who believes in human life more strongly than in spheres of influence.

It is impossible, in the mid-seventies, to shake off the feeling that something has gone terribly wrong and that things must get worse before they get better, if they ever do. We have been so wrong about so many things.

But throughout all of this the Norwegian Nobel Committee has gone on doling out prizes for peace . . .

1970 Neil Borlaug

1971 Willy Brandt

1972
Prize not awarded

1973 Henry Kissinger

1973
Le Duc Tho
[Declined prize]

1974 Sean MacBride

1974 Eisaku Sato

1975 Andrei Sakharov

1970

NORMAN ERNEST BORLAUG (1914–), United States: *Geneticist, plant pathologist and architect of the "green revolution," he developed a high-yield, short-strawed, disease-resistant wheat, ideally adapted for use in the developing nations of the Third World.*

IN THE CITATION for 1970, the Nobel Committee stated that it was awarding the prize to Dr. Norman Borlaug, a scientist, "because more than any other single person of his age, he has helped to provide bread for a hungry world. We have made this choice in the hope that providing bread will also give the world peace."

Norman Borlaug came from Norwegian farming stock in Cresco, Iowa, and initially studied forestry at the University of Minnesota. After working for a period for the US Forestry Service in Massachusetts and Idaho, he returned to the University of Minnesota to study plant pathology, receiving his doctorate in 1942.

From 1942 to 1944 he was a microbiologist on the staff of the Du Pont de Nemours Foundation, where he was in charge of research on industrial and agricultural fungicides and preservatives.

In 1944 he became a geneticist and plant pathologist with the Rockefeller Foundation, which had just launched an ambitious agricultural program in Mexico, in conjunction with the Mexican government, to increase and improve Mexico's food supplies. Here Dr. Borlaug and his assistants developed new breeds of grain which have resulted in unexpectedly dramatic improvements in the quality and quantity of the harvest. For twenty-seven years he collaborated with Mexican scientists on developing a new, high-yield, disease-free, dwarf wheat; and for the last ten of those years, worked with scientists from other countries, notably India and Pakistan, to adapt his new strains of wheat to their particular needs.

"I am impatient and do not accept the need for slow change and evolution to improve the agriculture and food production of the emerging countries," he wrote. "I advocate instead a 'yield-kick' or a 'yield blast-off.' There is no time to be lost considering the magnitude of the world food and population problem." Inevitably, with this attitude, he came up against red tape and the delays of bureaucracy. His comment: "Strangulation of the world by well-camouflaged bureaucracies is one of the great threats to mankind."

The older, long-bladed varieties of wheat gave increased yields but tended to snap when given an overdose of artificial fertilizer. The new dwarf varieties were capable of standing up to two or three times the regular dosage of fertilizer, which meant that the output per decare [$\frac{1}{10}$ of a hectare] could be increased from 450 to 800 kilos [990 to 1,760 lbs.]. They can also be used all over the world because they are not affected by varying periods of daylight and are highly resistant to the traditional enemies of wheat, like rust fungus.

By switching over to Borlaug's dwarf wheat, Mexico became self-supporting by 1956 and in more recent years has even become an exporter of grain. In 1959 Borlaug introduced the dwarf wheat in Pakistan, where there was a steady annual deficit, with yields as low as 100 kilos [220 lbs.] per decare. After a brief struggle to break down local prejudice against the new wheat—it was said to cause sterility, a questionable disadvantage, if true, in Pakistan—Borlaug persuaded the nation to import some of the Mexican seedcorn: within a very few years Pakistan was self-sufficient in wheat. In 1963 the "green revolution" spread to India, and five years later the highest output in the history of the country was achieved, an output high enough to rate a commemorative stamp marking "The Indian Wheat Revolution of 1968."

Since then, the new dwarf wheat has been tried out in Turkey, Afghanistan, Iran, Iraq, Tunisia, Morocco, Lebanon and the Soviet Union.

In her presentation speech, Mrs. Aase Lionaes, chairman of the Nobel Committee, pointed out that new technology in agriculture should also stimulate other branches of the economy, such as various kinds of construction work. The increase in crop yields would require the building of artificial fertilizer factories, roads, irrigation works, railways, warehouses, silos and mills, with the resultant spin-off in the form of more money to build schools and hospitals.

In his Nobel lecture, Dr. Borlaug said: "In the affluent, industrialized nations giant surpluses of wheat, maize and sorghum are commonplace; cattle, swine and poultry are fed and fattened on cereal grains; meat, milk eggs, fruit and vegetables are within the economic reach of most of the population; well-balanced diets are more or less automatically achieved, and cereal products constitute only a modest portion of the 'daily bread.' Consequently most of the people in such societies have difficulty in comprehending and appreciating the vital significance of providing high-yielding strains of wheat, rice, maize, sorghum and millet for the people of the developing nations. . . . They know that food comes from the supermarket, but only a few see beyond to the necessary investments, the toil, struggle and frustration on the farms and ranches that provide their daily bread. Since the urbanites have lost their contact with the soil, they take food for granted and fail to appreciate the tremendous efficiency of their farmers and ranchers who, although constituting only five per cent of the labor force in a country such as the United States, produce more than enough food for their nation."

"In most of the countries of Asia and Africa, however," he went on, "seventy to eighty percent of the population is engaged in agriculture, mostly at the subsistence level. The land is tired, worn out and depleted of nutrients; crop yields have been low, near starvation level, and stagnant for centuries. Hunger prevails and survival depends largely on the success or failure of the cereal crops. In these nations both undernutrition and malnutrition are widespread and a constant threat to survival and to the attainment of the genetic potential for mental and physical development. Animal proteins are so scarce and expensive as to be beyond the economic reach of the vast majority of the population.

"For the underprivileged billions in the forgotten world, hunger has been a constant companion, and starvation has all too often lurked in the nearby shadows. To millions of these unfortunates, who have long lived in despair, the green revolution seems like a miracle that has generated new hope for the future. . . . Never before in the history of agriculture has a transplantation of high-yielding varieties coupled with an entirely new technology and strategy been used on such a massive scale, in so short a period of time, and with such great success."

He ended his lecture, however, on a warning note: "Most people still fail to comprehend the magnitude and menace of the 'Population Monster.' . . . By the time of Christ, the world population had probably reached 250 million. . . . Between then and now, it has grown to 3.5 billion. . . . If it continues to increase at the present estimated rate of two percent a year, the world population will reach 6.5 billion by the year 2000. . . . Where will it all end?

"Since man is potentially a rational being, I am confident that within the next two decades he will realize the self-destructive course he steers along the road of irresponsible population growth and will adjust the growth rate to levels which will permit a decent standard of living for all mankind."

1971

WILLY BRANDT (1913–   ), West Germany: *As mayor of Berlin, minister of foreign affairs in West Germany's coalition government and then chancellor of West Germany (1969–1974), he was largely responsible for initiating Ostpolitik, a more active policy of détente in relation to the Soviet Union, East Germany and the Eastern European Countries generally.*

"MEN CANNOT LIVE without hope and faith," said Aase Lionaes of the Nobel Committee in making the presentation address to Willy Brandt. "So we would hope, so we would wish to believe that the reconciliatory hand extended by Willy Brandt across the old enemy frontiers will be accepted and seized in the same spirit of goodwill. If this hope of peace is realized, Willy Brandt will live in our history as the great German chancellor of peace and reconciliation."

Born in Lübeck in 1913, Willy Brandt grew up in Hitler's increasingly totalitarian Germany and was deeply affected by what he saw. In 1933, at the age of nineteen, he emigrated to Norway as a political refugee where he divided his time between working as a journalist and helping the victims of Naziism, both refugees and prisoners in concentration camps.

When Norway was invaded in 1940, Brandt, like so many others, fled to Sweden. He had been stripped of his German citizenship by the Nazi government, and now became a Norwegian citizen, though living in Sweden. While there, he continued to work for a democratic Germany and a free Norway and wrote several books and articles on Norway's struggle against the Germans. When the war ended, he received numerous offers from Norwegian and international newspapers and magazines, but after working for the Norwegian press for one year in Berlin, he decided to turn to the service of his country.

He began to work first for a free Berlin, because he was convinced that the defeat of Berlin carried in it the germ of a defeat for any hope of peace in Europe.

According to the Nobel Committee's presentation address: "As mayor of Berlin, at a time when the city was menaced by political pressures which eventually crystallized in the form of the Berlin Wall of 1961, Willy Brandt was, in critical situations, proof of a moderation and a courage, often a despairing courage, which saved Berlin from the risks of an immense catastrophe."

His career took him to Bonn and to the Bundestag. He became president of the Social Democratic party and in 1961 and 1965 was their candidate for federal chancellor, though he was unsuccessful.

In 1966 the Christian Democrats and the Social Democrats formed a coalition government in which Brandt was vice-chancellor and minister for foreign affairs. In 1969 he became chancellor, this time in a new coalition between the Social Democrats and Liberals. Like Conrad Adenauer, the first chancellor of the Federal Republic, Brandt believed that West Germany was part of Western Europe and eagerly sought military and economic cooperation with Germany's former enemies. Convinced that a strong Western Europe was necessary before confrontation could be turned into collaboration with Eastern Europe, he always fought for the introduction of new members, particularly the United Kingdom, to the European Economic Community (EEC), a policy which before his emergence had been implacably opposed by France.

"The day will arrive," he had written in *After the Victory* (1944), "when the inevitable hate of wartime will be forgotten. It must then become a reality, this Europe in which we can all live as Europeans."

The first concrete result of Brandt's efforts to create a climate of détente in his relations with the Soviet Union came in August 1970 with the signing of the nonaggression pact in Moscow. In December of the same year, an agreement to regularize relations between West Germany and Poland was concluded. In Warsaw he said: "I have a feeling that this is a difficult journey. It will have its importance for the future of peace. The Warsaw agreements will put an end to the sufferings and sacrifices of a somber past. They will create a climate of conciliation between two states and two peoples. They will allow dispersed families to be reunited as our frontiers separate us less than in the past."

Brandt also worked hard to ease the regulations regarding the right of East Berliners to visit their relatives in the West, and succeeded in getting a measure of agreement. "The terms of the Berlin agreement," he said, "naturally cannot resolve all the problems of the city on a long-term basis. This will not be possible until we are a little nearer a peaceful European control. The wall still exists. But at least it is more open."

In his Nobel lecture, Willy Brandt stressed the importance of the concept of a pan-European federation. "A good German cannot be a nationalist," he said. "A good German knows that he cannot be other than a good European. Through Europe, Germany has discovered her true identity. . . . Under the threat of self-destruction, coexistence is no longer one of many acceptable possibilities, but our only chance of survival."

He talked briefly about the division of Germany and the Berlin Wall—"the absurd division of that which remained of a great city, with all the regrettable consequences, not only for those who lived there but for the peace of the world."

"The Western powers stood by, without faltering, for the protection of West Berlin; but whether they liked it or not, they had to accept the fact that East Berlin was controlled entirely by one power. The four-power status could not alter the fact that the wall became a dividing line between the atomically equipped super powers, and no one with any sense of responsibility expected the Western powers to use their military strength and risk a war in order to recover their share of what had originally been a collective responsibility. Passionate protests were justified, even necessary, but they did nothing to change the situation. The wall remained. The impeding of traffic on the approach road to Berlin remained. The ditch which divided Germany from Lübeck on the Baltic to the Czechoslovak frontier remained and became even deeper. We had to make a new approach to political possibilities if we were to make peace more secure. The Cuban crisis showed dramatically, and with far higher stakes at risk, the changing relationship between the atomic giants. The Cuban crisis was resolved by taking a calculated risk. This was an important experience and a turning point. . . .

"Having had a glimpse into the abyss which would have resulted from a global war, we then realized that there were other problems of global dimensions which threaten us—hunger, population explosion, pollution, the wastage of our natural resources. . . . It is no longer a question of the contrasts between ideologies and social systems. It is rather a question of the future of all mankind—indeed, whether mankind even has a future. We are faced with problems which go far beyond the boundaries of states and even continents. . . . We need peace today not only in the sense of a situation free from conflict and violence, but also as the prerequisite for the cooperative effort we must make to solve all the other problems which face us. But, just as these problems demand peace as a prerequisite, their solution can also contribute towards peace, for where there are people working together to help one another, there is peace, and with time, trust will grow more and more.

"My country is no longer a great power and can never be one again but we are an economic and a scientific power [and we are prepared] to work together with other nations at any time, anywhere.

"Ideological contrasts create and have created frontiers and will continue to create them, but it is a big step forward when more importance is attached to mutual interests than differing ideologies. It is encouraging when dialogue takes the place of monologue in East-West relations. Mutual solving of problems means creating new alliances and ties through constructive cooperation over and beyond the frontiers of power blocs.

This in turn leads to the creation of trust by practical and functional means, and this trust can become a new basis for the resolution of old, unsolved problems. If we take this chance, it could be Europe's chance in a world which has demonstrated that it cannot be ruled by Washington, or Moscow, or even Peking. Our world is in a state of great change; the weight of even the small nations counts in the big game.

"The Federal Republic of Germany knows its limitations but at the same time we are conscious that we are a power and that we have power. Above all, we know that we can play a great role as peacemakers. . . .

"Peace is far more than the mere absence of war . . . a lasting and just peace would mean equal chances of development for all the peoples of the world."

1972

Prize not awarded.

1973

HENRY ALFRED KISSINGER (1923–   ), United States: *The fifth American secretary of state to win the award, though the first to do so while in office, he was instrumental in arranging a cease-fire in Vietnam in January 1973 after discussions that had gone on for nearly two years.*

LE DUC THO (1910–   ), North Vietnam: *Founder of the Vietminh in 1945, a delegate to South Vietnam in 1949 and subsequently secretary-general of the Vietminh. He was chief adviser to the North Vietnamese delegation to the Paris Peace talks of 1969–72, and, with Kissinger, was responsible for arranging the 1973 cease-fire.*

"THE BIGGEST SURPRISE in the history of the prize" was the comment of one Swedish newspaper on the announcement that the Peace Prize for 1973 was to be divided between Henry Kissinger and Le Duc Tho. Another Swedish newspaper claimed that the Nobel Committee in Oslo "had disgraced itself again. . . . Kissinger has shown that he is a tough negotiator. . . . He has been said to give Nixonian thoughts an intellectual setting; but he has never produced anything which coincides with the peace ideals of Nobel. . . . And the same goes for Le Duc Tho—a tough negotiator for a small power which has become known because it has learned how to protect its interests by force."

Newspapers all over the world attacked the decision, largely on the grounds that it was inappropriate to award a prize for peace to two negotiators alleged to have achieved a cease-fire which had never in fact taken place. The *New York Times* said that the award was, at the very least, premature: "The truce agreement they achieved . . . was promptly met by an intensive new combat in Laos and Cambodia." The Italian newspaper *La Stampa* said it was "an encouragement to those who would declare war only to be able to stop it again."

There were demonstrations in Oslo when Mr. Thomas Byrne, the American ambassador, arrived to accept the prize on behalf of Dr. Kissinger, who was unable to attend, and snowballs—some reports say stones—were thrown at his car, and even at that of King Olav.

Le Duc Tho was not present, as he had already turned down the prize on the grounds that he could not accept it until peace had really been restored in Vietnam.

In her speech of presentation to Dr. Kissinger, Aase Lionaes, chairman of the committee, began by briefly recapping events in Vietnam. Never since the conclusion of World War II, she said, had the people of Vietnam enjoyed unbroken peace. After the war, when France was faced in Vietnam with a well-armed resistance movement under Communist leadership, all attempts to negotiate an independant Vietnamese state foundered. Although the French troops were 400,000 strong, France was defeated at Dien-Bien Phu in 1954; two states emerged from the struggle, a Communist one in the north based on Hanoi and a non-Communist one in the south based on Saigon. In the south, however, a guerrilla movement opposed to the Saigon government and supported by North Vietnam came into being, which was known as the FLN (National Liberation Movement).

In 1964 decisions were made that resulted in the United States committing American armed forces to acts of war on Asian soil, both in the civil war in South Vietnam, and in the larger war between the two Vietnamese states. By March 1969, 541,500 American troops were involved, with a corresponding escalation on the other side. The war had proved a nightmare, not only to the people of Vietnam but to the entire world.

"Nevertheless," said Aase Lionaes; "the negotiations for a cease-fire and peace in Vietnam, initiated in Paris in 1969, suffered only minor interruptions. Finally, on January 23 [1973] the United States negotiator Henry Kissinger and the North Vietnam negotiator Le Duc Tho arrived at a cease-fire agreement which they were able to sign on January 27.

"The Nobel Committee of the Norwegian Storting was fully aware that a cease-fire and not a peace agreement was involved. They realized that peace has not yet come to Vietnam, and that the sufferings of the population of Vietnam are not at an end. They were also aware that events in Vietnam may yet endanger the détente in the world. The cease-fire agreement was only the first but a tremendously important step on the laborious road to full peace. . . .

"The two negotiators who were awarded the prize represent widely differing systems—one an essentially Western system . . . the other a Communist system. We are under no illusion that the differences between systems and ideologies can be ignored; but the Nobel Committee has been anxious to emphasize that in a world yearning for peace, no one can assume the right to force his particular system on others by armed might. Nations with different systems of government must be able to live together in peace and solve their controversies by negotiation."

HENRY A. KISSINGER was born in Germany of Jewish parents. He escaped with his family to the United States in 1938, where his father, who had been a teacher in Germany, worked in an office. Kissinger became an American citizen and was called up for military service in 1943. He was in Europe for the closing stages of the war and for a time was responsible for the administration of a small south German town.

In 1946 he won a scholarship to Harvard, where he later received a Ph.D. for a thesis on the European peace settlement following the Napoleonic wars. From 1954 until 1971 he was a member of the Harvard faculty, both in the Department of Government and at the Center of International Affairs. He was study director, nuclear weapons and foreign policy, for the Council of Foreign Relations (1955–1956); director of the Special Studies Project for the Rockefeller Fund (1956–1958); director of the Harvard International Seminar (1951–1971); and director of the Harvard Defense Studies Program (1958–1971). He also carried out research programs for President Eisenhower and President Kennedy, and helped to draw up Nelson A. Rockefeller's platform during his presidential campaign in 1968.

Kissinger's book *Nuclear Weapons and Foreign Policy* (1957) established him as the leading authority on strategic policy in America (a curious background, you would think, for a future Peace laureate) and is said to have influenced President Kennedy in his thinking.

Although he had not previously been a supporter of Nixon, Kissinger accepted appointment as an advisor to the president on national security affairs in 1968. He also became executive secretary of the National Security Council.

Before very long he emerged as the most influential figure in the Nixon administration, going far beyond his brief as special adviser on security matters to act as a sort of jet-age, whistle-stop, globetrotting diplomat, popping up unexpectedly and often almost momentarily in all the world's trouble spots.

As chief foreign policy adviser to Nixon, he initiated the Strategic Arms Limitation Talks (SALT) in 1969, achieved a new and more relaxed relationship with the USSR in 1972, established the anti-India policy in the Indian-Pakistan War of the early seventies, and developed a rapprochement between the United States and the People's Republic of China, which flowered into something approaching friendship when Nixon visited Chairman Mao in February 1972. Late in 1973 he became secretary of state following the resignation of William P. Rodgers.

He played a major role in Nixon's policy of Vietnamization—the program by which the US troops were progressively disengaged and replaced by South Vietnamese troops. On January 23, 1973, he initialed the agreement for a cease-fire in Vietnam after nearly two years of negotiations, during which, presumably on Kissinger's advice, the bombing of North Vietnam and the mining of North Vietnamese ports continued. The cease-fire was to have come at 24:00 GMT on January 27, 1973. Nixon announced it as a "peace with honor" and told the people and government of South Vietnam: ". . . by your courage, by your sacrifice, you have won the precious right to determine your own future and have developed the strength to defend that right. We look forward to working with you in the future, friends in peace as we have been allies in war."

At a press conference on January 24, Kissinger said: "We were looking for some expression which would make clear that the two parts of Vietnam would live in peace with each other and that neither side would impose its solution on the other by force. This is now explicitly provided."

Strangely enough, the fact that the fighting continued until the fall of Saigon in April 1975 did not seem to dampen Kissinger's ardor in any way. When the Yom Kippur War broke out in October 1973, very shortly after Kissinger became secretary of state, a visit to Moscow to see Soviet party leader Brezhnev, followed by a whirlwind tour of seven Middle East capitals in November and December, led to the signing of a cease-fire between Egypt and Israel. In February 1974 he announced from Cairo the resumption of full-scale diplomatic relations between the US and Egypt (which had been severed for six years) and the reopening of the Suez Canal, and in May a marathon 32-day flying "shuttle diplomacy" mission between Israel and Syria produced the first signed agreement between the two states since the armistice ending the 1948 war for Israeli independence. On May 19 Kissinger accompanied President Nixon on a tour of the Middle East during which the US agreed to provide Egypt with nuclear technology for peaceful purposes.

When President Nixon was forced to resign in the aftermath of Watergate in August 1974, Kissinger continued as secretary of state for the Ford administration, and in 1976 he turned his attention to the African continent.

Kissinger has written six books and more than fifty major articles on US foreign policy, international affairs and diplomatic history. Among the awards he has received are the Guggenheim Fellowship (1965–1966); the Woodrow Wilson prize for outstanding writing in the fields of government, politics and international affairs (1958); the American Institute for Public Service Award (1973); the International Platform Association Theodore Roosevelt Award (1973); the Veterans of Foreign Wars Dwight D. Eisenhower Distinguished Service Medal (1973); and the Hope Award for International Understanding (1973).

When informed that he had won the Peace Prize, Kissinger said he would continue to work "for a world in which this award will be irrelevant. . . . Nothing that has happened to me in public life has moved me more than this award, which represents the central objective of [President Nixon's] foreign policy—a lasting peace."

Kissinger has always believed that peace must be based on rules to which all states, at any rate the great powers, adhere in their conduct. It is not sufficient for one state, or a number of states, to do so. On the contrary, a dangerous situation might arise if some states desire peace at any price and fail to ensure that other states, too, adhere to the rules.

In his doctoral thesis he put it this way: "Whenever peace—conceived as the avoidance of war—has been the primary objective of a power or a group of powers, the international system has been at the mercy of the most ruthless member of the international community." A policy of this kind could lead us to war, he said, and the most frightening example was the Munich agreement of 1938, when the Western powers sacrificed Czechoslovakia to Hitler. There were people who believed that as a result of this deal, peace would be secured "in our time." What they failed to understand was that Hitler entirely ignored all the rules of the game in international relations.

Kissinger believes that it is precisely because the great powers have conflicting interests and different systems and ideologies that it has become imperative to seek a détente in the relationship between them; this is why reducing the danger of nuclear war is so vital. Détente provides governments with opportunities to show moderation.

Le Duc Tho, who refused his share of the Peace Prize that year, would probably argue that if Kissinger had advised his own government to show a bit of moderation back in 1973, a real peace might have been achieved in time to have avoided the tragic extent of the devastation of life, limb and property.

LE DUC THO, born in North Vietnam in 1910, founded the Communist party in Indochina in 1930. He was imprisoned and expelled to China in 1940, during the French regime in Indochina. He returned towards the end of the war and became a founding member of the Vietminh, serving as its delegate to South Vietnam in 1949. A member of the Lao-Dong party, he was made secretary-general and executive of the Central Committee of the Communist party. He joined the Politbureau in 1955 and was director of the party's training school from 1959 on. In 1961 he became a delegate to Russia and then to France in 1965. He was appointed special adviser to the North Vietnamese delegation when the Paris peace talks opened in 1969.

In May 1972 Le Duc Tho refused one of President Nixon's proposals to end the war and called on the United States to end the bombing of North Vietnam unconditionally. He said that he would remain in Paris nevertheless and was prepared to resume private discussions with the Americans, a gesture which he said constituted "a sign of good will" on his part in view of the fact that President Nixon was intensifying the war and ordering the mining of North Vietnamese ports.

When, after 202 public sessions at the international conference center in the Avenue Kléber and 24 private meetings with Kissinger, the cease-fire agreement was finally signed, Le Duc Tho said at a press conference: "For centuries Vietnam has been one: the Vietnamese nation has been one and indivisible. The Vietnamese people from north to south aspire with all their heart not only to a peaceful settlement of the Vietnam problem, but also to the reunification of their country. . . ."

Le Duc Tho rejected his share of the prize "because of violations of the Paris peace agreements by the United States and South Vietnam." He added that he would consider accepting the prize when peace had really been restored in South Vietnam—but apparently the matter has not come up since.

1974

EISAKU SATO (1901–1975), Japan: *Prime minister from November 1964 to June 1972, who believed that the renunciation of war, as set out in the 1947 Japanese constitution, must serve as the basis for the country's policy. He traveled throughout Asia to improve trade relations, increase aid to developing countries, and generally encourage greater cooperation. In 1961 he concluded a treaty with the United States securing the return of Okinawa and the Ogasawara Islands and the promise that nuclear arms would not be maintained on American bases on Okinawa.*

SEAN MACBRIDE (1904–   ), Ireland: *Journalist, lawyer and politician, he was one of the foreign ministers responsible for piloting the European Convention on Human Rights through the Council of Europe in 1950. Since 1961 he has been president of the International Board of Amnesty International.*

AWARE, NO DOUBT, that the choice of Eisaku Sato, former Japanese premier, would not be a popular one with those who remembered the surprise attack on Pearl Harbor and the treatment of prisoners of war in Japanese camps, Aase Lionaes, chairman of the Nobel Committee, began her presentation speech with what amounted to an apologia, almost a defense.

"It could hardly be expected," she said, "that the decisions of the committee would not give rise to discussion. This has been the case ever since the first award was made over seventy years ago. This proves how difficult it is to define the concept of peace. On previous occasions the Nobel Committee has selected laureates whose efforts on behalf of peace have covered a great many, varied fields; they have included statesmen negotiating around the conference table, defenders of human rights, experts on international law, rebels, humanists, idealists, pragmatists, dreamers. They have all been controversial figures. . . .

"Eisaku Sato is the first Asiatic who has accepted the prize. He comes to us today also as a representative of the only nation that has experienced the unspeakable horrors of nuclear war."

Sato studied law at Tokyo University and worked for the Ministry of Railways until 1948, when he became chief cabinet secretary of the second

Yoshida government in 1948. He was prime minister of Japan for nearly eight years, from 1964 to 1972, and his principal aim was to secure for Japan an influence in international politics consistent with the country's status as a major economic power (second after the United States and ahead of West Germany, in terms of gross national output since 1968).

Throughout these years Sato was deeply aware of a unique provision in Japan's postwar constitution—that "the Japanese people forever renounce war as a sovereign right of the nation and the threat or the use of force as a means of settling international disputes."

Although this provision was partially dictated by the American occupation force after World War II, Sato accepted it as a basis for his country's foreign policy, and in turn laid down three principles affecting his government's policy on nuclear arms: never to produce them, never to own them, and never to introduce them to Japan.

Sato was largely responsible for the return of Okinawa and the Ogasawara Islands, which the United States had occupied since the end of World War II. In 1961, after five years of patient negotiation, he succeeded; and what was particularly important to him and to the Japanese people was that the final agreement insisted that no nuclear arms would be maintained in the American bases still maintained on Okinawa. Today Japan's national security is safeguarded by a relatively small, conventional defense system; in fact, as the chairman of the Nobel Committee pointed out in the presentation speech, many small countries maintain military forces that are very much larger and stronger than those of Japan.

His next concern was the improvement of economic relations with other Asian countries. In 1965 he concluded a pact of friendship with South Korea. In 1967 he set off on a tour of Burma, Malaysia, Singapore, Thailand, Laos, Indonesia, Australia, New Zealand, the Philippines and South Vietnam. His principal aims were to strengthen diplomatic relations, improve economic connections, stimulate trade and, hopefully, to promote political and cultural cooperation. He firmly believed that if the Asian countries were better able to exploit their material and cultural resources, they would be less likely to make war on one another. Accordingly he embarked on a program of increased aid to developing countries in the East, and under his auspices Japan initiated a conference on economic development in Southeast Asia which resulted in the formation of the International Development Bank for Asia.

Japan's close relations with the United States caused a great deal of criticism in the East, especially during the Vietnam War. Sato, however, did not for a moment consider Japanese military intervention in Vietnam; on the contrary, he did his best to urge the two sides to come together without imposing any preconditions. A Japanese attempt to open a new peace initiative failed in the spring of 1966.

"In awarding the 1974 Peace Prize to Eisaku Sato," said Aase Lionaes, "the Nobel Committee wishes to emphasize the important role the Japanese people have played in promoting close and friendly cooperation with other nations. Japan's attitude has helped to strengthen peace in East Asia and to lay the foundation for economic growth and progress for many countries. By countering a tendency towards a nationalistic policy in Japan after the war, by constantly emphasizing the need for international cooperation and understanding, by playing the role of arbitrator and thus helping to iron out differences, Sato has made a major contribution to peace."

In his Nobel lecture, Sato made a point not emphasized by most of the laureates, who have tended to talk about peace in generalized, abstract terms. "If the attainment of peace is the ultimate objective of all statesmen," he said, "it is, at the same time, something very ordinary, closely tied to the daily life of each individual. In familiar terms, it is the condition that allows each individual and his family to pursue, without fear, the purpose of their lives. It is only in such circumstances that each individual will be able to devote himself, without the loss of hope for the future of mankind, to the education of his children, in an attempt to leave upon the history of mankind the imprint of his own creative and constructive achievements in the arts, culture, religion and other activities fulfilling social aspirations. This is the peace which is essential for all individuals, peoples, nations, and thus for the whole of humanity."

He referred to the return of Okinawa and the islands through peaceful diplomatic channels as "an event rarely witnessed in world history," and warned the nations which then possessed nuclear weapons that they had especially heavy responsibilities for assuring the peace and security of the world. He then turned to the utilization of nuclear energy for peaceful means, as "a source of potentially limitless energy which could well open up new vistas for the civilization of tomorrow":

"Several years ago I set down the three non-nuclear principles which gave concrete expression to the determination of the Japanese people to achieve peace . . . this was because the entire nation is against the use of thermonuclear energy as a means of killing their fellow men. However, I am entirely in favor of the peaceful utilization of nuclear energy. That is why I wish to express here three views on the peaceful uses of this energy.

"First of all, we need to create international safety standards; next, an international agreement on the exchange and allocation of nuclear fuel will have to be concluded, to avoid an unbridled race for the acquisition of nuclear fuels; and third, there must be international cooperation in research and development work on nuclear fusion, because the rapid development of a system for the effective use of thermonuclear energy seems to be beyond the capacity of a single nation, no matter how great its resources may be. . . . Japan has reached an advanced stage in science and technology. I have no doubt that, should an international research facility be created, young and able brains from among us will gladly volunteer to participate in this work.

"Japan is basically a difficult nation to understand," he concluded, "because the foundation of our culture differs so much from those of the West and of other Asian countries. Because this was so, we should have tried to make ourselves better understood. I cannot but admit that at a time when international understanding was required, our efforts to promote such understanding were inadequate. . . . I therefore plan to use the prize I received to further the links between our country and the rest of the world."

SEAN MACBRIDE, THE first Irishman to win a Peace Prize, was described by Aase Lionaes as "a citizen of a country that for many years has been the scene of a bitter, grievous conflict."

He was born in Paris in 1904, the son of the beautiful Maude Gonne MacBride—to whom W. B. Yeats, another Irish Nobel laureate (Literature, 1923) addressed many of his youthful poems—and of Major John MacBride, a British officer who fought *against* the English in the Boer War and was executed by a British firing squad for his part in the 1916 Easter Rising.

After working as a journalist for a number of years, MacBride studied law and was called to the bar in 1937. As a barrister he specialized in working for the legal rights of people suffering from any kind of persecution.

In the middle forties he went into politics, forming a new republican party which joined with a coalition of other minority parties to put de Valera's Fianna Fail government out of office after an unbroken run of sixteen years. MacBride, a fluent linguist, became foreign minister of this coalition government. At the Council of Europe in 1950, he was instrumental in securing acceptance of a European Convention on Human Rights. From then on, he devoted all his energies to the promotion of greater respect for basic human rights, not only in Western Europe but throughout the world.

In 1961 he was elected president of the International Board of Amnesty International—an organization set up to investigate allegations of torture—and he spent many years visiting countries all over the world to plead the cause of persecuted men and women, and to focus world attention on the torture and the inhumane treatment of prisoners. In the words of Aase Lionaes: "He mobilized the conscience of the world in the fight against injustice."

He was also active as secretary general of the International Commission of Jurists from 1963 to 1970. This was a commission set up in West Berlin in 1952, to record acts of injustice perpetrated in East Germany and other Eastern European countries, but as time went by it became involved in countering violations of human rights elsewhere.

MacBride has advocated the establishment of a universal Human Rights Court, with authority to deal with complaints from individuals who are being subjected to persecution in violation of the universally accepted principals of justice. He holds the opinion that no state can claim absolute sovereignty where basic human rights are concerned.

He has also been an active member of the Peace Bureau (which itself was awarded the Peace Prize in 1910); and in 1973 he was elected commissioner for Namibia by the General Assembly of the United Nations and given the rank of assistant secretary-general.

MacBride began his Nobel lecture by referring to the fundamental changes which had taken place in the course of the last thirty years—scientific developments, accompanied by radical changes in our social and political structure. "There has never been in the history of mankind a revolution so fundamental or far reaching. . . . Perhaps as a result of this scientific revolution . . . there has taken place a near collapse of public and private morality in practically every sector of human relationship. . . . Governments go to war directly or by proxy without declaring war. Force, or threat of force, are constantly used to dominate other countries. In these undeclared wars civilians, men, women and children, are bombed and massacred indiscriminately; chemical agents are used to destroy humans, animals and crops. Prisoners are not only ill-treated but are tortured systematically in a worse manner than at any barbaric period of history. In many cases this is done with the direct or tacit approval of governments that claim to be civilized or even Christian. . . . Secret services are used to assassinate political opponents or to provoke internal dissension in another country or to procure the overthrow of a democratically elected government. In other cases the overthrow of a government is followed by a massacre of its members and supporters. Again cases occur when one ethnic group seeks to supplant another in order to impose its domination, and for this purpose resorts to outright genocide. . . .

Addressing himself to the nuclear threat, he said: "Not only has man lost 'the capacity to see and to forestall the consequences of his own acts,' as Schweitzer put it, but he does not realize that knowledge without wisdom and idealism is dangerous. What does wisdom entail in this context? A realization that the world was not created by man and that in tampering with nature and creation man is endangering human survival. And what does idealism involve? An ethical belief in a duty to help human beings to survive and to benefit from the natural goodness and beauty with which Providence has surrounded humanity. It is clear that it is not man who has created the universe and—whether you believe in God, or in gods, or deny any divine presence—man cannot alter the laws that govern the universe without destroying it."

Turning to what could be done to secure world peace, he said that despite agreement on the objective of general and complete disarmament, the major powers are still engaged in the greatest arms race that has ever existed. Negotiations are only aimed at limiting the increase of nuclear weapons and this only because the armament race is so costly that it is bankrupting their economies.

"The arsenal of nuclear weapons is now such that there are enough nuclear missiles to destroy the world twenty times over. Despite conferences and 'Partial Disarmament Measures,' no progress has been made to outlaw nuclear weapons. . . . Nuclear warheads are spread all over the world in bases, aircraft, ships and submarines to a greater extent than ever before. The Nuclear Test Ban Treaty and the Non-Proliferation Treaty have been of little value, but . . . to defuse public anxiety."

Suggesting that the use of nuclear weapons should be completely outlawed, MacBride said that all kinds of issues, such as the problem of inspection, are raised merely to block or delay arguments. Why not begin quite simply by outlawing the use, manufacture, sale, transfer and stockpiling of all nuclear weapons and components thereof?

He then got down to the root of the problem: vested interests. "The issues of peace or war, or the armament race versus disarmament, are never put to the people. . . . Even parliaments are often bypassed on such issues, or only partially consulted. The real decisions . . . are taken behind closed doors by the joint chiefs of staff of the defense forces. It is they who are the 'experts' to whom all questions relating to armament, disarmament, nuclear weapons, war and peace are referred. They are the experts to whom governments turn for advice on all these vital questions on which depend the future of humanity. . . .

"Who are these experts? Military officers, often drawn from a particular caste or class of society, whose profession it is to prepare for war . . . their professional objectives must be to have the best army and armament possible. . . . Of course an atom bomb is more effective than a conventional one and therefore the experts do not want the use of atom bombs outlawed. Of course a fragmentation bomb will kill more people than an ordinary one, therefore it is desirable. Nerve gases and napalm are very effective killers, therefore we must use them. . . . So, the experts upon whom the governments rely for ultimate advice on disarmament are those whose profession it is to make war and who want bigger and more destructive arms. . . .

"In addition to the military experts . . . there are the financial interests which make money out of armament and also the industrial-military complex that lives by increased armament. To [them] the arms race is a boon. A war far away, such as in Southeast Asia or in the Middle East, means increased arms sales and more profits . . . it is not unwelcome. General and complete disarmament would spell disaster to the industrial-military complexes in the United States, France, Britain and Germany, to mention but a few of the countries that thrive on increased armament.

"The socialist countries do not have a profit-motivated industrial-military complex. They can therefore adjust more easily to disarmament. To them disarmament means an automatic switch from increased arms production to an increase in production for industrial development and for the consumer and export markets. They cannot lose by disarmament, they can only gain.

MacBride concluded his lecture by stressing the growing impact of informed public opinion on government policy. "The public can now be informed as to current events and policies . . . giving a much greater influence to public opinion in the world than it has ever had in the past. . . . It was American and world public opinion that forced the United States to withdraw from Vietnam. This was the first time that a country at war was stopped in its tracks by its own and by world opinion. Now, because the public can learn and see what its government is doing, it is able to curb the government. . . .

"If disarmament can be achieved it will be due to the untiring, selfless work of the nongovernmental sector. This is what Alfred Nobel appreciated in his days. It is more urgent than ever now. The big powers are traveling on the dangerous road of armament. The signpost just ahead of us is 'Oblivion.' Can the march on this road be stopped? Yes, if public opinion uses the power it now has."

1975

ANDREI SAKHAROV (1921–   ), USSR: *Nuclear physicist who, at thirty-two, became the youngest member of the Russian Academy of Scientists. He worked on the development of nuclear arms from 1950 to 1968. In 1968, he issued a manifesto appealing for worldwide cooperation in the control of nuclear power and urging that the US and the USSR achieve some measure of approximation between their political systems. In an attempt to institute constructive reforms for the protection of human rights within the framework of the law, he and two other scientists founded the Committee for Human Rights in 1970.*

THE FIRST RUSSIAN ever to be awarded a Peace Prize—after considerable lobbying by, among others, Alexander Solzhenitsyn, the 1970 Nobel Literary laureate—Sakharov was not at first likely to be a popular candidate. A nuclear scientist, he had worked on the development of Soviet nuclear armaments from 1950 to 1968. Sakharov himself has justified this work by saying that as the United States was far more advanced in nuclear technology than the USSR, it was important, *in the interest of peace,* to narrow this gap in order to establish a balance in the arms race which would be capable of deterring both parties from starting a war. It is a dangerous argument which could be used by any country as a justification for increasing its armaments.

In 1968 he underwent an abrupt change of heart. "Not without the influence of statements on this subject made throughout the world by such people as Albert Schweitzer (the 1951 Peace laureate), Linus Pauling (the 1962 laureate) and others, I felt myself responsible for the problem of radioactive contamination from nuclear explosions."

Sakharov made no secret of the fact that he had reached these conclusions, but explained his views to authorities in letters in which he set forth his ideas in full. As a result, he was removed from his research post and sent to work in the Physics Insitute in the Academy of Science.

Later that year he issued his famous "Manifesto on Progress, Coexistence and Intellectual Freedom." It deals principally with the threat of the total annihilation of civilization which would result from a nuclear war. In his view, this could be averted only by worldwide cooperation, transcending national and ideological boundaries. He was particularly concerned with relations between the United States and the USSR, and expressed the belief that peaceful coexistence between these powers could be achieved if some measure of approximation would take place between their divergent political systems. So far as his own country's contribution was concerned, he stressed the need for democratization, debureaucratization, demilitarization, and continued social and scientific progress. He also envisioned a joint approach to the problems of world hunger, overpopulation and pollution.

Sakharov acknowledges freely that he began his life by confronting global problems and only later on did he start to concentrate on more concrete, personal and human ones. This concern for human problems led to his founding the Committee for Human Rights in 1970. Among its chief aims are the abolition of secret trials, a free press, reforms in the prison system, amnesty for political prisoners, the abolition of the death penalty, open frontiers, and a ban on the use of psychiatric institutes for political ends.

Though couched in far vaguer and more general terms, perhaps, than Sakharov would have chosen, many of these ideas were incorporated in the Agreement on Security and Cooperation in Europe, signed by thirty-five nations in Helsinki in August 1975.

When it was announced that Sakharov had won the Peace Prize, the Moscow passport office informed him that he would not be allowed to leave Russia to go to Oslo to accept the prize. The Soviet government regarded the award as an act of "cold warfare," but the official reason given for refusing him a passport was that as a scientist he was in possession of state secrets and could not therefore be allowed to leave the country. His wife, Elena, who was already out of Russia receiving medical treatment in Florence, went to Oslo to accept the prize on his behalf.

In making the award, the chairman of the committee said: "Andrei Sakharov's great contribution to peace is this, that he has fought in a particularly effective manner and under highly difficult conditions, in the greatest spirit of self-sacrifice, to obtain respect for those values that the Helsinki Agreement declares to be its object. Sakharov's struggle for human rights, for disarmament and for cooperation between all nations has peace as its final goal. . . . The Nobel Committee deeply deplores the fact that Andrei Sakharov has been prevented from being present here today in person to receive the Peace Prize . . . a fate he shares with Carl von Ossietzky who forty years ago, in 1935, was awarded the prize."

In making this reference to von Ossietzky, the chairman was clearly drawing a parallel between personal freedoms in Russia today and those in Nazi Germany in the thirties.

Elena Bonner Sakharova not only accepted the prize on her husband's behalf, but also delivered his Nobel lecture. "I am convinced," he wrote, "that international confidence, mutual understanding, disarmament and international security are inconceivable without an open society with freedom of information, freedom of conscience, the right to publish and the right to travel and choose the country in which one wants to live."

Sakharov referred in his lecture to the new era of détente which seemed to have been ushered in with the Helsinki Agreement of that year, in which the question of international security was bound up with that of human rights, freedom of information and freedom of movement. Referring to his own country, he said that during the months since the Helsinki Agreement, there had been absolutely no real improvement in this direction; in fact, in some cases, attempts on the part of the hardliners had been made "to give the screw another turn."

"The Helsinki Agreement confirms yet again the principle of freedom of conscience," he wrote. ". . . In the Soviet Union today many thousands of people are persecuted because of their convictions, both by judicial and by nonjudicial organs, for sake of their religious beliefs and for their desire to bring their children up in the spirit of religion, for reading and disseminating, often only to a few acquaintances, literature which is unwelcome to the State, but which, in accordance with ordinary democratic practice, is absolutely legitimate—for example, religious literature—and for attempts to leave the country. On the moral plane the persecution of persons who have defended other victims of unjust treatment, who have worked to publish and in particular to distribute information regarding the persecution and trials of persons with deviant opinions, and of conditions in places of internment, is particularly important.

"It is unbearable to think that at this very moment . . . hundreds of thousands of prisoners of conscience are suffering from undernourishment as the result of year-long hunger, and of an almost total lack of proteins and vitamins in their daily food, of a shortage of medicines (there is a ban on sending vitamins to internees) and of overexertion. They shiver with cold, damp and exhaustion in ill-lit dungeons, where they are forced to wage a ceaseless war for their human dignity against the very destruction of their souls. . . .

"In struggling to protect human rights we must, I am convinced, first and foremost act as protectors of the innocent victims of regimes installed in various countries, without demanding the destruction or total condemnation of these regimes. We need reform, not revolution. We need a pliant, pluralist, tolerant community, which selectively and tentatively can bring about a free, undogmatic use of the experiences of all social systems. What is détente? What is rapprochement? We are concerned not with words, but with a willingness to create a better and more friendly society, a better world order. . . ."

Peace in Our Time?

THEY'VE HAD THEIR say, the champions of peace—fifty-six men, three women and the representatives of eight institutions. Is there anything that emerges from all that talk as a common denominator?

Curiously, the message that comes out most strongly is that somewhere along the line, mankind has lost all feeling for spiritual values. The laureates were not, however, lamenting the decline in the influence of established religions as such, but rather making the point that the staggering advances that man has made in science, in space travel, in technology, in medicine and in communications ought to have been accompanied by a corresponding progress in his attitude towards his fellow man.

Despite all the disarmament talks, agreements on the nonproliferation of nuclear weapons and treaties on the limitation of strategic arms, we are still sitting on a powder keg which could go up at the press of a button and destroy every living thing on this earth. Nuclear submarines prowl the oceans incessantly, bristling with missiles capable of wiping out entire cities. Planes patrol the upper atmosphere ceaselessly round the clock, carrying hydrogen bombs many thousands of times as destructive as those that instantaneously killed 71,000 people in Hiroshima and 80,000 people in Nagasaki (apart from the tens of thousands of people who died hours, weeks and even years later from the results of radioactive contamination).

Despite all the declarations and agreements on human rights, thousands of people are still being interned without trial, imprisoned, tortured and mutilated all over the world. In 1935 when Carl von Ossietzky was chosen for the Peace Prize, the Nazi government regarded the award as an insult to the German people and Ossietzky, who was in a concentration camp, was refused a passport to go to Oslo. In 1975 when the Russian dissident Andrei Sakharov was chosen for the prize, the USSR regarded it as an act of "cold warfare" and refused him a passport to go to Oslo. We have learned everything and nothing.

Leaving aside for a moment the wars and revolutions and outbreaks of racial violence and the widespread denial of basic human rights—with which the laureates have been principally concerned— we have been wrong in so many other ways.

To take one very narrow aspect of progress, we overestimated the growth in demand for transatlantic liners, with the result that the last of them were obsolete even before they were launched. The railroad companies overestimated the growth demand for rail travel with the result that networks everywhere were completed just about the time when people began to switch over to automobiles. In turn, most of the countries in the Western world have now ruined vast stretches of their landscapes to accommodate millions of cars which may now never be built because the fuel on which they operate is rapidly running out. The airlines in their turn have overestimated the growth demand for air travel.

It is beginning to look as if the real problem is going to be food—assuming, that is, that nobody presses any nuclear buttons. So will it come to the point where we will have to hack our way down through all that concrete—the highways and runways and launching pads—and try to reach and cultivate the good earth that lies beneath it, maintaining, perhaps, a few isolated cloverleaf intersections as monuments to our twentieth century which will be about as relevant and as useful as the ruins of the Mayan temples?

Three-quarters of the way through the twentieth century, we seem to have reached a crossroads.

Or is it a cul-de-sac?

THAT WE HAVE been so wrong about such relatively uncontroversial and fairly predictable developments should make us perhaps a bit more tolerant of the Nobel laureates who operate in the far less predictable field of war and peace. It is desperately easy, with hindsight, to cavil at the brave words, the noble sentiments, the confident optimism of the early champions of peace; but what emerges from their speeches is the fact that they were all deeply committed. They went on believing in the machinery of international arbitration, international courts of justice and the League of Nations long after it was clear that this machinery stood no chance at all against the warmongers; and they did so because, even if a vanishing hope, it was still the only hope. As Willy Brandt put it in his Nobel lecture, in relation to his own efforts in Berlin, "I learned that to make small steps forward is better than to make none at all."

This has, in some ways, been a depressing book to research and to write: for mankind to have come all this way, since 1901, and to have learned so little.

Paradoxically, the one ray of hope lies in the almost hopeless situation in which the world finds itself today. So many of the problems that beset us are global problems—overpopulation, the exhaustion of the planet's resources, the pollution of the environment—that it could just happen that by tackling these problems on a global, cooperative basis, men everywhere may discover that the things about which they differ, and will always differ, are rather less important than the things they have in common.

Bibliography

As I have already indicated in the Acknowledgments, a great deal of the material in this book came from the Nobel Institutes in Stockholm and Oslo. Anyone interested in reading more deeply into the subject can consult *The Nobel Lectures,* published in three volumes for the Nobel Foundation by the Elsevier Publishing Company (Amsterdam, London and New York). These volumes cover the years 1901 through 1970 and include the citations, the presentation addresses, the laureates' replies (whether delivered directly, by telegram, or by the ambassador of the country concerned), extracts from the speeches at the Nobel banquets and, where applicable, the Nobel lectures.

So far as Nobel's own life is concerned, the material is sparse. Most of the books available cover broadly the same ground and are clearly based on the Sohlman book of 1929. The most perceptive material is that by August Schou in *Nobel: The Man and His Prizes;* the best informed is that by Ragnar Sohlman, who was Nobel's chief assistant just before his death and was one of the executors of his will.

I list here the books I found most helpful:

Bergengren, Erik. *Alfred Nobel: The Man and His Work.* London: Thomas Nelson, 1962.

Evlanoff, Michael, and Fluor, Marjorie. *Alfred Nobel: The Loneliest Millionaire.* Los Angeles: The Ward Ritchie Press, 1969.

Moe, Reginald. *Le Prix Nobel de la Paix et de l'Institut Nobel Norvégien.* Oslo: Aschehoug and Co., 1932.

Nobel, Alfred. *Modern Blasting Agents.* Glasgow: Maclehose and Macdougall, 1875.

The Nobel Foundation, ed., and W. Odelberg, coordinating ed. *Nobel: The Man and His Prizes.* New York: American Elsevier Publishing Co., 1972.

Sohlman, Ragnar, and Schück, Henrik. *The Life of Alfred Nobel.* London: William Heinemann, 1929.

Stähle, Nils K. *Alfred Nobel and the Nobel Prizes.* Stockholm: The Swedish Institute for Cultural Relations, 1960.

Williams, Trevor H. *Alfred Nobel, Pioneer of High Explosives.* London: Priory Press, 1974.

Index

Note: For easy reference, the names of the Peace Prize laureates appear in boldface; the year in parentheses indicates when the award was made.